Immigrant Council of Ireland

A **Social Innovations** Ireland Initiative

HANDBOOK ON IMMIGRANTS' RIGHTS AND ENTITLEMENTS IN IRELAND

ACKNOWLEDGEMENTS

This handbook was compiled by: Catherine Kenny
Edited by: Orla Parkinson

The Immigrant Council of Ireland would like to thank all the following people who gave their time, energy and expertise through commentary and advice, in order to bring this book to completion:

Hilkka Becker, Nerilee Ceatha, Cathryn Costello, Rachel Collier, Oliver Donohoe, Geraldine Hegarty, Stanislaus Kennedy, Piaras MacÉinrí, Sara McNeice, Fidèle Mutwarasibo, Sr Pereka Nyirenda, Joan O'Shea, Siobhan Phelan, Nicole Roger, Barbara Salmon, Tanya Ward.

Sponsorship was provided for the production of this handbook by Comhairle, the Department of Social and Family Affairs, the Religious Sisters of Charity and Social Innovations Ireland.

Published by: Immigrant Council of Ireland
               42 Upper Dorset Street,
               Dublin 1, Ireland
               Tel: 01 865 6525
               E-mail: info@immigrantcouncil.ie
               Website: www.immigrantcouncil.ie

Design: Dermot O'Connor & Associates Ltd.

Cover
Photographs: Derek Speirs.

Printed by: Future Print

ISBN: 0-9545496-0-0

TABLE OF CONTENTS

FOREWORD

I welcome the publication of this guide which outlines the rights and entitlements of the various categories of immigrants now resident in Ireland. As a *céad míle fáilte* to our country, it is a significant publication providing a myriad of information across all areas of Irish life for a wide variety of immigrants ranging from international students to migrant workers and self-employed business people.

I hope it proves to be a practical support to all those people seeking information on their arrival in Ireland and indeed throughout their stay here.

The Department of Social and Family Affairs now has a very significant amount of dealings with non-nationals and the departmental staff throughout the regions are conscious of respecting the rights of minorities at all times in the delivery of our services.

In July 2000 the Government under the Strategic Management Initiative endorsed various Quality Customer Service Principles including a Principle of Equality and Diversity. My Department has endorsed these Principles under our own Action Plans.

I hope this handbook responds to the needs of immigrants in providing easy to understand, accessible and accurate information for all those who require it.

Mary Coughlan, T.D.,
Minister for Social and Family Affairs

PREFACE

Significant immigration to Ireland is a recent phenomenon, and we have neither a coherent immigration policy nor comprehensive legislation in this area. There have been legislative and procedural changes designed to a large extent to exclude rather than provide a clear route of access for immigrants to Ireland. The lack of clarity with regard to the rights and entitlements of immigrants, amongst both immigrants themselves and the people who are trying to provide services for them, was the main driving force behind the drawing up of this handbook.

This book, the first of its kind in Ireland, outlines the application process and the rights and entitlements of the various categories of immigrants now resident in or seeking to come to Ireland. It provides basic, practical information on immigration law and on the rights and entitlements of different categories of people who migrate to Ireland. (It does not contain information on the asylum process.)

The handbook is as up-to-date as we have been able to make it, but both the law and official procedures are constantly changing. In fact change is part and parcel of all matters relating to immigration in Ireland making it extremely difficult for everyone concerned to be fully aware of the rights and entitlements of immigrants at any time. Even as this handbook was going to print we had the Supreme Court's decision that non-national parents and siblings of children who are Irish citizens are not automatically entitled to residency in Ireland; this was followed almost immediately by a decision of the Department of Justice, Equality and Law Reform not to accept applications for residency on grounds of being parents of an Irish citizen.

Like most directories this handbook cannot be fully comprehensive, but it does provide very extensive and accessible information which has not been available before, both to immigrants themselves and to service providers. It should be used in conjunction with the various statutory and voluntary guides and directories that are listed throughout. The availability of good information in an accessible form is vitally important, particularly for immigrants who do not know the country and its systems, structures, or may not even know the English language. For this reason, this handbook is organised in such a way that specific categories of immigrants can easily find the information that relates to them. The information in this book will also be disseminated throughout the country in a variety of ways, including website, booklets and leaflets, and we hope also to make the information available in different languages.

We will be grateful for helpful comments from users of the handbook, particularly with regard to changes in the situation, and will use your comments to amend and improve future editions.

I wish to thank Catherine Kenny, who researched and compiled the handbook. Without her dedication and hard work it would not exist. I also wish to acknowledge the invaluable contribution of Hilkka Becker, ICI's legal consultant, who provided detailed information and legal advice and of Orla Parkinson for her meticulous editing. Thanks also to the numerous other people both inside and outside the agency who read, commented on and contributed to the production of this handbook.

Executive Chair
Stanislaus Kennedy RSC

INTRODUCTION

International migration has grown considerably in recent years. It is believed that towards the end of the twentieth century, the number of migrants world wide was in the region of 135 to 140 million, almost double the number in 1965 (75 million). The United Nations estimates that 97 million of these are migrant workers.[1] Migrants accounted for four-and-a-half per cent of the population of 'developed' countries in the 1990's.[2]

Many 'developed' countries, including Ireland are now experiencing acute labour shortages in certain sectors of the economy and have had to revise their existing policies of zero immigration.

Ireland has traditionally been a country of emigration rather than immigration. Until recently, the weakness of the Irish economy, characterised by high unemployment, meant that thousands of people had to leave Ireland to seek employment abroad. The economic situation was undoubtedly one of the main factors in keeping the numbers of immigrants low. In addition, Ireland's position at the edge of Europe and its lack of a colonial past meant that there was no tradition of immigration to Ireland.

Successive Irish governments maintained a policy of closure both in relation to migrant workers and asylum seekers. In their view, a policy of discouraging immigration was necessary to protect the labour market, and to protect the homogeneity of Irish society. Prior to the Second World War, there were less than 3,000 non-nationals in the State and with few exceptions, Ireland refused to accept persons fleeing the war. Between 1939 and 1945, only 588 non-nationals were permitted to enter Ireland.[3]

Ireland joined the European Union (EU)[a] in 1972, which meant that for the first time non-nationals (with the exception of those born in the United Kingdom (UK) who already were allowed) were permitted to reside and work in Ireland in any significant numbers. However, immigration from other EU Member States remained relatively low until the 1990's.

During the 1990's, the number of persons migrating to Ireland increased considerably. Since 1997, the total numbers of immigrants coming to Ireland each year has constantly exceeded 40,000.[b]

The Government recognises that, for the foreseeable future, Ireland will have to rely on workers from outside the State, if the economy is to continue to grow. To this end, it is developing policy and legislation with regard to immigration for labour.

The *Programme for Prosperity and Fairness,* 2000 states that immigration policy will be developed to meet the needs of the labour market.[4] An Inter-departmental/Agency Group on immigration policy was established which reported to the Government in March 2000. It recommended a 'skills-based approach' to immigration.[5]

In 2001, the Department of Justice, Equality & Law Reform announced that it would engage in a public consultation process on immigration as part of its

a Then called the EEC (European Economic Community).

b This figure includes asylum seekers.

development of immigration policy and legislation. In addition to the public consultation, the proposed development of immigration law and policy included:[6]

- the establishment of an inter-departmental group on immigration
- a study of international law and practice with regard to immigration[7]
- an internal review of the practices of the Immigration and Citizenship Division of the Department of Justice, Equality & Law Reform

In February 2000, it was announced that 200,000 skilled immigrants would be needed over the next six to seven years to achieve National Development Plan targets.[8] However, by 2001 a downturn in the economy and increasing unemployment led to concerns being raised about the level of immigration should the economy continue to decline. Politicians were anxious to reassure the public that migrant workers were here on a temporary basis, a 'safety valve' as the Tánaiste noted. There is a danger of migrant workers being seen as 'disposable' and of having their rights overlooked.

Ireland now has the opportunity to introduce immigration legislation which safeguards the rights of migrant workers and other migrants in accordance with international legal instruments and best practice. At EU level, measures are being adopted regarding immigration and Ireland should play a positive role in ensuring the rights of migrant workers and other migrants will be protected.

As immigration to Ireland is a recent phenomenon and to date no comprehensive legislation dealing with immigration has been enacted, there is often little awareness of the rights of immigrants among the immigrant communities, the host community and service providers. Indeed the term 'immigrant' is often used interchangeably with other terms.

What is this Handbook About?

This handbook details the application process and the rights and entitlements of the various categories of immigrants now resident in Ireland. It focuses on the rights and entitlements of those persons who immigrate voluntarily rather than those fleeing persecution and applying for refugee status in Ireland. It does not contain information on the asylum process, or give information to those with refugee status.[9]

How to Use this Handbook

The handbook is organised so that specific categories of immigrants can find the information that relates to them easily:

You are in this category	If you are a migrant who...	You should read...
Migrant worker	has permission to remain in the State on the basis of an employment permit granted to your employer, or on the basis of a work visa or work authorisation granted to you	Chapter 1 for information on international and domestic legislation on migrants, and Chapter 2 for information specific to migrant workers. You may also need to refer to the appendices.

You are in this category	If you are a migrant who...	You should read...
Self-employed/ business person	has permission to remain in the State on the basis of a business permission granted to you	Chapter 1 for information on international and domestic legislation on migrants, and Chapter 3 for information specific to migrants who are self-employed / business persons. You may also need to refer to the appendices.
International student	has permission to remain in the State on the basis of a student visa granted to you	Chapter 1 for information on international and domestic legislation on migrants, and Chapter 4 for information specific to migrants who are international students. You may also need to refer to the appendices.
Non-economically active person	has permission to remain in the State but does not have permission, or the financial need, to enter employment or establish a business, and does need to rely on public funds	Chapter 1 for information on international and domestic legislation on migrants, and Chapter 5 for information specific to migrants who are non-economically-active. You may also need to refer to the appendices.
Parent or a sibling of Irish citizen children	has permission to remain in the State as the parent, brother or sister, of an Irish citizen child	Chapter 1 for information on international and domestic legislation on migrants, and Chapter 6 for information specific to migrants who are parents or siblings of Irish citizen children. You may also need to refer to the appendices.
Person granted leave to remain on exceptional grounds	has permission to remain in the State at the discretion of the Minister of Justice, Equality & Law Reform temporarily	Chapter 1 for information on international and domestic legislation on migrants, and Chapter 7 for information specific to migrants who are persons granted leave to remain. You may also need to refer to the appendices.
A family member of a migrant or Irish national	either: • has permission to remain in the State as the family member of a migrant who is legally resident in Ireland • has permission to remain in the State as the family member of an Irish national	Chapter 1 for information on international and domestic legislation on migrants, and Chapter 8 for information specific to migrants who are family members of migrants or Irish nationals. You may also need to refer to the appendices.

You are in this category	If you are a migrant who...	You should read...
Person residing in the state without permission	either: • has entered the State without permission • has entered the State with permission for a specified period, but has remained on after that period without permission • has entered the State with permission, but has not registered with the Garda registration officer	Chapter 1 for information on international and domestic legislation on migrants, and Chapter 9 for information specific to migrants who are residing in the State without permission. You may also need to refer to the appendices.
Visitor	either: • has entered the State with permission for a specified period for the purpose of a visit to a person who is resident in Ireland, but do not have permission to enter employment, study or establish a business • has entered the State with permission for a specified period of time for the purpose of visiting Ireland as a tourist and who does not have permission to enter employment, study or establish a business	Chapter 1 for information on international and domestic legislation on migrants, and Chapter 10 for information specific to migrants who are visitors. You may also need to refer to the appendices.

The term 'non-national' is a legal term, which is why it is used throughout this manual. Usually, the Immigrant Council of Ireland prefers to refer to people by their own nationality.

Endnotes

1   United Nations Press Release, 15 December 2000 *http://www.un.org/news/press/docs/2000/200001215.pil305.doc.html*

2   UNHCR Discussion Paper 'Reconciling Migration Control and Refugee Protection in the European Union: A UNHCR Perspective'. October 2000 *http://www.unhcr.ch/cgi-bin/texis/vtx/home*

3   Ward, Eilis, 'Ireland and Refugees/Asylum seekers 1922 - 1996' in *The Expanding Nation: Towards a Multi-ethnic Ireland* Proceedings of a conference held in Trinity College Dublin 22-24 September 1998, p 41 *http://www.tcd.ie/sociology/mphil/dwnl/expanding_nation.pdf*

4   'Immigration policy will be developed as appropriate to address the needs of the labour market'. Programme for Prosperity and Fairness (available on the Citizens Information Database established by Comhairle *http://www.cidb.ie/*).

5   Department of Justice, Equality & Law Reform *Public Consultation on Immigration Policy* p. 6.

6   The Department of Justice, Equality & Law Reform *Report of the Public Consultation on Immigration Policy.* Available on the Department's website *http://www.justice.ie/*

7   International Organisation for Migration *International Comparative Study of Migration Legislation and Practice* commissioned by the Department of Justice, Equality & Law Reform, April 2002. Available from Government Publications, Molesworth Street, Dublin 1, or on the Department's website *http://www.justice.ie/*

8   *Irish Times* 1 March 2000 'Employers Back Plan to Bring 200,000 into State'.

9   For information relating to the asylum process and refugee status contact the Irish Refugee Council, 40 Lower Dominick Street, Dublin 1, telephone (01) 873 0042, website *http://www.irishrefugeecouncil.ie/*

What Legislation Relates to Migrants?

1.1 *What International Instruments Relate to Migrants?*

1.2 *What Domestic Legislation Relates to Migrants?*

WHAT LEGISLATION RELATES TO MIGRANTS?

1.1 What International Instruments Relate to Migrants?

While it must be acknowledged that the Irish State has the right to control the entry and residence of non-nationals, it is essential that immigration policy reflects Ireland's commitments under international law. This section describes briefly the principal international instruments relevant to immigration.

1.1.1 United Nations instruments

The *International Convention on the Protection of the Rights of All Migrant Workers and Members of their Families,* 1990, is the only UN instrument directly concerned with the rights of migrant workers. This Convention comes into force 1 July 2003. Ireland, in common with most countries that receive migrant workers, has not ratified the Convention.[a]

The Convention establishes minimum standards of protection for migrant workers. It is particularly significant because it recognises that migration is more than an economic phenomenon. Consequently, the families of migrant workers are also afforded rights under the Convention. The Convention defines a migrant worker as:

> ...*a person who is to be engaged, is engaged or has been engaged in remunerated activity in a State of which he or she is not a national.*[1]

The term 'migrant worker' encompasses several different types of worker: frontier worker,[b] seasonal worker, seafarer,[c] worker on an offshore installation, itinerant worker,[d] project-tied worker,[e] and self-employed worker.[f]

For the purposes of the Convention, members of the family of a migrant worker refers to:

> *Persons married to migrant workers or having with them a relationship that, according to applicable law, produces effects equivalent to marriage, as well as their dependent children and other dependent persons who are recognised as members of the family by applicable legislation or applicable bilateral or multilateral agreements between the States concerned.*[2]

a The Convention has been ratified by twenty-one States : Azerbaijan, Belize, Bolivia, Bosnia and Herzegovina, Cape Verde, Colombia, Ecuador, Egypt, El Salvador, Ghana, Guatemala, Guinea, Mexico, Morocco, Philippines, Senegal, Seychelles, Sri Lanka, Tajikistan, Uganda and Uruguay. For further details, see the website of the UN Commissioner for Human Rights *http://www.unhchr.ch/*

b According to Article 2 of the Convention, a frontier worker is "a migrant worker who retains his or her habitual residence in a neighbouring State to which he or she returns every day or at least once a week".

c According to Article 2 of the Convention, this category includes fishermen and is described as "a migrant worker employed on board a vessel registered in a State of which he or she is not a national".

d An itinerant worker is defined in Article 2 as a "migrant worker who, having his or her habitual residence in one state has to travel to another state or states for short periods owing to the nature of his or her occupation".

e The term 'project-tied worker' refers to a migrant worker admitted to a state of employment for a defined period, to work solely on a specific project being carried out in a State by his or her employer.

f According to Article 2, a self-employed worker is "a migrant worker who is engaged in a remunerated activity otherwise than under a contract of employment and who earns his or her living through this activity normally working alone or together with members of his or her family and to any other migrant recognised as self-employed by applicable legislation of the State of employment or bilateral or multilateral agreements".

Under the Convention, migrant workers and members of their families have the right to be fully informed by the State of origin or by the host State as appropriate "before their departure or at the latest at the time of their admission to the State of employment" about the conditions applicable to their admission, stay and work activities in the host State.[3] However, the Convention does not state that such information should be provided in a language the migrant understands.

Articles 22 and 56 of the Convention deal with the issue of expulsion from the State of employment. A decision to expel a migrant worker must be taken by the competent authority in accordance with law.[4] Such a decision must only be taken for reasons defined in the national legislation of the State of employment.[5] Article 22, paragraph 4 states that:

> *The person concerned shall have the right to submit the reasons why he or she should not be expelled and to have his or her case reviewed by the competent authority, unless compelling reasons of national security require otherwise.*

Ireland signed both Protocols that supplement the *UN Convention against Transnational Organised Crime* in December 2000, namely, the *Protocol to Suppress and Punish Trafficking in Persons Especially Women and Children* and the *Protocol Against the Smuggling of Migrants by Land, Sea and Air.*

Although the terms 'trafficking' and 'smuggling' are used interchangeably in the Protocols, there is a fundamental difference between them: 'trafficking' in persons is characterised by the exploitation of the victim and the abuse of power by the 'trafficker'.[6]

Trafficking is defined as:

> *...the recruitment, transportation, transfer, harbouring or receipt of persons, by threat or use of abduction, fraud, deception, coercion, or the abuse of power or by the giving or receiving of payments or benefits to achieve the consent of a person having control over another person, for the purposes of exploitation.[7]*

Smuggling is defined as:

> *...the procurement of the illegal entry into or illegal residence of a person in a State Party of which the person is not a national or permanent resident in order to obtain, directly or indirectly, a financial or other material benefit.[8]*

Persons who are trafficked usually work illegally in exploitative circumstances such as in sex work. The majority of trafficked persons are women and children. Smuggled persons are generally smuggled for the purposes of (illegal) employment or to seek international protection. In the latter case, people resort to smugglers due to the difficulty of travelling in a regular manner to another country such as visa restrictions, or the difficulty of obtaining valid documentation in their own country.

The issues of immigration and migrant workers have also been addressed at recent UN Conferences:

Recent UN Conference	Summary of what it said...
The World Conference on Human Rights Vienna, 1993	called on States to ratify the *International Convention on the Protection of the Rights of All Migrant Workers and Members of their Families* and encouraged them to protect the human rights of all migrant workers and their families. The Conference also emphasised the importance of creating conditions leading to greater harmony and tolerance between migrant workers and the host community in States of employment.
The International Conference on Population and Development, Cairo, 1994	addressed the issue of global migration and called for a comprehensive international approach to deal with it.
The World Summit for Social Development Copenhagen, 1995	called on States to ensure that migrant workers benefit from the protection they are afforded under international law, to ratify all relevant international instruments, and to take measures to ensure that migrant workers are not exploited. In addition, States were encouraged to combat illegal immigration and trafficking in persons while safeguarding the rights of undocumented migrants.
The Fourth World Conference on Women, Beijing, 1995	paid particular attention to the vulnerability of migrant women to violence and other forms of abuse and encouraged States to establish culturally appropriate services for women suffering gender-based violence.
The World Conference on Racism, Racial Discrimination, Xenophobia and Related Intolerance, Durban, 2001	urged States to facilitate family reunification expeditiously and acknowledged that such a measure would have a 'positive effect' on the integration of migrants and the host community. It also called for the

Recent UN Conference	Summary of what it said...
	humane treatment of migrants in detention regardless of their status in the host State, and emphasised the importance of providing effective legal protection and competent interpreting services for detained migrants.

The UN has further demonstrated its commitment to the rights of migrant workers and other migrants by appointing a Special Rapporteur on the human rights of migrants, and by the proclamation by the United Nations General Assembly of 4 December as International Migrants Day.

Also of relevance to migrant workers are:

Convention	Summary of what it says...
The *International Convention on the Elimination of All Forms of Racial Discrimination (ICERD)*	obliges States Parties to prohibit discrimination on the grounds of race, colour, descent or national or ethnic origin. However, it does not apply to: "distinctions, exclusions, restrictions or preferences made by a State Party...between citizens and non-citizens".[9] The convention is of limited use to migrants as the discrimination they encounter is often of this type. The convention has recently been ratified by Ireland.
The *UN Convention against Torture or Degrading Treatment or Punishment,* 1984	prohibits the return of a person to a state where they could face torture. Article 3 (1) of the Convention states: "No State Party shall expel, return ('refouler') or extradite a person to another State where there are substantial grounds for believing that he would be in danger of being subjected to torture."
The *UN Commission on Human Rights,* 2002	adopted a Resolution on the protection of migrants and their families,[10] which addresses several important issues including racism and access to remedies in situations where the rights of migrant workers have been infringed. The Commission also noted the treatment of migrants by immigration officials at borders, airports and ports of arrival and encouraged States to: "train public officials who work in these facilities and in border areas to treat migrants and their families respectfully and in accordance with the law".[11] Resolutions such as this are not binding on States, however.

1.1.2 *European instruments*

1.1.2.1 *Immigration from outside the EU*

Ireland joined the European Economic Community (EEC)[a] in 1973, at a time when Member States focused little attention on the issue of immigration. Since the creation of the EEC issues of immigration and asylum have gained increasing importance for Member States. Prior to the adoption of the Maastricht Treaty in 1992, asylum and immigration policy had been a matter for co-operation between the Member States. The Maastricht Treaty identified nine issues of common interest to Member States including asylum policy, rules governing crossing external borders and immigration policy and policy regarding third-country nationals. A number of instruments were adopted with regard to asylum and immigration, but for the most part these were not legally binding on Member States.[12] Thus, under the Maastricht Treaty asylum and immigration issues continued to depend on inter-governmental co-operation and not EU competence.[13]

In October 1997, the EU Heads of State and Government signed the Treaty of Amsterdam, which added a new Title IV on "visas, asylum, immigration and other policies relating to the free movement of persons" in the *EC Treaty*.[b]

Article 63 sets out measures to be adopted in the area of immigration with regard to:

- conditions of entry and residence and standards relating to the procedures for issuing long-term visas and residence permits including those for the purpose of family reunion
- illegal immigration and illegal residence including repatriation of illegal residents
- rights of third-country nationals resident in one Member State to reside in another Member State

To this end, the European Commission has adopted several proposed Directives that are now under consideration by the Council of the European Union or have been adopted by it.[c]

Also relevant to immigrants is the comprehensive non-discrimination provision, which was inserted into the *EC Treaty*. Article 13 of the *EC Treaty* states:

> *Without prejudice to the other provisions of this Treaty and within the limits of the powers conferred upon the community, the Council acting unanimously on a proposal from the Commission and after consulting the European Parliament, may take appropriate action to combat discrimination based on sex, racial or ethnic origin, religion or belief, disability, age or sexual orientation.*

a Later this became the European Union (EU).

b Unless otherwise stated, all references to the *EC Treaty* refer to the *EC Treaty* as amended by the Treaties of Amsterdam and Nice.

c With regard to immigration, the proposed directives deal with: family reunification, long-term residency, and economic migration. The Commission is currently working on a proposal dealing with students and persons coming to the EU for other purposes.

The Council has adopted two Directives implementing Article 13. The first prohibits discrimination on the basis of racial or ethnic origin,[14] and the second prohibits discrimination in employment on the basis of the grounds set out in Article 13.[15]

The EU has competence to conclude Readmission Agreements with third countries under Article 63(3)(b) of the *EC Treaty*. Readmission Agreements facilitate the expeditious expulsion of third-country nationals living in the host country without authorisation.[a] Individual Member States can also conclude bilateral Readmission Agreements, as Ireland has done.[b]

Several Protocols to the Amsterdam Treaty are noteworthy. From the Irish standpoint, the Fourth Protocol, under which Ireland may opt to participate in EU measures on immigration and asylum, is very significant. Article 1 states that:

> *Subject to Article 3 the United Kingdom and Ireland shall not take part in the adoption by the Council of proposed measures pursuant to Title IV of the Treaty establishing the European Community.*

Ireland can participate in adopted measures if it notifies the Presidency of the Council. Furthermore, it can decide that it no longer wishes to be covered by the Protocol.

The European Union has also concluded pre-accession agreements with a number of Central and Eastern European States.[c] Under these agreements, which are known as *Association Agreements*, nationals of these States are permitted to set up a business in a Member State and acquire residence there. The requirements for fulfilling criteria for setting up a business are governed by Member States themselves. Such persons do not have the right to travel freely within the European Union. However, most of them no longer require visas to travel to EU countries.

The issue of illegal immigration is of serious concern to EU Member States. Several initiatives are under consideration and the Council of the European Union agreed a Directive in May 2001, on the mutual recognition of decisions in the expulsion of third-country nationals. The provisions of this Directive apply to Ireland and it refers to expulsions based on a threat to public order or national security and safety in cases where a third-country national is convicted in a Member State of a crime, punishable by a term of imprisonment of at least one year, or if there are serious grounds for believing that the person has committed a serious crime, or if a third-country national contravenes entry and residence rules.[16]

---

a The 1999 Tampere Conclusions stated that: "The Amsterdam Treaty conferred powers on the Community in the field of readmission". The Commission invited the Council to conclude readmission agreements or to include standard clauses in other agreements between the European Community and relevant third countries or groups of countries. Consideration should also be given to rules on internal readmission. In September 2000, the Council authorised the Commission to negotiate readmission agreements on behalf of the EU with Russia, Morocco, Pakistan and Sri Lanka. In addition, standard readmission clauses are now included in association, partnership and stabilisation agreements concluded with third countries, for example with the states of the former Yugoslavia and the 2000 Cotonou agreements with the Asian, Pacific and Caribbean (APC) States.

b See Section 1.2.1.6 page 18.

c Czech Republic, Slovakia, Hungary, Poland, Bulgaria, Romania, Estonia, Lithuania and Latvia.

The aim of the Directive is to ensure greater effectiveness in enforcing expulsion decisions, and co-operation among States in recognising expulsion decisions made by other Member States.

In April 2002, the European Commission issued a Green Paper on a community return policy on illegal residents.

The Commission has drawn up a proposal for a Council Framework Decision on combating trafficking in human beings. This deals with both trafficking in persons for the purposes of labour exploitation and sexual exploitation. The Commission Proposal recognised that trafficked persons are not voluntary illegal immigrants, but have been brought to the host State by a variety of means including, deception, coercion, threats, and abduction. Rather than being criminals, they are victims. The Proposal requests that Member States:

> ...ensure that a victim of an offence provided for in this Framework Decision is given adequate legal protection and standing in judicial proceedings. In particular, Member States shall ensure that criminal investigations and judicial proceedings do not cause an additional damage for the victim.[a]

1.1.2.2 Free movement of nationals of EU Member States within the EU

Since the 1960's, several important Directives have been adopted providing for the free movement of EU nationals within the EU and their rights and entitlements.

The most significant of these are:

EU Directive	What it does...
The Council Directive of 15 October 1968, on the *Abolition of Restrictions on Movement and Residence within the Community for Workers of Member States and their Families* (68/360/EEC)	abolishes restrictions on the movement of nationals of the EU Member States who move to another EU State to take up employment. The Directive obliges Member States to permit such persons to enter their territory if they produce a valid passport or identity card.[17] In addition, Member States must grant them residence in their territory[18] and, as proof of residence, shall issue them with a 'residence permit for a National of a Member State of the EEC.[b]
The Council Directive of 21 May 1973, on the *Abolition of Restrictions on Movement and Residence within the Community for Nationals of Member States with Regard to Establishment and the Provision of Services* (73/148/EEC)	obliges States to remove restrictions on the movement and residence of EU nationals "who are established or who wish to establish themselves in another Member State in order to pursue activities as self-employed persons or who wish to provide services in that state". Such persons are permitted to reside in another Member State and shall be issued with a residence permit as in the case of workers, referred to above.

a The *Commission Proposal for a Council Framework Decision on Combating Trafficking in Human Beings,* Article 8. Although Ireland has legislation in place prohibiting trafficking in persons *(Illegal Immigrants (Trafficking) Act,* 2000), it provides no protections for the trafficked persons.

b European Economic Community (EEC). Later known as the European Union (EU).

EU Directive	What it does...
The Council Directive of 29 October 1993, on the *Right of Residence for Students* (93/96/EEC)	grants students the right of residence for the duration of their course in another Member State. If the course lasts more than one year, the student shall be issued with a residence permit which can be renewed annually.[19]

In addition, a series of Directives dealing with social policy and rights at work have been adopted including the Council Directive on the *Approximation of the Laws of Member States relating to the Application of the Principle of Equal Pay for Men and Women* (75/117/EC) under which Member States undertake to abolish all discrimination between men and women in relation to equal pay. A similar Directive obliges States to progressively implement the equal treatment of men and women in relation to social welfare.[20]

Other Directives relate to rights in the work place such as parental leave and organisation of working time.[21]

1.1.3 *Council of Europe instruments*

The Council of Europe was founded in 1949 and its aims are to guarantee democracy, human rights and the rule of law. Forty-four European States are currently members of the Council of Europe.

The principal Council of Europe instrument dealing with migrant workers is the *European Convention on the Legal Status of Migrant Workers* (1977). However, this is limited in application to nationals of a State Party, who have been permitted by another State Party to reside in its territory in order to take up employment. It has a much narrower scope than the *International Convention on the Protection of the Rights of All Migrant Workers and Members of their Families* since it does not apply to frontier workers, artists, seamen, persons undergoing training or seasonal workers who are carrying out specific work in a contracting state for a company whose registered office is not in that State.

States are required to provide migrant workers with information on:

> *...their residence, conditions and opportunities for family reunion, the nature of the job, the possibility of a new work contract being concluded after the first one has lapsed, the qualifications required, working and living conditions (including the cost of living, remuneration, social security, housing, food, the transfer of savings, travel and on deductions made from wages in respect of contributions for social protection and social security, taxes and other charges.*[22]

According to the Convention, migrant workers are entitled to family reunification but only in respect of their spouse and minor children.[23] Migrant workers and their families are entitled to education on the same basis as nationals of the host State and in general, they shall have the same rights with regard to social security[24] and social and medical assistance.[25]

Other Council of Europe Conventions that may afford additional rights to migrants are:

Council of Europe Convention	Summary of what it says...
The *European Convention on Establishment*, 1955	the Council of Europe was established with the aim of safeguarding and realising the ideals and principles which are the common heritage of its members and to facilitate their economic and social progress. The Council recognises the special character of the links between the member countries.
The *Convention on the Participation of Foreigners in Public Life at Local Level*, 1992	the Convention provides for different categories of measures. The "classical rights" of freedom of expression, assembly and association, including the right to form trade unions. The creation of consultative bodies at local level: participation in an advisory capacity in the deliberations of local authority commissions; consultative councils made up exclusively of foreigners. The right to vote in local elections, after five years residence in the host country, and to stand for election.
The *European Convention on Nationality*, 1997	embodies principles and rules applying to all aspects of nationality. It is designed to make acquisition of a new nationality and recovery of a former one easier, to ensure that nationality is lost only for good reason and cannot be arbitrarily withdrawn, to guarantee that the procedures governing applications for nationality are just, fair and open to appeal, and to regulate the situation of persons in danger of being left stateless as a result of state succession. It also covers multiple nationality, military obligations and co-operation between States Parties.
The *European Convention on Human Rights (ECHR)*, 1950	does not specifically address the issue of immigration but Article 3 (which prohibits torture and inhuman or degrading treatment or punishment) and Article 8 (which deals with the right of respect for the family and private life) are relevant as is the jurisprudence of the European Court of Human Rights in relation to these issues.[a]

a The Fourth Protocol to the ECHR, Article 4 also prohibits collective expulsion of non-nationals, both persons who are in the territory legally and those who are unlawfully resident.

Additionally, Article 14, of the ECHR provides that the rights afforded in the Convention shall be enjoyed without discrimination:

"The enjoyment of the rights and freedoms set forth in this Convention shall be secured without discrimination on any ground such as sex, race, colour, language, political or other opinion, national or social origin, association with a national minority, property, birth or other status."

Also of significance for migrants is the anti-discrimination provision contained in Protocol 12 to the ECHR, Article 1 of which states:

"1. The enjoyment of a right set forth by law shall be secured without discrimination on any ground such as sex, race, colour, language, religion, political or other opinion, national or social origin, association with a national minority, property, birth or other status.

2. No one shall be discriminated against by any public authority on any ground such as those mentioned in Part 1."

The EU *Revised Social Charter*, 1999

entered into force in July 1999, and will progressively replace the EU *Social Charter*, which guarantees social and economic rights.

The *Revised Social Charter* has been ratified by Ireland. Under Article 19 of the Charter "The right of migrant workers and their families to protection and assistance", ratifying States undertake to afford migrant workers and their families a wide range of rights in addition to those set out in Articles one to ten dealing with work and training. Among the most significant are that States must undertake:

"19.1. to maintain, or to satisfy themselves that there are maintained adequate and free services to assist such workers, particularly in obtaining accurate information, and to take all appropriate steps, so far as nationals laws and regulations permit, against misleading propaganda relating to emigration and immigration;

19.3. to promote co-operation, as appropriate between social services, public and private, in emigration and immigration countries;

Council of Europe Convention	Summary of what it says...
	19.6. to facilitate as far as possible the reunion of the family of a foreign worker permitted to establish himself in the territory;
	19.10. to extend the protection and assistance provided for in this article to self-employed migrants insofar as such measures apply;
	19.12. to promote and facilitate the teaching of the national language of the receiving state or, if there are several, one of these languages, to migrant workers and members of their families"

The Council of Europe has adopted several recommendations on immigration, which are not binding. They do, however, set out basic human rights that should be enjoyed by all immigrants and should form the basis for legislation and practice in this area. Among the most significant of these are two recent recommendations adopted by the Council of Europe Parliamentary Assembly:

Council of Europe Recommendation	Summary of what it says...
The *Recommendation on Homosexuals' Immigration and Asylum Rights*[26]	urges Council of Europe Member States "to ensure that homosexual partnerships and families are treated on the same basis as heterosexual partnerships and families", and "to take such measures as are necessary to ensure that bi-national lesbian and gay couples are accorded the same residence rights as bi-national heterosexual couples".[27]
The *Recommendation on the Security of Residence of Long-term Migrants*[28]	includes provisions on: the acquisition of secure residence for long-term migrants, the acquisition of nationality, the withdrawal of secure residence, and protection against expulsion.

The Parliamentary Assembly of the Council of Europe has warned States of the dangers of restrictions on immigration, in particular that:

"...draconian restrictions on lawful immigration introduced by European Countries increase the likelihood of persons illegally entering Europe since they encourage recourse to the services of unscrupulous traffickers of human beings, using increasingly sophisticated and inhuman means to make money out of clandestine migration".[29]

Most of the articles and recommendations of the Council of Europe do not have any legally-binding effect.

1.1.4 *International Labour Organisation instruments*

The International Labour Organisation(ILO) was founded after the First World War and is the only international organisation dedicated to the protection of workers' rights. The ILO Membership includes Non-governmental Organisations (NGOs) and trade unions.

The International Labour Organisation has recognised that migrant workers are more vulnerable to exploitation than other workers and require additional safeguards. To this end, it has concluded several Conventions directly related to migrant workers, in particular:

Convention	Summary of what it says...
Migration for Employment Convention (Revised) 1949, (No.97)	obliges States to maintain a free service to assist migrant workers with employment particularly in relation to providing them with accurate information. If the State itself does not provide such a service it must ensure that the service is provided.[30] States Parties must make available to the ILO on request information on issues relating to immigration, on national legislation and policy relating to both immigration and emigration, on special provisions relating to migration for employment and conditions of work for migrant workers.
	Moreover, States must treat immigrants equally to their own nationals, without discrimination in respect of nationality, race, religion or sex in relation to:
	• remuneration, including hours of work, overtime arrangements, holidays with pay and apprenticeships and training
	• membership of trade unions and the benefits of collective bargaining
	• accommodation
Migrant Workers (Supplementary Provisions) Convention 1975, (No. 143)	requires that States undertake to respect the fundamental rights of all workers.[31] The Convention deals mainly with the issue of illegal immigration and measures to combat it. However, it states in Article 8 that a migrant worker:
	"shall not be regarded as in an illegal or irregular situation by the mere fact of the loss of his employment, which shall not in itself imply the withdrawal of his authorisation of residence or, as the case may be, employment permit."

The Convention emphasises equality of opportunity and treatment for migrant workers. Each State must undertake to:

"...pursue a national policy designed to promote and to guarantee, by methods appropriate to national conditions and practice, equality of opportunity and treatment in respect of employment and occupation, of social security, of trade union and cultural rights and of individual and collective freedoms for persons who as migrant workers or as members of their families are lawfully within its territories."[32]

Furthermore, States must take all steps to assist and encourage migrant workers and their families to preserve their culture including the possibility of mother-tongue classes for the children of migrants.[33]

Prior to the adoption of Convention No. 143, the ILO preparatory report emphasised the importance of family reunion and the negative effects of the separation of migrant workers from their families in their home country:

"Prolonged separation and isolation lead to hardship and stress situations affecting both the migrants and the families left behind and prevent them from leading a normal life. The large numbers of migrant workers cut off from social relations and living on the fringe of the receiving community create many well-known social and psychological problems that, in turn, largely determine attitudes towards migrant workers."[34]

In addition, the ILO has issued two recommendations: *Recommendation Concerning Migrants for Employment* (No. 86) and *Recommendation Concerning Migrant Workers* (No. 151).

Although Ireland has ratified several ILO Conventions, which apply to all workers,[35] it has not ratified the Conventions relating specifically to migrant workers.

1.2 What Domestic Legislation Relates to Migrants?

This section describes briefly the principal domestic legislation relevant to immigration.

1.2.1 General Irish legislation

1.2.1.1 The Aliens Act, 1935

The *Aliens Act,* 1935, replaced the existing *Aliens Restriction Act,* 1914, and the *Aliens Restriction (Amendment) Act,* 1919, both pieces of legislation inherited from the British legal system. The *Aliens Act* grants wide powers to the Minister for Justice to regulate all aspects of the lives of non-nationals[a] in the State. This includes their entry to, departure from, movement around and residence in the State. Section 2 of the Act defines an alien as "a person who is not a citizen of Saorstat Eireann".[b]

Section 5 of the Act provides the Minister with extensive powers to make orders under the Act with regard to the control of non-nationals, including:

- prohibiting certain non-nationals from landing in, or entering the State
- entering the State including limiting such landing or prohibiting such entering or landing at a particular place
- leaving the State including prohibiting aliens from embarking on ships or aircrafts
- imposing restrictions and conditions on certain non-nationals with regard to landing in or entering the State
- prohibiting certain non-nationals from leaving the State

Penalties may be imposed in respect of non-nationals who act in contravention of an Aliens Order. Numerous Orders have been made under the Act, the most significant being those of 1946 and 1975. Under these Orders leave to land may be refused to a non-national in certain circumstances. Under the 1946 Order (as amended by the 1975 Order), an Immigration Officer who refuses leave to land, must as soon as possible inform the person in question in writing of the ground or grounds on which leave to land has been refused. It also provides that the 'alien' may be arrested and detained by an Immigration Officer or a member of the Gardaí.

Section 5 (1)(e) of the 1935 Act dealing with the deportation of non-nationals was found to be unconstitutional[36] and new legislation was enacted to provide for deportation. This new legislation is the *Immigration Act,* 1999.

1.2.1.2 The Immigration Act, 1999

The *Immigration Act,* 1999 in Section 3(1), provides that:

> *Subject to the provisions of Section 5 (prohibition of refoulement) of the Refugee Act, 1996, and the subsequent provisions of this section, the Minister may by order (in this Act referred to as a 'deportation order') require any non-national specified in the order to leave the State within such a period as may be specified in the order and to remain thereafter out of the State'.*

a Non-nationals are referred to as 'aliens' in the Act.

b This does not include a person born in the United Kingdom.

The Act lists the persons in respect of whom the Minister may make a deportation order and the matters the Minister shall consider when deciding whether to make a deportation order.

The *Immigration Act* also provided for amendments to be made to the *Refugee Act* in particular with regard to the functions of the Refugee Applications Commissioner and fingerprinting asylum seekers.

1.2.1.3 *Illegal Immigrants Trafficking Act, 2000*

The *Illegal Immigrants (Trafficking) Act,* 2000, prohibits trafficking of illegal immigrants. Section 2 of the Act states:

> *A person who organises or knowingly facilitates the entry into the State of a person whom he or she knows or has reasonable cause to believe to be an illegal immigrant or a person who intends to seek asylum shall be guilty of an offence...*

In addition, the Act permits the Gardaí to detain vehicles used by a person accused of trafficking and empowers the State to forfeit ships, aircraft and other vehicles.[a]

1.2.1.4 *The Irish Nationality and Citizenship Acts, 1956 - 2001*

These Acts set out the conditions under which non-nationals may apply for, and be granted, Irish citizenship. They also provide for the making of post-nuptial declarations by spouses of Irish nationals who got married to the Irish national on or before 29 November 2002, and continue to be in a subsisting marriage.
In general, the Minister for Justice, Equality & Law Reform may grant an application for a certificate of naturalisation at their discretion if they are satisfied that the applicant:

- is of full age
- is of good character
- has had one year of continuous residence in Ireland immediately prior to his/her application, and in the eight years immediately preceding that period, has had a total of four years of residence in Ireland
- intends in good faith to reside in Ireland after naturalisation
- has made a declaration of fidelity to the nation and loyalty to the State, either before a District Court Justice or in such other manner permitted by the Minister

In certain cases, the Minister has the power to dispense with the conditions of naturalisation.[b]

The *Irish Nationality and Citizenship Act*, 2001, which came into force 30 November 2002, has made substantial changes to the previous Acts; in particular, persons born in Ireland are no longer automatically Irish citizens, but are entitled to Irish citizenship if they do "any act which only an Irish citizen is entitled to do".[37] The Act does not specify what such acts may be, however.

In addition, the Act makes changes to the previous provisions dealing with the naturalisation of spouses of Irish citizens[38] and the calculation of the period of residence in relation to application for naturalisation for certain categories of non-nationals.[39]

a The Act also amends other legislation including the *Refugee Act 1996*, and the *Immigration Act 1999*.

b The *Irish Nationality and Citizenship Act 1956*, Section 16 (as amended by the *Irish Nationality and Citizenship Act 1986*, Section 5). This no longer applies to persons married to a naturalised Irish citizen or persons married to a person who is an Irish citizen (otherwise than by naturalisation).

1.2.1.5 Criminal Justice Act (UN Convention against Torture) Act, 2000[a]

This Act provides that a person shall not be returned to a country where:

> ...the Minister is of the opinion that there are substantive grounds for believing that the person would be in danger of being subjected to torture.

This provision is particularly relevant in the case of persons in respect of whom the Minister is considering making a deportation order and who have made representations under Section 3 of the *Immigration Act* to the Minister requesting permission to remain in Ireland, as they believe that they face torture should they be returned to their country.

1.2.1.6 Readmission Agreements

Readmission Agreements facilitate the return of persons residing without authorisation in another State, to their country of origin.

The Irish Government has concluded Readmission Agreements with the Governments of Romania (12 May 2000) and Nigeria (29 August 2001). Further Readmission Agreements are to be concluded with Poland and Bulgaria.

These Readmission Agreements provide for the:

- readmission to either State of citizens of the other State who are residing in the first State without authorisation

- readmission of citizens of a third country who arrived in either State from the other State without authorisation

- return of persons to a third country by transiting either State

The Readmission Agreements set out the repatriation procedures and the method of establishing nationality to be followed. Proof of nationality is usually established through official documents, including a passport, identity card, citizenship certificates and other official documents stating the person's citizenship. Other evidence that may be considered, include a driving licence, company identity card, statements made by witnesses and statements of the person concerned.

In circumstances where evidence to conclusively establish nationality cannot be obtained, but it is possible to presume nationality, the requesting State may request the assistance of diplomatic and consular officials in the requested State to help determine the nationality of the person. This will be done by means of an interview with the person concerned.[40]

---

a The main purpose of the Act is to create a statutory offence of torture and thus enable Ireland to ratify the *UN Convention Against Torture*, which it signed in 1992.

Endnotes

1   *The International Convention on the Protection of the Rights of All Migrant Workers and Members of Their Families* 1990, Article 2.1.

2   *Ibid,* Article 4.

3   *Ibid,* Article 37.

4   *Ibid,* Article 22, paragraph 2.

5   *Ibid,* Article 56, paragraph 5.

6   European Council for Refugees and Exiles (ECRE) *An Overview of Proposals Addressing Migrant Smuggling and Trafficking in Persons* ECRE Background Paper July 2001, ECRE, London (2001) http://www.ecre.org/policy/research/smuggle.shtml

7 *Ibid.*

8 *Ibid.*

9 *The International Convention on the Elimination of All Forms of Racial Discrimination* 21 December 1965, Article 1(2).

10 *United Nations Commission on Human Rights Resolution* 2002/59.

11 *Ibid.*

12 Immigration Law Practitioners Association (ILPA) and Minority Protection Group (MPG) *The Amsterdam Proposals* ILPA, London (2000).The ILPA and MPG proposed Directives on immigration and asylum.

13 For further information, see website http://migration.ucc.ie/bordersofotherness.

14 Council Directive 2000/43/EC, 29 June 2000 *Implementing the Principle of Equal Treatment Between Persons Irrespective of Racial or Ethnic Origin* OJ 2000 L180/22.

15 Council Directive 2000/78/EC, 27 November 2000 *Establishing a General Framework for Equal Treatment in Employment and Occupation* OJ 2000 L303/16.

16 Council Directive 2001/40/EC, 28 May 2001, Article 3 (1)(a), OJ 2001 L149/34.

17 Council Directive 68/360/EEC, 15 October 1968 on *Abolition of Restrictions on Movement and Residence within the Community for Workers of Member States and their Families* Article 3.

18 *Ibid* Article 4.

19 Other relevant Directives and Regulations are:
Council Regulation 68/1612/EEC, 15 October 1968, on *Freedom of Movement for Workers within the Community,* as amended by Regulation 76/312/EEC, OJ 1976 L39/2 (9 February 1976).
Council Directive 75/34/EEC, 17 December 1974, concerning the *Right of Nationals of a Member State to Remain in the Territory of Another Member State after Having Pursued Therein an Activity in a Self-employed Capacity.*
Council Directive 90/365/EEC, 28 June 1990, on the *Right of Residence of Employees and Self-employed Persons who have Ceased their Occupational Activity* OJ 1990 L180/28.

20 Council Directive 79/7/EEC, 19 December 1978 on the *Progressive Implementation of the Principle of Equal Treatment for Men and Women in Matters of Social Security* OJ 1979 L6/24.

21 Council Directive 93/104/EC, 23 November 1993 *Concerning Certain Aspects of the Organisation of Working Time* OJ 193 L307/18, and Council Directive 96/34/EC, 3 June 1996 on the *Framework Agreement on Parental Leave,* concluded by UNICE, CEEA and the ETUC. *The Organisation of Working Time Act,* 1997, and the *Parental Leave Act,* 1998, give effect to these Directives in Ireland, OJ 1996 L145/4.

22 *European Convention on the Legal Status of Migrant Workers* 1977.

23 *Ibid,* Article 12.

24 *Ibid,* Article 18.

25 *Ibid,* Article 19.

26 Council of Europe, Parliamentary Assembly, Recommendation 1470 (2000): *Situation of Gays and Lesbians and their Partners in Respect of Asylum and Immigration in the Member States of the Council of Europe.*

27 *Ibid,* Article 7(ii)(d) and (e).

28 Committee of Ministers Recommendation Rec 15 (2000) 13 September 2000 *Concerning the Security of Residence of Long-term Migrants.*

29 Council of Europe, Parliamentary Assembly Recommendations 1449 and 1467, (2000).

30 *ILO Migration for Employment Convention (Revised)* 1949 (No. 97), Article 2, available at http://www.ilo.org/.

31 *ILO Migrant Workers (Supplementary Provisions) Convention* 1975, (No. 143), Article 1, available at http://www.ilo.org/

32 *Ibid,* Article 10.

33 *Ibid,* Article 12(f).

34 International Labour Organisation (ILO) Migrant Workers, Report VII (1) International Conference, 59th Session, Geneva June, 1974, p. 27 quoted in the ILO *Report of the Committee of Experts,* p.188.

35 ILO Conventions ratified by Ireland include: *Freedom of Association and Protection of the Right to Organise Convention* 1948 (No 87), the *Equal Remuneration Convention* 1951 (No. 100) and the *Discrimination (Employment and Occupation) Convention* (No. 111).

36 *Laurentiu v Minister for Justice* (1999) 4 IR 26.

37 *Irish Nationality and Citizenship Act* 2001, Sections 6 (1) and 6 (2)(a).

38 *Irish Nationality and Citizenship Act* 1956, Section 15 A as amended by the *Irish Nationality and Citizenship Act* 2001, Section 5.

39 *Irish Nationality and Citizenship Act* 1956, Section 16 A as amended by the *Irish Nationality and Citizenship Act* 2001, Section 6.

40 *Agreement Between the Government of Ireland and the Government of the Federal Republic of Nigeria on Immigration Matters,* Article VI.

Migrant Workers

MIGRANT WORKERS

The rights and entitlements of migrant workers depend largely on two factors:

- Where they come from, that is whether they are a national of an EEA State[a] or Switzerland. EEA and Swiss nationals generally have more rights and entitlements than persons from outside the EEA; they do not require permission to work here and there are less formalities required for their entry to and residence in the State. In addition, Turkish workers are also entitled to certain rights under the terms of the EU-Turkey Association Agreement.[1]

- What they do, for example, non-EEA nationals as persons who are employed under the working visa/work authorisation scheme, which applies to highly-skilled workers, generally have more rights and entitlements than those employed under the employment permit scheme.

2.1 *EEA and Swiss Nationals*

2.1.1 *EU nationals*

The status of Citizenship of the Union was introduced by the Treaty of Maastricht (1992). Article 17 of the *EC Treaty*[b] states:

> *Citizenship of the Union is hereby established. Every person holding the nationality of a Member State shall be a citizen of the Union. Citizenship of the Union shall complement and not replace national citizenship.*
>
> *Citizens of the Union shall enjoy the rights conferred by this Treaty and shall be subject to the duties imposed thereby.*

Article 18(1) of the *EC Treaty* states:

> *Every Citizen of the Union shall have the right to move and reside freely within the territory of the Member States, subject to the limitations and conditions laid down by this Treaty and by the measures adopted to give it effect.*

The right to move and reside referred to in Article 18(1) may be subject to limits and conditions but the competent authorities and, where necessary, the national courts must ensure that these limitations and conditions are applied in compliance with the general principles of Community law and, in particular, the principle of proportionality.[2]

The Commission has proposed replacing these Directives with a general all-embracing Directive to deal with citizens' migration rights, but this not been adopted yet.[3] However, it is clear that the effect of Article 18(1) is such that once a Citizen of the Union is lawfully resident in the territory of another Member State, they are entitled to equal treatment with nationals of that State in most circumstances. For example, regarding welfare rights equal treatment extends to all EU migrants, regardless of whether they are workers, service providers or simply visitors, provided they are lawfully resident.[4] Regarding political rights, Citizens of the Union have the right to vote and stand in both municipal and European elections, when resident in another Member State.

---

a European Economic Area (EEA): EU Member States (Austria, Belgium, Denmark, Finland, France, Germany, Greece, Republic of Ireland, Italy, Luxembourg, Netherlands, Portugal, Spain, Sweden and the UK) and Norway, Iceland and Liechtenstein.

b Unless otherwise stated, all references to the *EC Treaty* refer to the *EC Treaty* as amended by the Treaties of Amsterdam and Nice.

The rights conferred by the Treaty also include freedom of movement for workers. Article 39 states that:

> *Such freedom of movement shall entail the abolition of any discrimination based on nationality between workers of the Member States as regards employment, remuneration and other conditions of work and employment.*

Employers are not required to obtain an employment permit when employing EU nationals.

2.1.2 EEA nationals

In 1994, the *European Economic Area Agreement* was signed between the European Union and Norway, Iceland and Liechtenstein. Nationals of these states enjoy certain rights within the EU and as a consequence can work in Ireland without an employment permit. This also applies to their non-EEA spouse and children under the age of 21, or dependent children over that age. EEA nationals do not need a visa to enter Ireland to take up employment or for any other purpose.

2.1.3 Swiss nationals

The *European Communities and Swiss Confederation Act*, 2001, came into force in June 2002. As a result, Swiss nationals now have the same rights as EEA nationals in Ireland. Therefore, Swiss workers can engage in employment without an employment permit or authorisation.[5] Swiss nationals do not need a visa to enter Ireland to take up employment or for any other purpose.

2.2 Non-EEA and Swiss Nationals[a]

Non-EEA and Swiss nationals, with the exception of persons in the categories listed in Section 2.2.2, page 26 may not work in Ireland without permission. This permission may take the form of an employment permit, work authorisation or working visa depending on the type of employment, and whether the applicant is required to possess a visa in order to travel to Ireland.

The *Employment Permits Act* restates the existing law regarding persons (not otherwise entitled to do so) working without a work permit (now to be called an employment permit). It creates a specific offence for both an employer and an employee where employment is entered into in the absence of a requisite permit. It also provides for penalties for non-compliance. Penalties range from €3,000 or 12 months in prison (or both) for a summary conviction, and up to €250,000 and 10 years in prison (or both) for conviction on indictment. The provision remedies a defect in the present legal basis on which the employment permit system operates, whereby there is no charge which can be brought against an employer who employs persons not entitled to work in the State without an employment permit, in the absence of such a permit.

---

a Turkish nationals should see Section 2.3, page 25, and nationals of the accession states joining the EU in 2004 should see Section 2.4, page 25.

2.2.1 *What types of work permissions for Non-EEA and Swiss nationals exist*

The following table outlines the types of work permissions for Non-EEA and Swiss nationals:

Type of permission	Rules
Employment permits	<ul><li>are not granted to migrant workers themselves</li><li>may be granted to employers who wish to recruit workers from outside the European Economic Area (EEA)</li><li>can cover periods of one month to one year and may be renewed</li><li>the employee is only permitted to change employment if the new employer has obtained an employment permit in respect of the person, prior to them entering the new employment</li></ul>In general, employment permits will not be granted (however, there may be room for discretion in certain cases) if:[a]<ul><li>the prospective employee is in the State illegally</li><li>the prospective employee has entered the State on the basis that they will not take up employment</li><li>the prospective employee has been deported or is in the process of being deported</li><li>the prospective employer is operating in Ireland without business permission from the Minister for Justice, Equality & Law Reform</li></ul>
Work authorisations	<ul><li>the person applying for a work authorisation must have an offer and contract of employment from an employer in Ireland in one of the designated sectors (see Section 2.5.5.1, page 31)</li><li>are issued to persons who hold a passport of a country whose nationals are not required to have a visa to travel to Ireland (see Appendix A).</li></ul>
Working visas	<ul><li>the person applying for a working visa must have an offer and contract of employment from an employer in Ireland in one of the designated sectors (see Section 2.5.5.1, page 31)</li><li>are issued to the holder of the passport of a country whose passport holders are required to possess a visa in order to travel to Ireland (see Appendix A)</li></ul>

a Employment permit and work authorisation schemes have no statutory basis.

2.2.2 Are there any Non-EEA or Swiss nationals who can engage in employment without these work permissions?

The following Non-EEA and Swiss nationals can engage in employment in Ireland without an employment permit, working visa/work authorisation:

- Persons who are recognised as refugees by the Minister for Justice, Equality & Law Reform.

- Asylum seekers who have made an application for refugee status before 26 June 1999. Asylum seekers who have arrived in Ireland since that date are not permitted to work.[a]

- Post-graduate students when the work is part of the course being undertaken. In such cases, a letter must be obtained from the college where the applicant is a student. This includes post-graduate doctors who are temporarily registered with the Irish Medical Council and dentists who are temporarily registered.

- Persons who are granted permission to remain as the spouse of an EEA national. Such persons must be granted leave to remain before taking up employment.

- Persons who are granted permission to remain as the parent of an Irish citizen. Such persons must be granted leave to remain before taking up employment.

- Persons whose application for refugee status has been refused but who are given temporary leave to remain. Such persons must be granted leave to remain before taking up employment.

- Non-EEA nationals who are legally employed in one EU Member State and who are temporarily sent on contract to another Member State.[6]

- Persons who are coming to Ireland for a period of training of up to three years at an Irish-based company.[b] Such persons need to satisfy Immigration Officers that they come within this category. Therefore, they must bring letters from the person's overseas employer and the Irish company where the training will take place with them, setting out the nature and duration of the training. The letters should relate only to the person concerned, and should not be general letters covering a number of trainees. These letters should be originals and must be given to the Immigration Officer.

- Persons who are sent on secondment or intra-company transfer to a company in Ireland, which is owned by a company or group, which has operations in more than one State.[c] The person concerned must be an existing employee of the company or group. Such persons will be required to satisfy Immigration Officers that they come within this category and should therefore, bring an original letter with them (relating only to the person concerned) from the company or group headquarters stating that the person in question is being posted to the Irish branch for the particular purpose and duration. The letter must be given to the Immigration Officer.

a The situation with regard to asylum seekers engaging in employment is unclear. While asylum seekers who applied for refugee status before 26 June 1999, were informed by the Department of Justice, Equality & Law Reform that they are permitted to work, the *Refugee Act, 1996* prohibits asylum seekers from engaging in employment. According to the *Refugee Act*, Section 9(4)(b) "An applicant [for Refugee Status] shall not seek or enter employment or carry on any business, trade or profession during the period before the final determination of his/her application for a declaration".

b The Non-EEA Trainee Scheme was suspended by the government 29 October 2002, following growing evidence of extensive misuse of the scheme (see press release on the Department of Trade and Enterprise website *http://www.entemp.ie/*)

c The Intra-Company Transfer Scheme was suspended by the government 29 October 2002, following growing evidence of extensive misuse of the scheme (see press release on the Department of Trade and Enterprise website *http://www.entemp.ie/*)

- Non-EEA national spouses and children of EEA and Swiss nationals in employment or self-employment in Ireland.[7]

- Persons to whom the EU Directive on posting of workers in the framework of the provision of services applies.[a]

Persons who may engage in employment in Ireland without an employment permit, must however, be in possession of a valid visa if they come from a country whose passport holders require a visa in order to travel to Ireland (see Appendix A).

2.3 Turkish Nationals

The *EU Association Agreement* of 1963 and the *Additional Protocol* of 1970, provide for the freedom of movement to workers.[8] Workers are afforded certain rights to reside in the EU under the terms of the Agreement and Protocol. Member States are not permitted to discriminate between Turkish and EU nationals with regard to work and remuneration.[9]

However, before a Turkish National can come to Ireland to work, they need to obtain a working visa, or find an employer to obtain permission to employ them, and obtain an entry visa prior to their arrival.

The main benefit under the Turkey Association Agreement is for those who have been admitted to Ireland in an immigration category that allows access to employment, for example, as a worker or spouse of an Irish/EEA national. Regulations, known as Decision 1/80 issued under the authority of the Turkish Association Council, state that after completing a period of one year in employment, a Turkish national has the right to a residence permit, allowing him/her to continue in that same employment for a further three years. On completion of the fourth year, a Turkish national in this situation acquires a right to a residence permit which will allow them to take up any employment.[10]

2.4 Nationals of Accession States Joining the EU in 2004

The Government has proposed[11] and the Oireachtas has recently passed the *Employment Permits Act* 2003, which will allow full freedom of access to the Irish labour market for nationals from the ten states which will become members of the EU from May 2004. This decision is in line with the approach being followed by Denmark, the Netherlands, Sweden, Spain, Greece, and the UK. These accession states are:

- Czech Republic

- Estonia

- Latvia

- Lithuania

- Hungary

a Directive 96/71/EC of the European Parliament and of the Council 16 December 1996, concerning the posting of workers in the framework of the provision of services. A 'posted' worker means "a worker who, for a limited period, carries out his work in the territory of a Member State other than the State where he normally works", OJ 1997 L18/1.

- Poland

- Slovenia

- Slovakia

- Cyprus (already provided for in Treaty of Accession)

- Malta (already provided for in Treaty of Accession)

Employment permits will not be required by citizens of the EU accession states once they have joined the EU. However, provision is made for the re-imposition of employment permits during the seven-year transition period if labour market conditions so require. While nationals of these countries will continue to need to apply for employment permits until that time, the Government has also decided[12] that they will be given preference over other applicants.

2.5 Applying for Employment Permits, Visas, and Working Visas / Work Authorisations

2.5.1 Applying for employment permits

Employment permits can only be applied for by, and be granted to, employers. All employers who wish to employ non-EEA nationals must advertise the vacancy or vacancies in Ireland.[a] The vacancy must also be advertised with FÁS CALLNET. The vacancies will then be put on the EURES and EEA websites; this can be done in parallel with the national advertising. If the employer is not successful in filling the vacancies in question, they must contact FÁS who will forward the relevant documentation to enclose with the employment permit application.

The Government has recently announced major changes in the employment permit scheme. Following consultations with FÁS, the Department of Enterprise, Trade & Employment will define, on a quarterly basis, those sectors which will be ineligible for employment permits. A very wide list of excluded sectors has been announced with immediate effect, and is listed in the following Section.

2.5.1.1 Occupational sectors ineligible for employment permits

The following sectors were ineligible for employment permits according to the Department of Enterprise, Trade & Employment's press release of 7 April 2003:

- clerical and administrative
- general labourers and builders
- operator and production staff
- sales staff including retail sales, sales representatives and management/ supervisory/specialist sales
- transport staff including drivers (bus, coach, car, taxi, forklift, HGV and so on)
- childcare workers including nursery/crèche workers, childminder/nanny
- hotel tourism and catering

---

a They should keep a record of the advertisements to submit with their application for an employment permit.

- reception staff and barpersons
- craft workers including mechanic (aircraft), bookbinder, bricklayer, cabinetmaker, carpenter/joiner, carton maker, fitter (construction plant) electrician, instrumentation craftsperson, fitter, tiler (floor/wall), mechanic (heavy vehicles) instrumentation craftsperson, metal fabricator, mechanic (motor), network administrator (IT) originator, painter and decorator, plumber, printer, refrigeration engineer, sheet metal worker, tool maker, vehicle body repairer, wood machinist.

When applying for an employment permit, an employer must send the following information to the Department of Enterprise, Trade & Employment:

- a completed application form which may be downloaded from the Department of Enterprise, Trade & Employment website at http://www.entemp.ie/
- two recent passport photographs of the prospective employee(s)
- relevant documentation from FÁS (Forms WP3 and WP6, referrals and copy of FÁS advertisement)
- the relevant fee[a]
- evidence of qualifications if the employee is required to hold certain qualifications
- a copy of the employee's passport
- evidence that the position has been advertised in Ireland

2.5.2 Renewing employment permits

An employer may apply for a renewal of an existing employment permit. To do this they must provide the Department of Enterprise, Trade & Employment with:

- an application form,[13] completed by the employer
- a copy of the employee's latest P60[b]
- a copy of the employee's passport
- the relevant fee[a]
- two passport photographs of the employee

When renewing employment permits, the employer will not have to produce documentation from FÁS.

The ability of an employer to renew an employment permit already issued will not be affected by the recent announcement of certain occupational sectors as ineligible for employment permits (see Section 2.5.1.1, page 28). Applications for the renewal of an employment permit must be made at least twenty-five days before the expiry of the current permit.

a The fees for employment permits are as follows: one month €65; two months €95; three months €125; four months €170; five months €210 and six months to one year €500 (as of 6 January 2003).

b At the end of each tax year the employer gives the employee a P60, which gives details of gross pay and all the deductions made during the year.

In circumstances where an employer applies for an employment permit for a former employee who has not left Ireland, or for an employee who previously worked in Ireland under the employment permit scheme but for a different employer, a new employment permit must be obtained.

For certain categories of employees, slightly different regulations apply when making an application for an employment permit:

Category of employee	Variation on employment permit requirements
Domestic staff	An application for an employment permit will only be granted where it has been established that the particular employee has been in employment abroad with the employer applying for the employment permit for at least one year.[14] Evidence that the applicable tax has been paid in respect of the employment abroad must also be provided.
'Ethnic' restaurant staff	Restaurants that provide speciality food may be granted several employment permits for each branch in respect of qualified chefs and catering staff, due to the specialised nature of the restaurants. The number of permits granted depends on the type of restaurant and the number of EEA nationals employed there.[15]

2.5.3 Applying for visas

Persons coming to Ireland to take up employment under the employment permit scheme, who are nationals of a state whose passport holders require a visa in order to travel to Ireland, must obtain a visa.[a] Applications can be made:

- through the Irish Embassy/Consulate in the applicant's country of residence
- through any Irish Embassy or Consulate if there is none in the applicant's country of residence
- by post, directly to the Visa Office, Department of Foreign Affairs, 13/14 Burgh Quay, Dublin 2, if there is no Irish Embassy or Consulate in the applicant's country of residence

Applicants must include the following documentation with their application:

- a completed visa application form
- a passport, which is valid to at least the date of expiry of the employment permit (or a full copy of the passport if the application is being made by post, or directly to the Department of Foreign Affairs)
- evidence that the applicant has been offered a job in Ireland and that their employer has obtained a employment permit for them
- the visa application fee[b]
- two passport photographs of the applicant

a Under the provisions of the *Aliens (Visas) Order* 2002 (SI No. 178 of 2002), certain non-nationals are not required to possess a visa to travel to Ireland. Persons from states not listed are required to have a visa (see Appendix A).

b Visa application processing fees are currently: €25 for a single journey and €50 for a multiple entry visa. Citizens of the following countries are exempt for the visa application fee: Bosnia, Bulgaria, Ecuador, Indonesia, Ivory Coast, Kirghizstan, Morocco, Peru, Slovak Republic, Sri Lanka, Tanzania, Tunisia, Uganda, Yugoslavia and Zambia (as of 1 January 2002).

If insufficient information is provided, the applicant may be asked to furnish the required information. However, some applications may be refused without any further information being sought. Therefore, it is advisable to submit evidence of the qualification of the employee together with their visa application.

In some circumstances, the applicant will be asked to provide the name of a person in Ireland who may be asked to supply further information. This person would normally be the employer to whom the employment permit, relevant for the applicant, has been granted.

2.5.4 *Appealing visa applications that have been refused*

A person whose application for a visa has been refused may apply to the Visa Section of the Department of Justice, Equality & Law Reform to have the application reviewed by a more senior official. Before doing so, they should request the reasons for the initial refusal of the visa application; these are not automatically provided but in most cases contain important information relevant to the appeal.

2.5.5 *Applying for working visas/work authorisations*

Working visas are issued to prospective employees who are nationals of states whose passport holders need a visa to travel to Ireland (see Appendix A). They must have a job offer and contract of employment from an employer in Ireland in one of the designated sectors listed below.

Work authorisations are issued to prospective employees who are nationals of states whose passport holders do not need a visa to travel to Ireland (see Appendix A). They must have a job offer and contract of employment from an employer in Ireland in one of the designated sectors listed below.

2.5.5.1 *Designated employment sectors*

- information and computing technologies professionals
- information and computing technologies technicians
- architects, including architectural technicians/technologists
- construction engineers, including engineering technicians
- quantity surveyors and building surveyors
- town planners
- medical practitioners
- registered nurses
- dentists
- the following health and social care professionals: audiologist, biochemist, cardiac catheterisation technician, diagnostic or therapeutic radiographer, dietician, ECG technician, hospital pharmacist, medical physicist, medical scientist, occupational therapist, orthoptist, neurophysiological measurement technician, psychologist, physiotherapist, speech and language therapist, and social worker.

Both working visas and work authorisations are granted initially for a period of two years and may be renewed.[a]

a See Section 2.5.6, page 33.

Applications for a working visa/work authorisation generally must be made outside Ireland. Once a working visa/work authorisation is granted, and the person has entered the state, they may change employers but must continue to work in the same skills category.

Applications can be made:

- through the Irish Embassy/Consulate in the applicant's country of residence
- through any Irish Embassy or Consulate if there is none in the applicant's country of residence
- by post directly to the Visa Office, Department of Foreign Affairs, 13/14 Burgh Quay, Dublin 2, if there is no Irish Embassy or Consulate in the applicant's country of residence

An application for a working visa or work authorisation should contain:

- a completed visa application form (in the case of working visas)[16]
- a job offer and contract from an employer in Ireland; this must correspond to the skills category in which the applicant is qualified and must include the starting date and the pay and must quote the employer's Registered Number for Tax Purposes and the applicant's passport number
- a passport or a full copy, which is valid at least until the expiry day of the relevant working visa or work authorisation
- two photographs of the applicant
- a visa application fee of €50, or the equivalent, or a work authorisation application fee of €50, or the equivalent; the visa application fee is not charged in the case of certain nationalities[a]

The following information must also be included with the application:[b]

Applicants who are...	Must..
IT and construction professionals	produce evidence of a relevant third-level education.
medical practitioners	present either a temporary or full registration certificate from the Medical Council of Ireland or a letter of acceptance for temporary or full registration from the Medical Council. A work authorisation/working visa will only be granted where the employer is one of the relevant authorised employers.[17]
dentists	present a letter confirming that they have full or temporary registration with the Dental Council. The employer must be one of the relevant, authorised employers; otherwise the application for the work authorisation/working visa will be rejected.

a Citizens of the following countries are exempt from the visa application fee: Bosnia, Bulgaria, Ecuador, Indonesia, Ivory Coast, Kirghizstan, Morocco, Peru, Slovak Republic, Sri Lanka, Tanzania, Tunisia, Uganda, Yugoslavia and Zambia (as of 1 January 2002, Visa Section, Department of Justice, Equality & Law Reform)

b Full details regarding registration and recognition of qualifications may be obtained from the relevant professional body (see Appendix E).

Applicants who are...	Must..
health and social care professionals	present a letter of validation or certificate of registration issued by the relevant professional body in Ireland. The employer must be one of the relevant authorised employers.
nurses	present a full or temporary registration certificate issued by An Bord Altranais (The Irish Nursing Board).

2.5.6 Renewing working visas/work authorisations

Working visas/work authorisations may be extended for a further period. Holders of such working visas/work authorisations, must apply to the registration officer in the area where the person resides. The local registration officer is a member of the Gardaí. Applicants should inquire at their local Garda station for the location of the registration officer for the area in which they reside. In Dublin this is the Garda National Immigration Bureau. They should present the following documents:

● a valid passport

● a valid Certificate of Registration

● their current P60

● a letter from the applicant's employer stating that the employment is in the skills category under which the person received the original permission to work in the State, and also stating that the employer continues to require the skills of the person

If an extension is granted, it is usually for an additional two-year period and the same conditions apply.

2.6 What are the Rules Governing Entry to the State for Migrant Workers?

2.6.1 UK nationals

Ireland and the UK[a] share a Common Travel Area. This means that UK nationals coming to Ireland to take up employment (or for any other purpose) are not subject to immigration controls at Irish airports and ports. Since June 1997, as a result of an order made under the *Aliens Act*, 1935,[18] Immigration Officers may carry out checks on persons arriving from the UK. UK nationals should carry their passport or some other form of identification to satisfy Immigration Officers that they are in fact UK nationals.

2.6.2 EEA and Swiss nationals

EEA and Swiss nationals are not required to possess a visa to travel to Ireland. They must possess a passport or national identity card, which should be shown to Immigration Officers at the port or airport of entry.

---

a This includes the Isle of Man and the Channel Islands.

In accordance with the *European Communities (Aliens) Regulations*, 1977, EEA and Swiss nationals may only be refused leave to land if: "… his or her personal conduct has been such that it would be contrary to public policy or would endanger public security",[19] or if the person is suffering from a scheduled disease.[a]

2.6.3 Non-EEA and Swiss nationals

Persons coming to work in Ireland from outside the EEA to take up employment must possess a valid passport, and either:

- evidence that their prospective employer has obtained an employment permit in respect of them, or a work authorisation or a working visa

- a visa if they come from a country whose passport holders are required to have a visa to travel to Ireland (see Appendix A)

A visa is not an entitlement to enter and remain in Ireland.[20]

2.6.3.1 Refusal of leave to land

Persons who arrive in Ireland must fulfil certain criteria before they are allowed to enter the country; otherwise they may be refused leave to land.[b] The *Aliens Order,* 1946 (as amended) lists the grounds on which a non-national may be refused leave to land.[c]

Persons who intend to take up employment will be refused leave to land if they are required to possess an employment permit, work authorisation or working visa and do not do so.

A person who is refused leave to land must be informed of the reasons for refusal. They may be arrested and detained until such time as they may be removed from the State.[21] A deportation order may be made in respect of them by the Minister for Justice, Equality & Law Reform.[22] The person will be notified of the Minister's intention to make such order and informed that they must either:

- make representations to the Minister within 15 working days, setting out the reasons why they should not be deported

- leave Ireland voluntarily within 15 working days (if the person agrees to leave, they must inform the Minister of their arrangements)

- consent to the making of the deportation order within 15 working days

2.7 Registering with the (Garda) Registration Officer[23]

2.7.1 EEA and Swiss nationals

The *European Communities (Aliens) Regulations*, 1977, apply to EEA and Swiss nationals, who are coming to Ireland to take up employment.[24] They may apply for a residence permit within three months of arrival in Ireland if they intend to remain in Ireland for more than three months. Regulation 5(1)(c) states:

---

a See Appendix B for details.

b To 'land' means "to arrive or enter by any means including over a land frontier" (from Northern Ireland). *Aliens Order* 1946 Section 3.

c See Appendix C for details.

A person to whom these Regulations apply and who:... is in employment in the State...may apply for a permit (which shall be known and is in these Regulations referred to as a 'Residence Permit') for a national of a Member State of the European Communities to the registration officer of the registration district in which he is a resident.

Although a residence permit is not obligatory for EEA nationals in employment in Ireland, it is recommended that they should apply for one. From 1 December 2002, when the relevant section of the *Irish Nationality and Citizenship Act*, 2001, came into force, if an EEA or Swiss national applies for a certificate of naturalisation, the period during which they lived in Ireland without a residence permit will not be counted.[25]

An application for a residence permit should be made to the registration officer in the area where the person resides. The local registration officer is a member of the Gardaí. Applicants should inquire at their local Garda station for the location of the registration officer for the area in which they reside. In Dublin this is the Garda National Immigration Bureau. A residence permit for an EEA national who came to Ireland to take up employment may be withdrawn or not renewed in certain circumstances. If the holder of a residence permit is unemployed for at least one year and applies to renew their residence permit, the duration of the new permit may be limited to twelve months. If, at the end of that period the person is still unemployed, an extension of the residence permit may be refused.[26]

2.7.2 *Non-EEA and Swiss nationals*

Non-EEA and Swiss nationals who come to Ireland to engage in employment must report to the registration officer in the area where the person resides. The local registration officer is a member of the Gardaí. Applicants should inquire at their local Garda station for the location of the registration officer for the area in which they reside. In Dublin this is the Garda National Immigration. They will be required to produce their passport and documentation relating to the purpose of their arrival in Ireland. In the case of employees, this would be an employment permit, work authorisation or working visa.

The person is then issued with a Certificate of Registration by the registration officer. The Certificate of Registration contains a photograph of the holder and states the duration of their permission to remain in Ireland. It also contains a stamp,[a] the number of which indicates the basis on which the Certificate of Registration was provided.

2.8 *What Rights and Entitlements Do Migrant Workers Have?*

2.8.1 *What are the rights of migrant workers in the work place?*

Non-national employees are entitled to the same rights in the work place as Irish employees.[27]

---

a Stamp No. 1 refers to people who are entitled to work if they are in possession of a work permit/work visa/work authorisation. Stamp A refers to medical practitioners entitled to work without a work permit (see Appendix D).

2.8.1.1 What taxes and social contributions do migrant workers pay?

All employees must pay tax on their earnings, known as 'pay as you earn' or PAYE and PRSI 'pay-related social insurance'.[a] These are deducted from employees' salaries each week or month. All employees are required to have a Personal Public Service Number (PPS No.), and persons who do not have a PPS No.[b] should contact the Department of Social Community and Family Affairs.[28] This number should be quoted in all contact with the Tax Office and the Department.

In addition, persons who are commencing their first employment in Ireland should complete a Certificate of Tax Credits and Standard Rate Cut-Off Point (Form 12A).[29] The Revenue Commissioners usually grant married tax credits even if the worker's spouse is not resident in the State.

2.8.1.2 How can migrant workers find employment?

EEA and Swiss nationals coming to Ireland need not have organised their employment before coming to Ireland.

Persons coming to Ireland to take up employment who are nationals of non-EEA states or Switzerland must have their employment organised before they arrive. However, once in Ireland those who require employment permits may change employment provided their new employer has obtained an employment permit for them. Persons holding a work visa/work authorisation, can change employment provided the new job is in the same sector as that for which their work visa/work authorisation applies.

All persons seeking employment through an employment agency should only approach registered agencies. The agency should not charge fees to the person seeking employment solely for agreeing to seek employment for them.

2.8.1.3 What details of employment are migrant workers entitled to receive?

Within two months of starting employment, the employer is required to provide the employee[c] with a written statement of certain details of the terms of employment.[30]

These include:

- name and address of employer
- place of work
- job title and nature of work
- date of commencement of employment
- nature of contract (temporary or fixed term)
- rate of pay
- pay intervals
- hours of work (including overtime)
- paid leave

a There are some exceptions to this, for example, low-paid workers.

b This replaces the old RSI Number.

c The term 'employee' covers those working under contract of employment or apprenticeship; those employed through an employment agency and those employed in the service of the State.

- arrangements for when the employee is unable to work due to sickness or injury
- pensions and pension schemes
- notice entitlements
- collective agreement/s, and the parties to the agreement/s

If the particulars contained in the statement change, the employer must notify the employee within one week.

If an employer has either failed to provide a written statement, or failed to notify the employee of changes that have taken place regarding the particulars contained in the statement, the employee may complain to a Rights Commissioner. If either party is dissatisfied with the recommendation of the Rights Commissioner, they may appeal to the Employment Appeals Tribunal.[a]

2.8.1.4 What is the minimum rate of pay for migrant workers?

- All employees over the age of 18 who have worked for at least two years since turning 18 are entitled to a minimum rate of pay. This is currently €6.35 per hour since 1 October 2002.[31] Persons who have not worked for two years must generally be paid 80 per cent of the minimum wage in the first year, and 90 per cent in the second year.[32]

- With their wages, employees must receive a written statement of the gross pay and deductions made.[33]

- Employees have the right to a readily negotiable mode of wage payment such as by cheque, credit transfer, cash, postal order or bank draft.

- Employers may only make deductions in certain circumstances[b] that are agreed with the employee.[c]

2.8.1.5 What are the rules governing working hours?

- Employees must not be required to work in excess of the maximum hours permitted each week. This is an average of 48 hours per week averaged over four, six or 12 months depending on the nature of the employment.[d]

- Employees are entitled to breaks and rest time as follows:

  - 11 hours rest per 24 hour period

  - one period of 24 hours rest per week preceded by a daily rest period (11 hours)

  - 15 minutes break after working four-and-a-half hours and another break of 15 minutes after six hours, or 30 minutes after six hours if the 15 minutes break was not taken after four-and-a-half hours[e]

a See Section 2.8.1.13, page 40 for details of the procedure for referring a complaint to the Rights Commissioner. In addition, the Rights Commissioner can investigate grievances or claims under most of the legislation dealing with rights in the workplace including: *Payment of Wages Act 1991*; *Terms of Employment Act 1994*; *Organisation of Working Time Act 1997*; *Parental Leave Act 1998* and *National Minimum Wages Act*, 2000.

b When the deductions are required by law; when they are provided for in the contract of employment and when they are made with the written consent of the employee.

c For example, VHI, BUPA, Union Dues, Pension Plan and so on.

d Four months for employees generally, six months for seasonal workers and workers who are directly involved in ensuring continuity of service or production, and twelve months for employees who have entered a collective agreement with their employer.

e The break cannot be taken at the end of the work period.

2.8.1.6 What holidays are migrant workers entitled to?

Full-time workers are entitled to four working weeks annual leave[34] and nine public holidays per year.[a] These are: 1 January, St Patrick's Day, Easter Monday, First Monday in May, First Monday in June, First Monday in August, Last Monday in October, Christmas Day and St Stephen's Day.

Part-time workers are entitled to annual leave consisting of eight per cent of the hours they work up to a maximum of four weeks and to public holidays if they have worked at least 40 hours in the five weeks preceding the public holiday.

2.8.1.7 What compensation for Sunday work are migrant workers entitled to?

Employees are entitled to be compensated for Sunday work. This can be extra pay[b] or time off in lieu.[35] For persons working in the retail sector, there is a *Code of Practice on Sunday Working in the Retail Trade.*[c]

2.8.1.8 What maternity leave are migrant workers entitled to?

- A pregnant employee is entitled to maternity leave from employment for a period of at least 14 weeks.[36]

- To be entitled to maternity leave, the employee must notify her employer and produce a medical certificate confirming the pregnancy and expected week of confinement. The notice must be given at least four weeks before the commencement of maternity leave and must be in writing.[37]

- An employee can choose the period of maternity leave. However, maternity leave must be taken at least four weeks before the end of the expected week of confinement and shall end not earlier than four weeks after the end of the expected week of confinement.[38]

- The employee has the right to return to work when the period of maternity leave has expired. Employees who have taken maternity leave are entitled to return to the:
  - same employer
  - job the employee held immediately before commencement of leave
  - same contract and conditions of employment[39]

2.8.1.9 What parental leave are migrant workers entitled to?

- Persons who have at least one year's continuous employment and are the parents of children (natural or adopted) may take up to a total of 14 weeks unpaid leave (for each child) to take care of their children who are no older than five years.[40]

---

a The employer has four alternatives with regard to the public holidays. They may give the employee: the day of the holiday off with pay, a paid day off within a month, an extra day of annual leave or an extra day's pay.

b With premium payment (that is, above normal payment).

c This was drawn up by the Labour Relations Commission and is based on the entitlements set out in the *Organisation of Working Time Act* 1997. It is available on the Department of Enterprise, Trade & Employment website *http://www.entemp.ie/*

- Employees who have taken parental leave are entitled to return to the:
  - same employer
  - job the employee held immediately before commencement of leave
  - same contract and conditions of employment[41]

2.8.1.10 What force majeure leave are migrant workers entitled to?

- Employees may also take *force majeure* leave in the case of sudden injury or illness to an immediate family member, where the dependant needs the worker to be present.[42]

- An 'immediate family member' of the employee is a child, spouse/partner, person to whom the employee is in *loco parentis*, brother, sister, parent or grandparent.[43]

- An employee may take three days in any consecutive 12 months or five days in any 36 consecutive months[44]

- *Force majeure* leave is paid leave[45]

2.8.1.11 What laws protect migrant workers from unfair dismissal?

Employees who have over 12 months continuous employment,[a] are protected by law from unfair dismissal. Dismissals may be regarded as unfair where they have resulted wholly or mainly from:

- the employee's trade union membership or activities

- the religious or political beliefs of the employee

- the race, skin colour or sexual orientation of the employee

- legal proceedings against the employer if the employee is a party or a witness

- the employee's pregnancy

- the employee taking leave provided for under the *Maternity Protection Act*, 1994

A dismissal will usually be considered fair if it is based wholly or mainly on one of the following:

- the employee's capability, competence or qualifications for the job

- the employee's conduct

- the employee's redundancy

- if continuation of the employment would contravene other legal requirements

Both 'actual' unfair dismissals and 'constructive' dismissals are prohibited by legislation. Constructive dismissal can occur where the employee's conditions of employment are made so difficult that they have no alternative but to leave.

a Two fixed terms of six months would qualify.

2.8.1.12 What claims for redress[a] exist for migrant workers who consider they have been unfairly dismissed?

An employee who considers that they have been unfairly dismissed (this includes 'actual' and 'constructive' dismissal) and who wishes to make a claim for redress must do so within six months.[b]

The employee must give formal notice of his/her claim in writing to a Rights Commissioner or to the Employment Appeals Tribunal. The claim is considered by the Employment Appeals Tribunal where the employee or the employer have notified a Rights Commissioner that they object to the claim being heard by a Rights Commissioner.

Persons who are employed through an employment agency must make their claim against whoever is paying their wages (this could be the actual 'employer' or the agency).

2.8.1.13 How can migrant workers take a claim to the Rights Commissioner?

Rights Commissioners are appointed by the Minister for Enterprise, Trade & Employment on the recommendation of the Labour Relations Commission. They are independent of the Minister in carrying out their functions. The procedure for persons wishing to make an appeal to the Rights Commissioner is described below:

● Persons wishing to make an appeal to a Rights Commissioner must:

 - notify their former employer that they intend to take a case to the Rights Commissioner

 - complete the standard form[46] (full details of the complaint must be given)

● The Rights Commissioner hears the case as soon as possible. The hearing takes place in private.

● Both parties can be represented at the hearing by a lawyer or trade union representative (in the cases of the employee).

● Both parties have the opportunity to present their case.

● The Rights Commissioner makes a recommendation, which may be appealed to the Employment Appeals Tribunal (EAT).

2.8.1.14 What is the minimum notice[47] period for migrant workers?

Employees who are in continuous employment with the same employer for 13 weeks or more and who normally work at least eight hours per week are entitled to a minimum period of notice from their employer if they intend to dismiss them.

The period of notice depends on the length of service. For persons who have served from 13 weeks to two years the minimum notice period is one week.

a Redress in the case of unfair dismissal can be any of the following:

  ● re-instatement in the employee's old job

  ● re-engagement in the old job or a suitable alternative

  ● financial compensation

b In exceptional circumstances, this can be twelve months.

Employees must also give notice if they intend to leave the job. If the employee is in employment for 13 weeks or over, they must give the employer at least one week's notice. If the contract of employment requires further notice to be given, they must adhere to the terms of the contract.

The Employment Appeals Tribunal considers disputes between employers and workers regarding minimum notice.

2.8.1.15 What redundancy payments[a] are migrant workers entitled to?

Employees are entitled to a lump sum redundancy payment when their employment is ended due to redundancy providing they:

- have 109 weeks continuous service
- are aged between 16 and 66
- are normally expected to work at least eight hours per week

The redundancy pay is calculated in the following manner:

- a half week's pay for each year of employment up to 41 years' service
- one week's pay for each year over 41 years' service
- one week's pay irrespective of the length of service

2.8.1.16 What rules govern discrimination in employment?

Discrimination against employees on grounds of age, gender, marital status,[48] family status,[49] race,[50] religion,[51] sexual orientation,[52] disability[53] and membership of the Travelling Community is prohibited under the *Employment Equality Act, 1998*.[b] The Act prohibits:

- direct and indirect discrimination
- discrimination in access to employment, conditions of employment, promotion, training and classification of posts[54]

The Equality Authority may provide legal advice, assistance and representation to persons who consider that they have a complaint under the legislation.[55]

A person who considers that they have been discriminated against on any of the nine grounds listed above can refer their complaint to:

Authority	Employees refer to this body if they...
the ODEI - the equality tribunal	are still in employment
the Labour Court	have already been dismissed (including 'actual' and 'constructive' dismissal)

a Redundancy payments are dealt with under the *Redundancy Payments Acts* 1967 -1991. Redundancy occurs when the employee's job ceases to exist, there is insufficient work, the firm closes down or the firm re-organises.

b The *Employment Equality Authority Act* 1998 came into force 18 October 1999, and only incidents of discrimination occurring on, or after that date can be dealt with under the Act. Incidents of discrimination on grounds of sex or marital status can be investigated by the ODEI - the equality tribunal under earlier legislation.

2.8.1.17 How can migrant workers bring a claim to the equality tribunal?

The ODEI - the equality tribunal (referred to as the equality tribunal in this handbook) is an independent body established to investigate claims of discrimination under the *Employment Equality Act*, 1998 and the *Equal Status Act*, 2000. The equality tribunal also offers a mediation service.

Persons wishing to refer their complaint to the equality tribunal must complete the complaint form (Form ODEI 1).[a] Persons who have difficulty in completing the form due to disability, language or other difficulties, should contact the equality tribunal immediately, and if appropriate, other arrangements will be made to enable the person to refer their complaint.

The person making the complaint (the complainant) may write to the person they believe has discriminated against them (the respondent), to request information in order to ascertain more fully, what actually took place. The complainant must use the standard form provided by the equality tribunal (Form ODEI 3).[56]

If the respondent does not reply promptly, the complainant may refer their complaint to the equality tribunal.

When the complaint is received, the Director of Equality Investigations will refer it to an Equality Officer within the equality tribunal.

2.8.1.18 How can migrant workers bring a claim to the Labour Court?

Persons who have been dismissed from their employment on grounds of discrimination or victimisation, may bring their claim to the Labour Court.

- The person can send a questionnaire to the former employer to obtain information. The employer can also give their version of what occurred through this procedure. The Questionnaire Form may be downloaded from the Labour Court website.[57]

- The application must be made within six months from the incident of discrimination or victimisation taking place. If there were a series of incidents, the application must be made six months from the last one taking place.

- The application may be made by completing the application form, which can be downloaded from the Labour Court website.

2.8.1.19 What are the rules governing the victimisation of migrant workers who bring claims?

If a person making a complaint to the equality tribunal is penalised in any manner by the person against whom they made the complaint or another person because they made the complaint, this is regarded as victimisation. Victimisation also occurs if the person in good faith lawfully opposed any act of discrimination or victimisation or gave evidence in any proceedings under the Act.

Victimisation is also prohibited under the *Employment Equality Act* and a person who considers that they were victimised may make a complaint to the equality tribunal in the manner described above for other types of discrimination.

---

a The forms, and all the other form to be used in this process, may be downloaded from the ODEI - the equality tribunal website *http://www.odei.ie/* or from the ODEI - the equality tribunal, 3 Clonmel Street, Dublin 2, telephone (01) 477 4100.

2.8.2 What types of accommodation can migrant workers access?

Some migrant workers coming to Ireland will have their accommodation already arranged by their employers. The alternatives for persons who have to find their own accommodation are:

- private rented accommodation
- local authority accommodation
- purchase

2.8.2.1 Private rented accommodation

Persons wishing to rent a house or apartment from a private landlord can do so directly themselves by replying to advertisements in newspapers or seek the assistance of a letting agency. Finding accommodation can be expensive and time-consuming, particularly in big cities. Prospective tenants should:

- Inspect the property before agreeing to move in and record the condition of the property and its contents in writing. Houses and apartments to let should comply with certain minimum standards.[58]

- Agree the amount of deposit and rent to be paid and the time of payment. A receipt should be obtained for all money paid to the landlord. The deposit should be returned to the tenant when s/he leaves the accommodation. However, the landlord may retain some or all of the deposit if: the tenant gives insufficient notice, damages the property or leaves without paying bills or rent.

- Find out whether the rent covers such items as electricity, gas and bin charges (where relevant).

- Agree on who is responsible for any repairs that need to be carried out in the future.

Tenants should be aware of their rights and duties as a tenant.
The most important of these are:

- The landlord must provide a rent book. The rent book should contain the name and address of the landlord, amount of deposit paid, the amount of rent and the time and method of payment. All rent payments should be entered in the rent book. The rent book should also include the terms of the tenancy.

- The landlord is not permitted (except in cases of emergency) to enter the accommodation without making an appointment with the tenant.

- The landlord must give a minimum of four weeks notice in writing if they require the tenant to leave the accommodation. This is referred to as a 'notice to quit'. If the tenant does not leave by the end of the four-week period, the landlord can go to court to apply for an eviction order.

- The tenant must also provide notice to the landlord if they decide to move out.

2.8.2.2 Local authority (council or corporation) Housing

Local authority housing is available, generally for persons who do not have sufficient resources to provide their own accommodation. Practice with regard to eligibility for local authority housing varies. Priority is usually given to low-income families with children and to older persons. However, there is usually a long waiting list of people for local authority housing.

Persons who are interested in being considered for local authority housing should:

- Contact their nearest local authority (see Appendix E for a full list of local authorities in Ireland), and obtain a copy of the authority's scheme of letting priorities. This sets out the rules for the allocation of accommodation including such matters as how applicants are prioritised and what type of accommodation may be provided to different categories of applicants.

- If the person is still interested in local authority accommodation, they should complete the application form, which is provided by the local authority.

- There is no requirement to live in the area for a certain time in order to qualify for local authority housing. It is possible to apply to more than one local authority, but not all local authorities accept applications from outside their area.

- Non-nationals who wish to apply for local authority accommodation may be required to provide evidence that they intend, and are entitled, to live in Ireland permanently. The practice varies with regard to this requirement and persons should contact their local authority.

- When the application has been received, an official from the local authority or health board will usually visit the applicant. (However, practice varies between local authorities and they may visit the applicant only when suitable accommodation is available.)

- As most local authorities have insufficient accommodation to meet the demand, they will put the applicant's name on a list. Some local authorities have a 'points system' to assist them in determining the greatest need for accommodation among applicants. An applicant will be awarded points for issues such as overcrowding.

2.8.2.2.1 *Offer of accommodation:*

If the person is offered a house or flat by the local authority and decides to take it, they must sign a tenancy agreement.

- The tenancy agreement is legal document and both the tenant and the local authority must adhere to the terms of the agreement.

- In the case of a married couple or partners, the tenancy is usually in joint names.

- The amount of rent to be paid per week is based on the income of the household.

- It is important to ensure that rent is paid up to date as the tenant may be issued with a notice to quit if arrears of rent have built up.

- Tenants can apply to transfer to another area.

2.8.2.3 Purchase

There are no restrictions on non-nationals buying private residential property in Ireland.[a] However there are requirements under the Land Acts and additional documents may be required. There are some restrictions with regard to farmland.[b]

However, persons should be aware that house purchase can be a lengthy and costly process, therefore, for some migrant workers renting a property may be a better option. It is important to note that a person's employment permit, working visa or work authorisation will not be extended simply because the person has bought property in Ireland, or is in the process of purchasing property.

Persons interested in buying a private house or apartment may find a suitable property through an auctioneer/estate agent or through advertisements in local and national newspapers.

- Persons who cannot afford to buy a property from their own resources need to get a mortgage from a building society or bank.
- Houses/apartments should be viewed and in the case of a second-hand house or apartment, a survey should be carried out to ensure that it is structurally sound.
- If the person is satisfied that they have found a property they wish to buy, they should make an offer, if the property is for sale by private treaty. If the property is for sale by auction, they must attend the auction and the highest bidder purchases the property.
- Generally, estate agents do not charge a fee to purchasers of property.
- The purchase of property can be complicated, and prospective buyers should always engage a solicitor to act for them.

2.8.2.4 What laws govern discrimination in the provision of accommodation?

The *Equal Status Act*, 2000, prohibits discrimination on the grounds of gender, marital status, family status, sexual orientation, religious belief, age, disability, "race" and membership of the Traveller Community in the provision of goods and services, the disposal of property and access to education. Discrimination on the nine grounds listed in the Act is prohibited in both the public and private sectors. The process for referring complaints is similar to that under the *Employment Equality Act*, 1998. Further information is available from the equality tribunal.[59]

2.8.3 What medical services are migrant workers entitled to?

Migrant workers coming to Ireland have two options with regard to medical care:

- public health care
- private health care

2.8.3.1 Public health care

The public health care system, including primary and hospital services, can be accessed by any person resident in Ireland including those on employment permits, working visas and work authorisations. This system can be accessed for a nominal charge or free of charge for medical card holders.

a The *Aliens Act*, 1935 states that "Real and personal property of every description in Saorstat Eireann or subject to the law of Saorstat Eireann may be taken, acquired, held and disposed of by an alien in like manner and to the like extend as such property may be taken, acquired, held or disposed of by a citizen of Saorstat Eireann".

b These restrictions apply to non-EU nationals wishing to buy land over five acres in size. They should contact the Department of Agriculture, Food and Rural Development, Agriculture House, Kildare Street, Dublin 2, telephone (01) 607 2000, Lo-call 1890 200 510.

2.8.3.1.1 What services can be accessed for a nominal charge?

A range of services are available including:

- General Practitioner (GP) services (family doctor) with a charge of between €30 and €50 per consultation
- in-patient hospital treatment in a public ward subject to a daily charge of €40[a]
- all other out-patient services including consultants
- visits to hospital Accident and Emergency Departments subject to a charge of €40 (persons who are referred by their GP will not be charged)
- maternity and infant care

2.8.3.1.2 Who can access medical services free of charge?

To access free medical care in Ireland, a person needs a medical card. Generally, migrant workers will not qualify for the medical card as their income normally exceeds the means test limit.

2.8.3.1.3 Who is entitled to a medical card?

Entitlement to a medical card in Ireland is based on a person's residence and means. To be fully eligible for a medical card a person must:

- be 'ordinarily resident' in Ireland; this means that they must intend to live in Ireland for at least one year and be permitted to do so
- satisfy the means test; a person will only be eligible for free medical care (Category A entitlement, that is medical card holders) if their gross income, less PRSI contributions is less than €138 and in the case of a married couple or single parent €200.[b]

2.8.3.1.4 What does a medical card entitle you to?

A medical card entitles you to the following free medical services:

- General Practitioner (GP) services (but you must register with a GP)
- prescribed medicines
- in-patient hospital treatment in a public ward
- out-patient hospital treatment
- dental, ophthalmic and aural services
- community care services

---

a Up to a maximum of €400 in any twelve-month period (as of 1 January 2003).

b A married couple or a single parent must earn less than €200. These rates apply to persons under sixty-six years of age. Persons applying for the medical card are permitted to have the following amounts over the income level and still qualify for the medical card, as of 1 January 2003:

- €25 for each child under 16 years of age
- €26 for each child over 16 years of age with no income maintained by applicant
- the amount by which the rent or mortgage paid each week exceeds €25
- the amount by which the costs of travelling to and from work each week exceeds €22
- weekly expenditure on medicines

2.8.3.2 Private Health Care

Persons can also take out private health insurance.[a] This insurance covers private care in public or private hospitals. There are two private health insurers in Ireland, VHI and BUPA.[60] Medical insurance will not cover pre-existing medical conditions and the cover may not, in any event, take effect for an initial period.

2.8.4 What social welfare entitlements do migrant workers have?

Irish social welfare legislation does not distinguish between nationals and non-nationals. Essentially, any person from outside the State who complies with the relevant laws covering entry, living and working here is entitled to seek social welfare payments in compliance with the normal conditions. For further information, contact the Information Service of the Department of Social and Family Affairs on (01) 704 3000.

2.8.5 What education can migrant workers access?

2.8.5.1 EEA and Swiss nationals

2.8.5.1.1 EU nationals

All EU citizens are entitled to equal treatment in the educational sector in Ireland on the same basis as Irish citizens. Thus for example, migrant EU students are entitled to the same fee level (or none as the case may be) and maintenance grants as national students.[61]

2.8.5.1.2 EEA and Swiss Nationals

EEA and Swiss nationals are generally entitled to education on the same basis as Irish nationals. However, EEA nationals (other than those belonging to the EU) and Swiss nationals are not entitled to local authority/VEC education grants. Third-level education fees vary between educational institutions. Employees are also entitled to 'training in vocational schools and retraining centres'.[b]

2.8.5.2 Non-EEA and Swiss nationals

Persons who are employed in Ireland may not generally change their status in the State. If they wish to take up full-time study in the State (for example, after the expiry of their employment permit, working visa or work authorisation) they must normally return to their country of origin and apply for a place in the educational institution in which they wish to study. They should possess a letter of acceptance from the college and a visa (if one is required)[c] before coming to Ireland to study. Non-EEA nationals will be charged the full international economic fee rate for third-level education. Third-level education fees vary between educational institutions.

Non-EEA employees in Ireland may attend part-time courses and classes if they can cover the fees and other expenses from their own resources. However, non-EAA migrant workers can avail of basic education (including literacy) free of charge from the Adult Literacy Service.

---

a Persons who wish to avail of private health care and who have not taken out private health insurance will be required to pay for hospital treatment.

b Council Regulation 68/1612/EEC, 15 October 1968, on *Freedom of Movement for Workers within the Community* (as amended by Regulations 312/76, Article 7.3).

c See Appendix A for details.

2.8.5.3 Children of migrant workers

All children and young people under the age of 18 in Ireland have the same rights irrespective of the child's or parent's/parents' or legal caregivers' race, colour, sex, language, religion, political or other opinion, national, ethnic or social origin, property, disability, birth or other status.[62] Children of non-EEA nationals can therefore access services on the same basis as an Irish child. Children of non-EEA nationals are registered on their parent's/parents' or legal caregivers' Certificate of Registration until the age of 16. However, children's birth certificates are usually required for identification and other purposes. Thereafter, they must register themselves with the registration officer in the area where the person resides. The local registration officer is a member of the Gardaí. Applicants should inquire at their local Garda station for the location of the registration officer for the area in which they reside. In Dublin this is the Garda National Immigration Bureau.

All children and young people in Ireland must engage in full-time education until they are 16 years old. At first and second level, there are two main education sectors: primary school (first level), and post-primary and vocational training (second level).

Schools are managed by the State (Comprehensive, Vocational Education Committees [VECs]) and religious bodies (Catholic, Protestant, Muslim, Jewish) and governed by their own ethos/philosophy. Lists of schools are available from the Department of Education and Science.[63]

Children with language needs are generally placed in classes with other children/young people of a similar age. Government support is provided to allow schools to offer limited language support programmes for bilingual and multilingual children.

To apply to a school or education centre parents or legal caregivers follow the process below:

- The parents/legal caregivers contact the local school/education centre of choice by writing or telephoning the school principal or manager to arrange a meeting.

- At the first meeting, the parents/legal caregivers are provided with the formal school/education centre policy which outlines the ethos, selection criteria and other matters.

- The parents/legal caregivers are required to provide the school/education centre with basic information on the student.

- An informal education and linguistic assessment of the student may take place but there is no State interpretation facility for this process. Schools/education centres cannot refuse access to a student on the basis of their level of English.

- If there are no places, or if the school/education centre is unsuitable for the student, the school/education centre recommends another school/education centre in the locality.

- If the student is offered a place in a school, the parents/legal caregivers should obtain a letter of acceptance from the school/education centre.

2.8.6 What family reunification rights do migrant workers have?

2.8.6.1 EEA and Swiss nationals

EEA and Swiss national employees are permitted to be joined in Ireland by certain members of their family[64] (this applies also to family members who are non-EEA nationals):

- spouses, children aged under 21, and children over 21 if they are dependent on the employee
- spouses of any children of the employee and their spouse
- dependent parents and grandparents of the employee and their spouse
- other dependent relatives in the ascending line of the employee and their spouse

Section 2(2) of the *European Communities (Aliens) Regulations*, 1977, defines dependants as:

> *the person's spouse, children under 21 years of age of the person and the spouse, other children of the person and the spouse if such other children are dependent on the person, the spouses of any children of the person, and the spouse and dependent direct lineal ancestors and descendants of the person and the spouse.*

The dependent relatives as defined above may take up employment in Ireland[65] and children of the worker are entitled to attend educational courses, including apprenticeships and vocational training on the same basis as Irish nationals.[66]

2.8.6.1.1 Entry to the State

The family members of EEA and Swiss nationals employed in Ireland must produce a passport or national identity card, as in the case of the migrant worker. They will only be refused leave to land by Immigration Officers, if they are suffering from a scheduled disease or their conduct has been such that it would be contrary to public policy or endanger public security.[67]

If the family members are not themselves nationals of Switzerland or an EEA Member State and if they come from a country whose nationals are required to possess a visa to travel to Ireland, they will have to obtain a visa prior to arrival. In either case, they should travel with sufficient evidence establishing that they are married to, or dependent on, an EEA or Swiss national who is resident and employed in Ireland.

2.8.6.1.2 Residence permits

Family members of EEA and Swiss nationals may apply for a residence permit.[68] If the family members are not EEA or Swiss nationals, they may apply to the registration officer in their local registration district[69] for a residence permit. The local registration officer is a member of the Gardaí. Applicants should inquire at their local Garda station for the location of the registration officer for the area in which they reside. In Dublin this is the Garda National Immigration Bureau. Family members may remain in the State for three months without applying for a residence permit.[70]

2.8.6.2 Non-EEA and Swiss nationals

In general, non EEA/Swiss nationals may apply for family reunification if they can support their family members without relying on public funds. However, in the case of workers from states whose nationals require a visa to travel to Ireland, they are generally not permitted to be joined by their family until they are in Ireland a year and have been offered a contract for another twelve months.[71]

2.8.7 How can migrant workers acquire Irish citizenship?

Migrant Workers who are legally resident in Ireland can become Irish citizens in three ways:

- naturalisation
- post-nuptial citizenship
- by descent

The *Irish Nationality and Citizenship Acts* 1956, 1986, 1994 and 2001 set out the criteria under which Irish citizenship is granted.

2.8.7.1 Acquiring citizenship by naturalisation

A person wishing to apply for a certificate of naturalisation must fulfil certain conditions including having legally resided in Ireland for five years out of the previous nine-year period. The Minister for Justice, Equality & Law Reform may grant an application for a certificate of naturalisation at their discretion if they are satisfied that the applicant:

- is of full age
- is of good character
- has had a period of one year's continuous residence in Ireland immediately prior to their application, and in the eight years immediately preceding that period has had a total residence of four years in Ireland
- intends in good faith to continue to reside in Ireland after naturalisation
- has made a declaration of fidelity to the nation and loyalty to the State, either before a District Court Justice or in such other manner permitted by the Minister

The Minister for Justice, Equality & Law Reform may waive these conditions in certain circumstances specified in the Acts. The number of circumstances in which the Minister may waive the conditions, has been reduced by the 2001, Act.[a]

---

a *Irish Nationality and Citizenship Act* 1956, Section 16 (as amended by *Irish Nationality and Citizenship Act,* 1986, Section 5). Since the coming into force of the 2001 Act, this no longer applies to persons married to a naturalised Irish citizen or persons married to a person who is an Irish citizen otherwise than by naturalisation.

2.8.7.2 *Acquiring post-nuptial citizenship*

A non-national who married an Irish national on or before 29 November 2002, and has been in a subsisting marriage with that person for a minimum of three years, may become an Irish citizen by making a post-nuptial declaration of citizenship. However, this is not possible if the Irish spouse has acquired citizenship by naturalisation, post-nuptial declaration, or was granted citizenship as a token of honour. Any such declarations will have to be made before 30 November 2005.

In the case of spouses of Irish nationals who got married on or after 30 November 2002, the Minister may at his/her 'absolute discretion' grant an application for a certificate of naturalisation to the spouse of an Irish citizen if the applicant:

● is of full age

● is of good character

● is married to an Irish citizen for at least three years

● is in a subsisting marriage, recognised as being in accordance with Irish legislation

● is living together with the Irish citizen as husband and wife (the applicant must submit an affidavit to that effect to the Minister)

● has lived in Ireland for at least one year continuously prior to the application

● has been resident in Ireland for at least two years of the four years immediately preceding that period

● intends in good faith to continue to reside in Ireland after naturalisation

● has made a declaration of 'fidelity to the nation and loyalty to the State' in whatever manner may be prescribed[72]

The Minister for Justice, Equality & Law Reform may waive certain of the above conditions if satisfied that the applicant would suffer serious consequences in respect of his or her bodily integrity or liberty if not granted Irish citizenship.[73]

2.8.7.3 *Acquiring citizenship by descent*

Persons whose father or mother was an Irish Citizen at the time of their birth are automatically Irish citizens. However, if a person is born outside Ireland, and the parent through whom they are claiming citizenship was also born outside Ireland, they will not be entitled to citizenship except in certain limited circumstances.[74] Persons whose grandparents were Irish citizens can become Irish citizens by registering in the Foreign Births Register in the Department of Foreign Affairs or, if residing outside Ireland, at the nearest Irish Embassy or Consulate.

2.8.7.4 *Acquiring permission to remain without condition as to time*

Persons who have been legally resident in Ireland for ten years and who have not applied for naturalisation may obtain a residence stamp giving them 'permission to remain without condition as to time'.[75]

2.8.8 What do migrant workers need to open a bank account?

Many employees are paid through their bank account. Banks require new customers to produce the following documents when opening a bank account:

- photo identification (a passport satisfies this requirement)
- proof of address in Ireland, for example a utility bill (electricity, gas or other utility) or lease agreement
- letter from employer giving details of the type and duration of the employment
- although not officially documented as a requirement, banks often request applicants to provide a personal introduction from an existing customer

2.8.9 Can migrant workers vote in elections?

Non-national residents in Ireland over 18 years of age may vote in some elections:

Citizens of...	Permitted to vote at...
The UK	Dáil, European and local elections
EU states apart from the UK	European and local elections
Non-EU states	Local elections only

Those permitted to vote must have their name included in the Electoral Register if they want to vote. Application forms are available in post offices, libraries and council and corporation offices.

Endnotes

1   *Agreement Establishing an Association Between Turkey and the European Economic Community*, 1963.

2   Case C-413/99 *Baumbast*, 17 September 2002.

3   Proposal for a European Parliament and Council Directive 29 June 2001 on the *Right of Citizens of the Union and their   Family Members to Move and Reside Freely within the Territory of the Member States* COM(2001) 257 final [2001] OJ C270 E/23.

4   Case C-85/96 *Maria Martinez Sala v Freistaat Bayern* [1998] ECR I-2691.

5   For further information see the Department of Justice, Equality & Law Reform information leaflet *New Immigration Procedures in Relation to Swiss Nationals* available on the Department's website at *http://www.justice.ie/*

6   *Vander Elst v. Office des Migrations Internationales* [1994] ECR I-3803 .

7   Regulation (EEC) No 1612/68 of the Council, 15 October 1968, *Freedom of Movement for Workers within the Community* OJ L257/2 (as Amended by Regulation 312/76 Article 11 OJ L 39/2 (9/2/76)).

8   *Additional Protocol of the Agreement Establishing an Association between Turkey and the European Economic Community,* Article 36 states that "...freedom of movement of workers between Member States of the Community and Turkey shall be secured by progressive stages in accordance with the principles set out in Article 12 of the Agreement of Association between the end of the twelfth and twenty-second year after the entry into force. The Council of Association shall decide on the rules necessary to that end". Dec 1/80 of Council of Association, Art 10.

9   *Ibid,* Article 37.

10 Duran Seddon (Ed.) *Joint Council for the Welfare of Immigrants, Immigration, Nationality & Refugee Law Handbook* 2002 Edition, p. 480.

11 Harney Mary (An Tánaiste) Press Release, *Tánaiste Announces New Immigration Rules for Accession Countries* 24 March 2003 *http://www.entemp.ie/press03/240303.htm*

12 Department of Enterprise, Trade & Employment, Press Release *Department of Enterprise, Trade & Employment and FÁS Clarify Operational Arrangements of Work Permit Procedures* Department of Enterprise, Trade & Employment(2003) *http://www.entemp.ie/press03/070403a.htm*

13 The form *Renewal Application for a Work Permit to Employ a Non-EEA National* can be obtained from the Department   of Enterprise, Trade & Employment, Davitt House, Adelaide Road, Dublin 2, or may be downloaded from their website *http://www.entemp.ie/*

14 See the Department of Enterprise, Trade & Employment website *http://www.entemp.ie/*

15 *Ibid.*

16 The *Working Visa Application Form* is available from the Department of Foreign Affairs *http://www.irlgov.ie/iveagh/services/toireland/visaapplication.pdf*

17 The holders of working visas/work authorisations may only take up employment with one of the authorised employers under the scheme for medical practitioners, dentists, and health and social care practitioners. A list of the authorised employers can be downloaded from the website of the Department of Enterprise, Trade & Employment *http://www.entemp.ie/*

18 *Aliens (Amendment)* (No.3) Order 1997, SI No. 277.

19 *European Communities (Aliens) Regulations* 1977, Regulations 4 (i) and 4 (ii), SI No. 393.

20 The *Aliens Order* 1946, Section 5 (1) (as amended by the *Aliens Amendment Order* 1975 Section 3) states that:

    "An alien coming from any place outside the State other than Great Britain shall on arrival in the State, present himself to an Immigration Officer for leave to land."

21 The *Aliens Order* 1946 (as amended), Section 5.

22 The *Immigration Act* 1999, Section 3 (1)(g).

23 This is provided for in the *Aliens Order* 1946, Section 11.

24 These Regulations give effect to several EU Directives including Council Directive 68/360/EEC, 15 October 1968, on the *Abolition of Restrictions on Movement and Residence within the Community for Workers of Member States and their Families.* This Directive deals with the rights of EU nationals (and members of their families) to take up employment and residence in another EU Member State. It provides for the issue of residence permits as proof of the right of residence. SI No. 393 of 1977.

25 Section 16A(1) of the Act states that:

    "When calculating a period of residence in the State for the purposes of an application for a certificate of naturalisation

    (a) in the case of a non-national who is a person to whom the *European Communities (Aliens) Regulations* 1997 (SI No. 393 of 1977) apply, no period shall be reckoned in relation to which the non-national was not the holder or subject of a residence permit or document granted under those Regulations or the *European Communities (Right of Residence for Non-Economically Active Persons) Regulations* 1997 (SI No. 57 of 1997)."

26 *European Communities (Aliens Regulations)* 1977, Regulation 9(2).

27 The Department of Enterprise, Trade & Employment have produced a *Guide to Labour Law* which may be downloaded from their website *http://www.entemp.ie/* The Department also provide an information service, the Employment Rights Information Unit, which is contactable at Room G05, Davitt House, 65a Adelaide Road, Dublin 2, telephone (01) 631 3131, Lo-call 1890 201 615, or e-mail erinfo@entemp.ie. All employees are entitled to join a trade union and they are often a useful source of information on employee rights.

28 Department of Social, Community and Family Affairs, Gandon House, Amiens Street, Dublin 1, telephone (01) 874 8444, website *http://www.welfare.ie/* The Department's leaflet SW100 *Personal Public Service Number* provides additional information on obtaining a PPS.

29 Further information may be obtained on Revenue Publication RES 2 *Coming to Live in Ireland* *http://www.revenue.ie/*

30 *Terms of Employment (Information) Act* 1994.

31 *National Minimum Wages Act* 2000.

32 This is provided for in the *National Minimum Wages Act* 2000, Section 15(1):

    "Subject to subsection (2) and Sections 16, 17 and 18, a person who:

    (a) enters employment for the first time after attaining the age of 18 years or

    (b) having entered into employment before attaining the age of 18 years, continues in employment on attaining that age

    shall be remunerated by his or her employer in respect of his or her working hours in any pay reference period at an hourly rate of pay that on average is not less than :

    (i) in the case of an employee commencing employment for the first time after attaining the age of 18 years:

(I) in his or her first year after commenced employment, 80% and

(II) in his or her second year after having commenced employment, 90%

(ii) in the case if an employee having entered into employment before attaining the age of 18 years and continuing in employment on attaining that age

(I) in his or her first year after having attained the age of 18 years, 80%

(II) in his or her second year after having attained that age, 90%

of the national minimum hourly rate of pay, notwithstanding that the employee, if he or she has changed his or her employer during the relevant period, may have been remunerated at a higher rate by the previous employer."

33 *Payment of Wages Act* 1991.

34 *Organisation of Working Time Act* 1997, Section 19.

35 *Ibid,* Section 14(1).

36 *Ibid,* Section 8.

37 *Ibid,* Section 9(1)(a) and (b).

38 *Ibid*, Section 10.

39 *Ibid*, Section 26.

40 *Parental Leave Act* 1998 Section 7 (1).

41 *Ibid*, Section 19 (3)(c).

42 *Ibid*, Section 13 (1).

43 *Ibid*, Section 13 (2).

44 *Ibid*, Section 13 (4).

45 *Ibid*, Section 13 (1).

46 This form may be downloaded from the Labour Relations Commission website *www.lrc.ie/lrc_services/rights_commissioner.htm* or can be obtained from the Secretariat, Rights Commissioner Service, Labour Relations Commission, Tom Johnson House, Haddington Road, Dublin 4, telephone: (01) 613 6700.

47 Minimum notice is provided for in the *Minimum Notice and Terms of Employment Act* 1973, as amended by the *Work Protection (Regular Part-Time Employees) Act* 1991.

48 According to the *Employment Equality Act* 1998,Section 2(1), (dealing with interpretation), 'marital status' means "single, married, separated, divorced and widowed".

49 'Family status' is described in Section 2(1) of the Act as "responsibility

(a) as a parent or as a person *in loco parentis* in relation to a person who has not attained the age of 18 years, or

(b) as a parent or the resident primary carer in relation to a person of or over that age with a disability which is of such a nature as to give rise to the need for care or support on a continuing, regular or frequent basis".

50 Discrimination on the basis of 'race' is described in the *Employment Equality Act* 1998, Section 6 (2)(h) as "between any two persons that are of a different 'race', 'colour', nationality or ethnic or national origins".

51 'Religious belief' as defined in the *Employment Equality Act* 1998, includes religious background or outlook.

52 The *Employment Equality Act* 1998, Section 2(1) defines 'sexual orientation' as meaning "heterosexual, homosexual or bisexual orientation".

53 'Disability' is defined in the *Employment Equality Act* 1998, Section 2(1) as:

"(a) the total or partial absence of a person's bodily or mental functions, including the absence of a part of the person's body,

(b) the presence in the body of organisms causing, or likely to cause, chronic disease or illness,

(c) the malfunction, malformation or disfigurement of a part of a person's body,

(d) a condition or malfunction which results in a person learning differently from a person without the condition or malfunction, or

(e) a condition, illness or disease which affects a person's thought processes, perception of reality, emotions or judgement which results in disturbed behaviour,

and shall be taken to include a disability which exists at present, or which previously existed but no longer exists, or which may exist in the future or which is imputed to a person".

54 *Employment Equality Act* 1998,Section 8(1).

55 The Equality Authority may be contacted at 2, Clonmel Street, Dublin 2, telephone (01) 417 3333, fax (01) 417 3366, email *info@equality.ie*

56 The respondent must also use the form provided by the ODEI - the equality tribunal to reply (Form ODEI 4). If the correct forms are not used, the provisions in the *Employment Equality Act* 1998, permitting the director to draw inferences from failure to supply information, do not apply.

57 *http://www.labourcourt.ie/labour/labour.nsf/LookupPageLink/formsDownload*

58 Details of these can be obtained from Threshold, 21 Stoneybatter, Dublin 7, email *advice@threshold.ie*

59 Further information is available from the ODEI - the equality tribunal, 3 Clonmel Street, Dublin 2, telephone (01) 477 4100, website *http://www.odei.ie/*

60 Voluntary Health Insurance (VHI), VHI House, Lower Abbey Street, Dublin 1, telephone (01) 874 4499, Lo-call 1850 444 444.

BUPA Ireland, Mill Island, Fermoy, Co. Cork, telephone (021) 42121, or 12 Fitzwilliam Square, Dublin 2, telephone (01) 6627 662, Lo-call 1890 700 890.

61 Case C-184/99 *Grzelczyk v CPAS* [2001] ECR I-6193.

62 Refer to the *International Convention on the Rights of the Child* 1989, Article 2(1), signed by Ireland, 30 September 1990 and ratified 28 September 1992.

63 Department of Education and Science, Marlborough Street, Dublin 1, telephone (01) 873 4700, website *http://www.education.ie/*

64 *European Communities (Aliens) Regulations* 1977, Regulation 2.

65 Council Regulation 68/1612/EEC, 15 October 1968, on *Freedom of Movement for Workers within the Community Articles* 10 and 11.

66 *Ibid,* Article 12.

67 See Appendix B.

68 *European Communities (Aliens) Regulations* 1977 Regulation 5(1).

69 *Ibid,* Regulation 5(2).

70 *Ibid,* Regulation 5(4).

71 Ingoldsby, Brian *Regular Migration to Ireland* paper delivered at the Incorporated Law Society Seminar 'Right to Reside in Ireland' 14 May 2002 at Blackhall Place, Dublin 7.

72 *Irish Nationality and Citizenship Act* 1956, Section 15A (1), as amended by the *Irish Nationality and Citizenship Act* 2001, Section 5.

73 *Irish Nationality and Citizenship Act* 1956, Section 15A (2), as amended by the *Irish Nationality and Citizenship Act* 2001, Section 5.

74 *Irish Nationality and Citizenship Act* 1956, Section 7 (3), as amended by the *Irish Nationality and Citizenship Act* 2001, Section 5.

75 Further information available on the Department of Justice, Equality & Law Reform website *http://www.justice.ie/*

Self-employed/Business Persons

SELF-EMPLOYED/BUSINESS PERSONS

The right of non-nationals to engage in business or be self-employed in Ireland is largely dependent on where they come from.

3.1 *EEA and Swiss Nationals*

3.1.1 *EU Nationals*

The status of Citizenship of the Union was introduced by the Treaty of Maastricht (1992). Article 17 of the *EC Treaty*[a] states:

> Citizenship of the Union is hereby established. Every person holding the nationality of a Member State shall be a citizen of the Union. Citizenship of the Union shall complement and not replace national citizenship.
>
> Citizens of the Union shall enjoy the rights conferred by this Treaty and shall be subject to the duties imposed thereby.

Article 18(1) of the *EC Treaty* states:

> Every Citizen of the Union shall have the right to move and reside freely within the territory of the Member States, subject to the limitations and conditions laid down by this Treaty and by the measures adopted to give it effect.

The right to move and reside referred to in Article 18(1) may be subject to limits and conditions but the competent authorities and, where necessary, the national courts must ensure that these limitations and conditions are applied in compliance with the general principles of Community law and, in particular, the principle of proportionality.[1]

The Commission has proposed replacing these Directives with a general all-embracing Directive to deal with Citizens' migration rights, but this has not been adopted yet.[2] However, it is clear that the effect of Article 18(1) is such that once a Citizen of the Union is lawfully resident in the territory of another Member State, they are entitled to equal treatment with nationals of that State provided they are lawfully resident.[3] For example, regarding political rights, Citizens of the Union have the right to vote and stand in both municipal and European elections, when resident in another Member State.

Self-employed persons have the right to free movement within the EU in accordance with Article 43 of the *EC Treaty*. In addition, Article 49 prohibits restrictions on the provision of services.[b]

The European Communities (Aliens) Regulations, 1977,[4] apply to EU nationals (and also to other EEA and Swiss nationals) who wish to reside in another Member State as a self-employed person.

EEA and Swiss nationals do not require a business permission to establish a business in Ireland and are not required to possess a visa.

---

a Unless otherwise stated, all references to the EC Treaty refer to the *EC Treaty* as amended by the Treaties of Amsterdam and Nice.

b *EC Treaty*, Article 49 states: "Within the framework of the provisions set out below, restrictions on freedom to provide services within the Community shall be prohibited in respect of nationals of Member States who are established in a State of the Community other that that of the person for whom the services are intended."

3.2 Non-EEA and Swiss Nationals

There are two categories of non-EEA nationals:

3.2.1 Nationals of Europe Agreement countries

Nationals from the following ten countries may establish a business in Ireland under the terms of the *Association Agreements*, also known as the *Europe Agreements*, concluded by the EU with the applicant states:

- Poland
- Hungary
- Bulgaria
- Czech Republic
- Romania
- Slovakia
- Lithuania
- Latvia
- Estonia
- Slovenia

As a result, individuals who are nationals of these states have the right to establish a business in the Member States.[a] They have the right to:

- pursue economic activities as self-employed persons and to set up and manage undertakings, in particular companies which they effectively control.
- take up and pursue economic activities by means of setting up and managing subsidiaries, branches and agencies (in regard to companies) and in order to do this, to send key personnel, as defined in the agreements.[5]

However, nationals of *Europe Agreement* countries require a business permission to establish a business in Ireland.

There are several organisations that can provide assistance to business persons wishing to establish a business in Ireland including the Industrial Development Authority (IDA)[b] and Enterprise Ireland.[c]

a Poland and Hungary from 1 Feb 1994, Bulgaria, Czech Republic, Romania and Slovakia from 1 Feb 1995 and Lithuania, Latvia, Estonia and Slovenia from 31 December 1999. The right of establishment for individuals from Slovenia has been delayed until six years after entry into force of the *Association Agreements* with Slovenia. Guild, Elspeth *A Right to the Establishment under the Europe Agreements* Bailey, Shaw and Gillett, London (1996), p5.

b The IDA sources overseas investment for Ireland *http://www.ida.ie/*

c Enterprise Ireland is an enterprise development agency dealing mainly with the food, drink and timber industries *http://www.enterprise-ireland.ie/*

3.2.2 Turkish Nationals

Under the Turkey Association Agreement, the European Court of Justice recently decided in the case of *Savas*[6] that the Agreement contained a 'stand-still' provision which prevented signatory states from introducing more restrictive immigration regulations for self-employed persons than were in place when the Agreement became effective in that Member State. The meaning of this judgment is yet to be tested in Ireland. For the UK, which was bound by the Agreement 1 January 1973, it is likely to mean that the requirement to invest St£200,000 and certain other requirements cannot be applied to Turkish nationals. This means that the rights of entry and residence for self-employed Turkish nationals may become similar to those extended to the nationals of CEEC countries under the Europe Agreements.[7]

3.2.3 Other Non-EEA and Swiss nationals

Non-EEA and Swiss nationals can establish a business in Ireland, but they require a business permission.

There are several organisations that can provide assistance to business persons wishing to establish a business in Ireland including the Industrial Development Authority (IDA)[b] and Enterprise Ireland.[c]

3.3 What Is a Business Permission?

A business permission is a written permission from the Minister allowing the person or persons concerned to establish and engage in a business in Ireland for a certain duration. Such persons are granted residency in Ireland for the duration of the validity of the business permission. A business permission is usually granted for one year initially.

3.3.1 Are there any Non-EEA or Swiss Nationals who can establish a business without a business permission?

The following Non-EEA or Swiss nationals can establish a business in Ireland without a business permission:

- persons who have been recognised as a refugee by the Minister for Justice, Equality & Law Reform
- persons who are granted leave to remain as the spouse of an Irish or EEA/Swiss national
- persons who are granted leave to remain as the parent of an Irish citizen
- persons whose application for refugee status has been refused but who are given temporary leave to remain.

3.4 Applying for Business Permissions
3.4.1 What are the requirements for business permissions?

Before a non-EEA national may be granted a business permission, certain criteria must be fulfilled:

- the proposed business must result in capital exceeding €300,000 being transferred to the State (see Section 3.4.2 page 62 for exceptions to this requirement)

---

b The IDA sources overseas investment for Ireland *http://www.ida.ie/*

c Enterprise Ireland is an enterprise development agency dealing mainly with the food, drink and timber industries *http://www.enterprise-ireland.ie/*

- the proposed business must create employment for at least two Irish or EEA/Swiss nationals or at least maintain employment in an existing business (see Section 3.4.2 below for exceptions to this requirement)
- the proposed business should add to the commercial activity and competitiveness of Ireland
- the proposed business should, if possible, manufacture or otherwise substitute Irish goods which are currently being imported
- the proposed business must have sufficient turnover to enable the applicant to support themselves and any dependants without having to avail of social welfare payments or entering paid employment (for which an employment permit would be required)
- the applicant must be of good character and in possession of a valid passport or national identity document

3.4.2 Are there any exceptions to these requirements?

The requirements to employ at least two Irish or EEA/Swiss nationals and to invest capital in excess of €300,000 do not have to be met in the following cases where the applicant:

- is seeking the right to establish a business under the *Association Agreements*, also known as the *Europe Agreements*, between the EU and Central and Eastern European States[a]
- has been legally resident in Ireland for at least five years, has been in employment and has not breached immigration legislation
- is an artist, writer or crafts person; the Department of Justice Equality & Law Reform should be contacted separately

3.4.3 What documentation is required?

Applicants for business permissions need to submit the following documentation to the Immigration Division of the Department of Justice, Equality & Law Reform:

- a valid passport or national identity document
- a Certificate of Registration (if the person is already legally resident in Ireland)
- a statement that the applicant is of good character to be obtained from the police authorities in each country that the applicant has resided for six months or more during the past ten years
- a business plan (the plan must address the criteria which need to be met before a business permission can be granted and should be endorsed by a firm of accountants or other relevant professionals)

a Poland and Hungary from 1 Feb 1994, Bulgaria, Czech Republic, Romania and Slovakia from 1 Feb 1995 and Lithuania, Latvia, Estonia and Slovenia from 31 December 1999. (The right of establishment for individuals from Slovenia has been delayed until six years after entry into force of the *Association Agreements* with Slovenia).

3.5 Appealing Business Permissions that have Been Refused

Persons who are refused a business permission will be informed of the reasons for the refusal in writing. The decision may be appealed within one month of the date of refusal.

3.6 Renewing Business Permissions

Persons wishing to renew an existing business permission should do so one month before the permission is due to expire. The applicant must enclose with their application audited accounts and evidence that the business has complied with taxation requirements. The applicant must also demonstrate that the business continues to meet the required criteria. If the application meets the relevant criteria, the applicant will be granted a renewal for a further year. Further renewals may be for a period of up to five years.

3.7 Applying for Visas

Persons coming to Ireland to establish a business, who are nationals of a state whose passport holders require a visa in order to travel to Ireland, must obtain a visa.[a] Applications can be made:

- through the Irish Embassy/Consulate in the applicant's country of residence
- through any Irish Embassy or Consulate if there is none in the applicant's country of residence
- by post, directly to the Visa Office, Department of Foreign Affairs, 13/14 Burgh Quay, Dublin 2, if there is no Irish Embassy or Consulate in the applicant's country of residence

Applicants must include the following documentation with their application:

- a completed visa application form
- a valid passport (or a full copy of the passport, if the application is being made by post, or directly to the Visa Office of the Department of Foreign Affairs)
- evidence that the applicant has been granted a business permission by the Minister for Justice, Equality & Law Reform
- a visa application fee[b]
- two passport photographs of the applicant

3.8 Appealing Visa Applications that Have Been Refused

A person whose application for a visa has been refused may apply to the Visa Section of the Department of Justice, Equality & Law Reform to have the application reviewed by a more senior official. Before doing so, they should request the reasons for the initial refusal of the visa application; these are not automatically provided but in most cases contain important information relevant to the appeal.

---

a Under the provisions of the *Aliens (Visas) Order* 2002 ,SI No. 178 of 2002, certain non-nationals are not required to possess a visa to travel to Ireland. Persons from states not listed are required to have a visa (see Appendix A).

b Visa Application Processing Fees are: €25 for a single-journey and €50 for a multiple-entry visa. Citizens of the following countries are exempt for the visa application fee: Bosnia, Bulgaria, Ecuador, Indonesia, Ivory Coast, Kirghizstan, Morocco, Peru, Slovak Republic, Sri Lanka, Tanzania, Tunsia, Uganda, Yugoslavia and Zambia (as of 1 January 2002).

3.9 What Rules Govern Entry to the State for Self employed/ Business Persons?

3.9.1 UK nationals

Ireland and the UK[a] share a Common Travel Area. This means that UK nationals coming to Ireland to establish a business (or for any other purpose) are not subject to immigration controls at Irish airports and ports. Since June 1997, as a result of an order made under the *Aliens Act*, 1935,[8] Immigration Officers may carry out checks on persons arriving from the UK. UK nationals should carry their passport or some other form of identification to satisfy Immigration Officers that they are in fact UK nationals.

3.9.2 EEA and Swiss nationals

EEA and Swiss nationals are not required to possess a visa to travel to Ireland. They must possess a passport or national identity card, which should be shown to Immigration Officers at the port or airport of entry.

In accordance with the *European Communities (Aliens) Regulations*, 1977, EEA and Swiss nationals may only be refused leave to land if: "... his or her personal conduct has been such that it would be contrary to public policy or would endanger public security",[9] or if the person is suffering from a scheduled disease.[b]

3.9.3 Non-EEA and Swiss nationals

Non-EEA and Swiss nationals coming to Ireland to establish a business are required to possess a valid passport and visa, if required.[c] They should possess their business permission and be in a position to satisfy Immigration Officers that they have sufficient funds to support themselves and their family until the business has been established.

3.9.3.1 Refusal of leave to land

Persons who arrive in Ireland must fulfil certain criteria before they are allowed to enter the country, otherwise they may be refused leave to land.[d] The *Aliens Order*, 1946 (as amended) lists the grounds on which a non-national may be refused leave to land.[e]

A person who is refused leave to land must be informed of the reasons for refusal. They may be arrested and detained until such time as they may be removed from the State.[10] A deportation order may be made in respect of them by the Minister for Justice, Equality & Law Reform.[11] The person will be notified of the Minister's intention to make such an order and informed that they must either:

---

a This includes the Isle of Man and the Channel Islands.

b See Appendix B for details.

c See Appendix A for details.

d To 'land' means "to arrive or enter by any means including over a land frontier" (from Northern Ireland). *Aliens Order* 1946 Section 3.

e See Appendix C for details.

- make representations to the Minister within 15 working days, setting out the reasons why they should not be deported
- leave Ireland voluntarily within 15 working days (if the person agrees to leave, they must inform the Minister of their arrangements)
- consent to the making of the deportation order within 15 working days

3.10 Registering with the (Garda) Registration Officer[12]

3.10.1 EEA and Swiss nationals

The European Communities (Aliens) Regulations, 1977, apply to EEA and Swiss nationals, who are coming to Ireland to establish a business.[13] They may apply for a residence permit within three months of arrival in Ireland if they intend to remain in Ireland for more than three months. Regulation 5(1)(c) states:

> *A person to whom these Regulations apply and who:... is in employment in the State...may apply for a permit (which shall be known and is in these Regulations referred to as a 'residence permit') for a national of a Member State of the European Communities to the registration officer of the registration district in which he is a resident.*

Although a residence permit is not obligatory for EEA nationals in self-employment in Ireland, it is recommended that they apply for one. From 1 December 2002, when the relevant section of the *Irish Nationality and Citizenship Act*, 2001, came into force, if an EEA or Swiss national applies for a certificate of naturalisation, the period during which they lived in Ireland without a residence permit will not be counted.[14]

An application for a residence permit should be made to the registration officer in the area where the person resides. The local registration officer is a member of the Gardaí. Applicants should inquire at their local Garda station for the location of the registration officer for the area in which they reside. In Dublin this is the Garda National Immigration Bureau.

The duration of the residence permit granted to EEA and Swiss nationals is five years and it is renewable.

3.10.2 Non-EEA and Swiss Nationals

Non-EEA and Swiss nationals who come to Ireland to establish a business must report to the registration officer in the area where they reside. The local registration officer is a member of the Gardaí. Applicants should inquire at their local Garda station for the location of the registration officer for the area in which they reside. In Dublin this is the Garda National Immigration Bureau. They will be required to produce their passport and documentation relating to the purpose of their arrival in Ireland, for example, their business permission.

The person is then issued with a Certificate of Registration by the registration officer. The Certificate of Registration contains a photograph of the holder and states the duration of their permission to remain in Ireland. It also contains a stamp,[a] the number of which indicates the basis on which the Certificate of Registration was provided.

---

a Stamp No. 1 refers to people who are entitled to work if they are in possession of an employment permit/work visa/work authorisation. Stamp A refers to medical practitioners entitled to work without an employment permit (see Appendix D).

3.11 Registering for Tax

All self-employed persons coming to Ireland should notify the tax office when starting business. They are required to register for the payment of tax by completing one of the following forms:

Category...	Should complete form...
Sole trader	STR to register for Income Tax, PRSI/PAYE and Value Added Tax (VAT).
Partnership between two or more business persons	TR1 to register for Income Tax, PRSI/PAYE and Value Added Tax (VAT).
Limited company	TR2 to register for Corporation Tax, Employers PRSI/PAYE and Value Added Tax (VAT)

All persons who have a business permission, and a business with a turnover exceeding €25,500 are obliged to register for VAT.

3.11.1 Requesting a visit from a revenue official

The tax system for business persons can appear rather complex and the Tax Office provides assistance to business persons in complying with their obligations. Business persons may request a 'New Business Visit' from a revenue official who will assist with operating the tax system.[a]

3.12 What Rights and Entitlements Do Self-employed/Business Persons Have?

3.12.1 What types of accommodation can self-employed/business persons access?

Business persons coming to Ireland have three options with regard to accommodation:

- private rented accommodation

- local authority accommodation

- purchase

3.12.1.1 Private rented accommodation

Persons wishing to rent a house or apartment from a private landlord can do so directly themselves by replying to advertisements in newspapers or seek the assistance of a letting agency. Finding accommodation can be expensive and time-consuming, particularly in big cities. Prospective tenants should:

---

a This service can be requested from the local tax office if living outside the Dublin area, or the Taxes Central Registration Office (Telephone: (01) 865 5000) if within the Dublin area.

- Inspect the property before agreeing to move in and record the condition of the property and its contents in writing. Houses and apartments to let should comply with certain minimum standards.[15]

- Agree the amount of deposit and rent to be paid and the time of payment. A receipt should be obtained for all money paid to the landlord. The deposit should be returned to the tenant when s/he leaves the accommodation. However, the landlord may retain some or all of the deposit if: the tenant gives insufficient notice, damages the property, or leaves without paying bills or rent.

- Find out whether the rent covers such items as electricity, gas and bin charges (where relevant).

- Agree on who is responsible for any repairs that need to be carried out in the future.

Tenants should be aware of their rights and duties as a tenant. The most important of these are:

- The landlord must provide a rent book. The rent book should contain the name and address of the landlord, amount of deposit paid, the amount of rent and the time and method of payment. All rent payments should be entered in the rent book. The rent book should also include the terms of the tenancy.

- The landlord is not permitted (except in cases of emergency) to enter the accommodation without making an appointment with the tenant.

- The landlord must give a minimum of four weeks notice in writing if they require the tenant to leave the accommodation. This is referred to as a 'notice to quit'. If the tenant does not leave by the end of the four-week period, the landlord can go to court to apply for an eviction order.

- The tenant must also provide notice to the landlord if they decide to move out.

3.12.1.2 Local authority (council or corporation) Housing

Local authority housing is available, generally for persons who do not have sufficient resources to provide their own accommodation. Practice with regard to eligibility for local authority housing varies. Priority is usually given to low-income families with children and to older persons. However, there is usually a long waiting list of people for local authority housing.

Persons who are interested in being considered for local authority housing should:

- Contact their nearest local authority (see Appendix E for a full list of local authorities in Ireland), and obtain a copy of the authority's scheme of letting priorities. This sets out the rules for the allocation of accommodation including such matters as how applicants are prioritised and what type of accommodation may be provided to different categories of applicants.

- If the person is still interested in local authority accommodation, they should complete the application form, which is provided by the local authority.

- There is no requirement to live in the area for a certain time in order to qualify for local authority housing. It is possible to apply to more than one local authority, but not all local authorities accept applications from outside their area.

- Non-nationals who wish to apply for local authority accommodation may be required to provide evidence that they intend, and are entitled, to live in Ireland permanently. The practice varies with regard to this requirement and persons should contact their local authority.

- When the application has been received, an official from the local authority or health board will usually visit the applicant. (However, practice varies between local authorities and they may visit the applicant only when suitable accommodation is available).

- As most local authorities have insufficient accommodation to meet the demand, they will put the applicant's name on a list. Some local authorities have a 'points system' to assist them in determining the greatest need for accommodation among applicants. An applicant will be awarded points for issues such as overcrowding.

3.12.1.2.1 *Offer of accommodation:*

If the person is offered a house or flat by the local authority and decides to take it, they must sign a tenancy agreement.

- The tenancy agreement is legal document and both the tenant and the local authority must adhere to the terms of the agreement.

- In the case of a married couple or partners, the tenancy is usually in joint names.

- The amount of rent to be paid per week is based on the income of the household.

- It is important to ensure that rent is paid up to date as the tenant may be issued with a notice to quit if arrears of rent have built up.

- Tenants can apply to transfer to another area.

3.12.1.3 *Purchase*

There are no restrictions on non-nationals buying private residential property in Ireland.[a] However, there are requirements under the Land Acts and additional documents may be required. There are some restrictions with regard to farmland.[b]

However, persons should be aware that house purchase can be a lengthy and costly process, therefore, for some self-employed/business persons renting a property may be a better option. It is important to note that a person's business permission will not be extended simply because the person has bought property in Ireland, or is in the process of purchasing property.

---

a The *Aliens Act*, 1935 states that "Real and personal property of every description in Saorstat Eireann or subject to the law of Saorstat Eireann may be taken, acquired, held and disposed of by an alien in like manner and to the like extend as such property may be taken, acquired, held or disposed of by a citizen of Saorstat Eireann".

b These restrictions apply to non-EU nationals wishing to buy land over five acres in size. They should contact the Department of Agriculture, Food and Rural Development, Agriculture House, Kildare Street, Dublin 2, telephone (01) 607 2000, Lo-call 1890 200 510.

Persons interested in buying a private house or apartment may find a suitable property through an auctioneer/estate agent or through advertisements in local and national newspapers.

- Persons who cannot afford to buy a property from their own resources need to get a mortgage from a building society or bank.
- Houses/apartments should be viewed and in the case of a second-hand house or apartment, a survey should be carried out to ensure that it is structurally sound.
- If the person is satisfied that they have found a property they wish to buy, they should make an offer, if the property is for sale by private treaty. If the property is for sale by auction, they must attend the auction and the highest bidder purchases the property.
- Generally, estate agents do not charge a fee to purchasers of property.
- The purchase of property can be complicated, and prospective buyers should always engage a solicitor to act for them.

3.12.1.4 What laws govern discrimination in the provision of accommodation?

The *Equal Status Act*, 2000, prohibits discrimination on the grounds of gender, marital status, family status, sexual orientation, religious belief, age, disability, "race" and membership of the Traveller Community in the provision of goods and services, the disposal of property and access to education. Discrimination on the nine grounds listed in the Act is prohibited in both the public and private sectors. The process for referring complaints is similar to that under the *Employment Equality Act*, 1998. Further information is available from the equality tribunal.[16]

3.12.2 What medical services are self-employed/business persons entitled to?

Self-employed/business persons coming to Ireland have two options with regard to medical care:

- public health care
- private health care

3.12.2.1 Public health care

The public health care system, including primary and hospital services, can be accessed by any person resident in Ireland including those on business permission. This system can be accessed for a nominal charge, or free of charge for medical card holders.

3.12.2.1.1 What services can be accessed for a nominal charge?

A range of services are available including:

- General Practitioner (GP) services (family doctor) with a charge of between €30 and €50 per consultation
- in-patient hospital treatment in a public ward subject to a daily charge of €40[a]

---

a Up to a maximum of €400 in any twelve-month period (as of 1 January 2003).

- all other out-patient services including consultants
- visits to hospital Accident and Emergency Departments subject to a charge of €40 (persons who are referred by their GP will not be charged)
- maternity and infant care

3.12.2.1.2 Who can access medical services free of charge?

To access free medical care in Ireland, a person needs a medical card. Generally, self-employed/business persons do not qualify for the medical card as their income normally exceeds the means test limit.

3.12.2.1.3 Who is entitled to a medical card?

Entitlement to a medical card in Ireland is based on a person's residence and means. To be fully eligible for a medical card a person must:

- be 'ordinarily resident' in Ireland; this means that they must intend to live in Ireland for at least one year and be permitted to do so

- satisfy the means test; a person will only be eligible for free medical care (Category A entitlement, that is medical card holders) if their gross income, less PRSI contributions is less than €138 and in the case of a married couple or single parent €200.[a]

3.12.2.1.4 What does a medical card entitle you to?

A medical card entitles you to the following free medical services:
- General Practitioner (GP) services (but you must register with a GP)
- prescribed medicines
- in-patient hospital treatment in a public ward
- out-patient hospital treatment
- dental, ophthalmic and aural services
- community care services

3.12.2.2 Private health care

Persons can also take out private health insurance.[b] This insurance covers private care in public or private hospitals. There are two private health insurers in Ireland, VHI and BUPA.[17] Medical insurance will not cover pre-existing medical conditions and the cover may not, in any event, take effect for an initial period.

---

a A married couple or a single parent must earn less than €200. These rates apply to persons under 66 years of age. Persons applying for the medical card are permitted to have the following amounts over the income level and still qualify for the medical card, as of 1 January 2003:

- €25 for each child under 16 years
- €26 for each child over 16 years with no income maintained by applicant
- the amount by which the rent or mortgage paid each week exceeds €25
- the amount by which the costs of travelling to and from work each week exceeds €22
- weekly expenditure on medicines

b Persons who wish to avail of private health care and who have not taken out private health insurance will be required to pay for hospital treatment.

3.12.3 What social welfare entitlements do self-employed/business persons have?

Irish social welfare legislation does not distinguish between nationals and non-nationals. Essentially, any person from outside the State who complies with the relevant laws covering entry, living and working here is entitled to seek social welfare payments in compliance with the normal conditions.

Self-employed persons and business persons are generally not entitled to social welfare payments. They are expected to have sufficient funds to maintain themselves while their business is being established.

Furthermore, a business permission is unlikely to be renewed once a businessperson has had to rely on the social welfare system in order to maintain themselves financially.

For further information, contact the Information Service of the Department of Social and Family Affairs on (01) 704 3000.

3.12.4 What education can self-employed/business persons access?

3.12.4.1 EEA and Swiss nationals

3.12.4.1.1 EU nationals

All EU citizens are entitled to equal treatment in the educational sector in Ireland on the same basis as Irish citizens. Thus for example, migrant EU students are entitled to the same fee level (or none as the case may be) and maintenance grants as national students.[18]

3.12.4.1.2 EEA and Swiss Nationals

EEA and Swiss nationals are generally entitled to education on the same basis as Irish nationals. However, EEA nationals (other than those belonging to the EU) and Swiss nationals are not entitled to local authority/VEC education grants. Third-level education fees vary between educational institutions.

3.12.4.2 Non-EEA nationals

Persons who are self-employed in Ireland may not generally change their status in the State. If they wish to take up full-time study in the State (for example, after the expiry of their business permission) they must normally return to their country of origin and apply for a place in the educational institution in which they wish to study. They should possess a letter of acceptance from the college and a visa (if one is required[a]) before coming to Ireland to study. Non-EEA nationals will be charged the full international economic fee rate for third-level education. Third-level education fees vary between educational institutions.

a See Appendix A for details.

3.12.4.3 Children of self-employed/business persons

All children and young people under the age of 18 in Ireland have the same rights irrespective of the child's or parent's/parents' or legal caregivers' race, colour, sex, language, religion, political or other opinion, national, ethnic or social origin, property, disability, birth or other status.[19] Children of non-EEA nationals can therefore access services on the same basis as an Irish child. Children of non-EEA nationals are registered on their parent's/parents' or legal caregivers' Certificate of Registration until the age of 16. However, children's birth certificates are usually required for identification and other purposes. Thereafter, they must register themselves, in their own name, with the registration officer in the area where reside. The local registration officer is a member of the Gardaí. Applicants should inquire at their local Garda station for the location of the registration officer for the area in which they reside. In Dublin, this is the Garda National Immigration Bureau.

All children and young people in Ireland must engage in full-time education until they are 16 years old. At first and second level, there are two main education sectors: primary school (first level), and post-primary and vocational training (second level).

Schools are managed by the State (Comprehensive, Vocational Education Committees [VECs]) and religious bodies (Catholic, Protestant, Muslim, Jewish) and governed by their own ethos/philosophy. Lists of schools are available from the Department of Education and Science.[20]

Children with language needs are generally placed in classes with other children/young people of a similar age. Government support is provided to allow schools to offer limited language support programmes for bilingual and multilingual children.

To apply to a school or education centre, parents or legal caregivers follow the process below:

- The parents/legal caregivers contact the local school/education centre of choice by writing or telephoning the school principal or manager to arrange a meeting.

- At the first meeting, the parents/legal caregivers are provided with the formal school/education centre policy which outlines the ethos, selection criteria and other matters.

- The parents/legal caregivers are required to provide the school/education centre with basic information on the student.

- An informal education and linguistic assessment of the student may take place but there is no State interpretation facility for this process. Schools/education centres cannot refuse access to a student on the basis of their level of English.

- If there are no places, or if the school/education centre is unsuitable for the student, the school/education centre recommends another school/education centre in the locality.

- If the student is offered a place in a school, the parents/legal caregivers should obtain a letter of acceptance from the school/education centre.

3.12.5 What family reunification rights do self-employed/business persons have?

3.12.5.1 EEA and Swiss nationals

EEA and Swiss national employees business persons are permitted to be joined in Ireland by certain members of their family[21] (this applies also to family members who are non-EEA nationals):

- spouses, children aged under 21, and children over 21 if they are dependent on the self-employed/business person
- spouses of any children of the self-employed/business person and their spouse
- dependent parents and grandparents of the self-employed/business person and their spouse
- other dependent relatives in the ascending line of the self-employed/business person and their spouse

Section 2(2) of the *European Communities (Aliens) Regulations*, 1977, defines dependants as:

> *the person's spouse, children under 21 years of age of the person and the spouse, other children of the person and the spouse if such other children are dependent on the person, the spouses of any children of the person, and the spouse and dependent direct lineal ancestors and descendants of the person and the spouse.*

The dependent relatives as defined above may take up employment in Ireland[22] and children of the self-employed/business person are entitled to attend educational courses, including apprenticeships and vocational training on the same basis as Irish nationals.[23]

3.12.5.1.1 Entry to the State

The family members of EEA and Swiss nationals self-employed in Ireland must produce a passport or national identity card, as in the case of the self-employed/business person. They will only be refused leave to land by Immigration Officers, if they are suffering from a scheduled disease or their conduct has been such that it would be contrary to public policy or endanger public security.[a]

If the family members are not themselves nationals of Switzerland or an EEA Member State and if they come from a country whose nationals are required to possess a visa to travel to Ireland, they will have to obtain a visa prior to arrival. In either case, they should travel with sufficient evidence establishing that they are married to, or dependent on, an EEA or Swiss national who is resident and employed in Ireland.

---

a See Appendix B for details.

3.12.5.1.2 Residence permits

Family members of EEA and Swiss nationals may apply for a residence permit.[24] If the family members are not EEA or Swiss nationals, they may apply to the registration officer[25] for a residence permit. The local registration officer is a member of the Gardaí. Applicants should inquire at their local Garda station for the location of the registration officer for the area in which they reside. In Dublin, this is the Garda National Immigration Bureau. Family members may remain in the State for three months without applying for a residence permit.[26]

3.12.5.2 Non-EEA and Swiss nationals

Self-employed/business persons from outside the EEA and Switzerland have no statutory rights to family reunification. However, if they are in a position to support their family, without recourse to public funds, family members may be permitted to join them in Ireland.

3.12.6 How can self-employed/business persons acquire Irish citizenship?

Self-employed/business persons in Ireland can become Irish citizens in three ways:

- naturalisation
- post-nuptial citizenship
- by descent

The *Irish Nationality and Citizenship Acts* 1956, 1986, 1994 and 2001 set out the criteria under which Irish citizenship is granted.

3.12.6.1 Acquiring citizenship by naturalisation

A person wishing to apply for a certificate of naturalisation must fulfil certain conditions including having legally resided in Ireland for five years out of the previous nine-year period. The Minister for Justice, Equality & Law Reform may grant an application for a certificate of naturalisation at their discretion if they are satisfied that the applicant:

- is of full age
- is of good character
- has had a period of one year's continuous residence in Ireland immediately prior to their application, and in the eight years immediately preceding that period has had a total residence of four years in Ireland
- intends in good faith to continue to reside in Ireland after naturalisation
- has made a declaration of fidelity to the nation and loyalty to the State, either before a District Court Justice or in such other manner permitted by the Minister

The Minister for Justice, Equality & Law Reform may waive these conditions in certain circumstances specified in the Acts. The number of circumstances in which the Minister may waive the conditions, has been reduced by the 2001, Act.[a]

---

a *Irish Nationality and Citizenship Act* 1956, Section 16 (as amended by *Irish Nationality and Citizenship Act*, 1986, Section 5). Since the coming into force of the 2001 Act, this no longer applies to persons married to a naturalised Irish citizen or persons married to a person who is an Irish citizen otherwise than by naturalisation.

3.12.6.2 Acquiring post-nuptial citizenship

A non-national who married an Irish national on or before 29 November 2002, and has been in a subsisting marriage with that person for a minimum of three years, may become an Irish citizen by making a post-nuptial declaration of citizenship. However, this is not possible if the Irish spouse has acquired citizenship by naturalisation, post-nuptial declaration, or was granted citizenship as a token of honour. Any such declarations will have to be made before 30 November 2005.

In the case of spouses of Irish nationals who got married on or after 30 November, 2002, the Minister may at his 'absolute discretion' grant an application for a certificate of naturalisation to the spouse of an Irish citizen if the applicant:

- is of full age

- is of good character

- is married to an Irish citizen for at least three years

- is in a subsisting marriage, recognised as being in accordance with Irish legislation

- is living together with the Irish citizen as husband and wife (the applicant must submit an affidavit to that effect to the Minister)

- has lived in Ireland for at least one year continuously prior to the application

- has been resident in Ireland for at least two years of the four years immediately preceding that period

- intends in good faith to continue to reside in Ireland after naturalisation

- has made a declaration of 'fidelity to the nation and loyalty to the State' in whatever manner may be prescribed[27]

The Minister for Justice, Equality & Law Reform may waive certain of the above conditions if satisfied that the applicant would suffer serious consequences in respect of his or her bodily integrity or liberty if not granted Irish citizenship.[28]

3.12.6.3 Acquiring citizenship by descent

Persons whose father or mother was an Irish Citizen at the time of their birth are automatically Irish citizens. However, if a person is born outside Ireland, and the parent through whom they are claiming citizenship was also born outside Ireland, they will not be entitled to citizenship except in certain limited circumstances.[29] Persons whose grandparents were Irish citizens can become Irish citizens by registering in the Foreign Births Register in the Department of Foreign Affairs or, if residing outside Ireland, at the nearest Irish Embassy or Consulate.

3.12.6.4 Acquiring permission to remain without condition as to time

Persons who have been legally resident in Ireland for ten years and who have not applied for naturalisation may obtain a residence stamp giving them 'permission to remain without condition as to time'.[30]

3.12.8 What do self-employed/business persons need to open a bank account?

Banks require new customers to produce the following documents when opening a bank account:

- photo identification (a passport satisfies this requirement)

- proof of address in Ireland, for example a utility bill (electricity, gas or other utility) or lease agreement

- although not officially documented as a requirement, banks often request applicants to provide a personal introduction from an existing customer

3.12.9 Can self-employed/business persons vote in elections?

Non-national residents in Ireland over 18 years of age may vote in some elections:

Citizens of...	Permitted to vote at...
The UK	Dáil, European and local elections
EU states apart from the UK	European and local elections
Non-EU states	Local elections only

Those permitted to vote must have their name included in the Electoral Register if they want to vote. Application forms are available in post offices, libraries and council and corporation offices.

Endnotes

1   Case C-413/99 *Baumbast*, 17 September 2002.

2   Proposal for a European Parliament and Council Directive 29 June 2001 on the *Right of Citizens of the Union and their   Family Members to Move and Reside Freely within the Territory of the Member States* COM(2001) 257 final [2001] OJ C270 E/23.

3   Case C-85/96 *Maria Martinez Sala v Freistaat Bayern* [1998] ECR I-2691.

4   These Regulations give effect to several EU Directives including Council Directive 68/360/EEC,15 October 1968, on the *Abolition of Restrictions on Movement and Residence within the Community for Workers of Member States and their Families.* This Directive deals with the rights of EU nationals (and members of their families) to take up employment and residence in another EU Member State. It provides for the issue of residence permits as proof of the right of residence. SI No 393 of 1977.

5   Guild, Elspeth and Staples, Helen 'Inside Out and Outside In: Third-country Nationals in European Law and Beyond' in European Union Law and Policy on *Immigration and Asylum* Universite Libre de Bruxelles, Brussels (2001).p. 192.

6   *Savas*, C-37/98, [2000], All ER (EC) 627.

7   Duran Seddon (Ed.) *Joint Council for the Welfare of Immigrants, Immigration, Nationality & Refugee Law Handbook* 2002 Edition, p. 481.

8   *Aliens (Ammendment) (No.3) Order* 1997, SI No. 277.

9   *European Communities (Aliens) Regulations* 1977, Regulations 4 (i) and 4 (ii), SI No. 393.

10 The *Aliens Order* 1946 (as amended), Section 5.

11 The *Immigration Act* 1999,Section 3 (1)(g).

12 This is provided for in the *Aliens Order* 1946, Section 11.

13 These Regulations give effect to several EU Directives including Council Directive 68/360/EEC,15 October 1968, on the *Abolition of Restrictions on Movement and Residence within the Community for Workers of Member States and their Families.* This Directive deals with the rights of EU nationals (and members of their families) to take up employment and residence in another EU Member State. It provides for the issue of residence permits as proof of the right of residence. SI No. 393 of 1977.

14 Section 16A(1) of the Act states that:

"When calculating a period of residence in the State for the purposes of an application for a certificate of naturalisation

(a) in the case of a non-national who is a person to whom the European Communities (Aliens) Regulations 1997 (SI No. 393 of 1977) apply, no period shall be reckoned in relation to which the non-national was not the holder or subject of a residence permit or document granted under those Regulations or the European Communities (Right of Residence for Non-Economically Active Persons) Regulations 1997 (SI No. 57 of 1997)."

15 Details of these can be obtained from Threshold, 21 Stoneybatter, Dublin 7, email advice@threshold.ie.

16 Further information is available from the ODEI - the equality tribunal, 3 Clonmel Street, Dublin 2, telephone (01) 477 4100, website *http://www.odei.ie/*

17 Voluntary Health Insurance (VHI), VHI House, Lower Abbey Street, Dublin 1, telephone (01) 874 4499, Lo-call 1850 444 444.

BUPA Ireland, Mill Island, Fermoy, Co. Cork, telephone (021) 42121, or 12 Fitzwilliam Square, Dublin 2, telephone (01) 6627 662, Lo-call 1890 700 890.

18 Case C-184/99 *Grzelczyk v CPAS* [2001] ECR I-6193.

19 Refer to the *International Convention on the Rights of the Child* 1989, Article 2(1), signed by Ireland, 30 September 1990 and ratified 28 September 1992.

20 Department of Education and Science, Marlborough Street, Dublin 1, telephone (01) 873 4700, website *http://www.education.ie/*

21 *European Communities (Aliens) Regulations* 1977, Regulation 2.

22 Council Regulation 68/1612/EEC, 15 October 1968, on *Freedom of Movement for Workers within the Community* Articles 10 and 11.

23 *Ibid,* Article 12.

24 *European Communities (Aliens) Regulations* 1977, Regulation 5 (1).

25 *Ibid*, Regulation 5(2).

26 *Ibid*, Regulation 5(4).

27 *Irish Nationality and Citizenship Act* 1956, Section 15A (1), as amended by the Irish Nationality and Citizenship Act 2001, Section 5.

28 *Irish Nationality and Citizenship Act* 1956, Section 15A (2), as amended by the *Irish Nationality and Citizenship Act* 2001, Section 5.

29 *Irish Nationality and Citizenship Act* 1956, Section 7 (3), as amended by the *Irish Nationality and Citizenship Act* 2001, Section 5.

30 Further information available on the Department of Justice, Equality & Law Reform website *http://www.justice.ie/*

International Students

INTERNATIONAL STUDENTS

The rights and entitlements of international students depend mainly on where they come from and to a lesser extent, the duration of their course of study in Ireland.

According to the Department of Education and Science statistics division, there were 3,377 non-national second-level and 7,413 third-level students in the academic year 1999/2000.[a] The Higher Education Authority provides statistics for third-level students according to nationality. In the academic year 2000/2001, students from over 120 countries were engaged in full-time education in Irish universities and colleges. Thirty-six per cent of these were from North America,[b] 34 per cent from Europe, 28 per cent from Asia and 5 per cent from Africa. The largest single nationality were from the United States of America(1,779 students), with sizeable numbers from Britain (732) and Malaysia (608).

4.1 EEA and Swiss Nationals

4.1.1 EU nationals

The status of Citizenship of the Union was introduced by the Treaty of Maastricht (1992). Article 17 of the *EC Treaty*[c] states:

> *Citizenship of the Union is hereby established. Every person holding the nationality of a Member State shall be a citizen of the Union. Citizenship of the Union shall complement and not replace national citizenship.*
>
> *Citizens of the Union shall enjoy the rights conferred by this Treaty and shall be subject to the duties imposed thereby.*

Article 18(1) of the *EC Treaty* states:

> *Every Citizen of the Union shall have the right to move and reside freely within the territory of the Member States, subject to the limitations and conditions laid down by this Treaty and by the measures adopted to give it effect.*

The right to move and reside, referred to in Article 18(1), may be subject to limits and conditions. For non-economically active migrants which may include students, these conditions include various financial conditions set out in a series of Community Directives.[1] However, the competent authorities and, where necessary, the national courts must ensure that these limitations and conditions are applied in compliance with the general principles of Community law and, in particular, the principle of proportionality.[2]

The Commission has proposed replacing these Directives with a general all-embracing Directive to deal with Citizen's migration rights, but this has not been adopted yet.[3] However, it is clear that the effect of Article 18(1) is such that once a Citizen of the Union is lawfully resident in the territory of another Member State, they are entitled to equal treatment with nationals of that State in most circumstances. Thus for example, migrant EU students are entitled to the same fee levels (or none as the case may be) and maintenance grants as national students.[4] Similarly, regarding welfare rights, equal treatment extends to all EU

a The most recent year for which statistics were available. Both figures include EU and non-EU nationals.

b North America includes Central America and the West Indies.

c Unless otherwise stated, all references to the *EC Treaty* refer to the *EC Treaty* as amended by the Treaties of Amsterdam and Nice.

migrants, regardless of whether they are workers, service providers or simply visitors, provided they are lawfully resident.[5] Regarding political rights, Citizens of the Union have the right to vote and stand in both municipal and European elections, when resident in another Member State.

In addition, students are entitled to access education in other Member States in a 'non-discriminatory' manner and to reside in another Member State for the duration of their course.[6]

A residence permit shall be issued to a student who is a national of an EU Member State if the Minister for Justice, Equality & Law Reform is assured by the student that they have sufficient resources to support themselves, their spouse and any accompanying dependants.[7]

4.1.2 EEA nationals

In 1994 the European Economic Area Agreement was signed between the European Union and Norway, Iceland and Liechtenstein. Nationals of these states enjoy certain rights within the EU similar to those of EU nationals. EEA nationals do not need a visa to enter Ireland to study or for any other purpose.

4.1.3 Swiss nationals

The *European Communities and Swiss Confederation Act,* 2001, came into force in June 2002. As a result, Swiss nationals now have the same rights as EEA nationals in Ireland. Swiss nationals do not need a visa to enter Ireland to study or for any other purpose.

4.2 Non-EEA and Swiss Nationals

Non-EEA and Swiss nationals may study in Ireland if they fulfil certain criteria.[a] Persons who wish to study in Ireland may obtain permission to enter and remain as a student if they can establish that they have enrolled in private education, have paid the relevant fees and have sufficient funds to support themselves during the course of their studies.

Non-EEA and Swiss nationals who have permission to remain in Ireland as students are entitled to take up 'casual employment', that is up to 20 hours per week or full-time work during holiday periods. An employment permit is not required. This only applies during the course of their studies. Should former students wish to continue to work in Ireland, an employment permit will be required. However, a change of status is not normally permitted[b] and persons wishing to take up employment here after they have completed their course of study will usually be required to return to their country of origin and apply from there.

4.3 Applying for Schools and Colleges

Students may study in Ireland at first-, second- and third-level schools and colleges, or at English language schools, and the application process for these different categories is outlined below.

a See criteria in Section 4.5 page 85. In general, they must have a letter of acceptance from a recognised educational institution, sufficient funding to maintain themselves for the duration of their course, full medical insurance and so on.

b It may be permitted where the work follows 'logically' from their course of study, for example.

4.3.1 Applying to first and second-level schools/education centres

At first and second level, there are two main education sectors: primary school (first level), and post-primary and vocational training (second level).

Schools are managed by the State (Comprehensive, Vocational Education Committees [VECs]) and religious bodies (Catholic, Protestant, Muslim, Jewish) and governed by their own ethos/philosophy. Lists of schools are available from the Department of Education and Science.[8]

All children and young people in Ireland must engage in full-time education until they are 16 years old.

The Department of Education and Science funds resource teachers for non-English speaking students at both first and second level.

To apply to a school or education centre, follow the process below (alternatively parents/legal caregivers may contact an organisation to make the necessary arrangements on their behalf):[9]

- Contact the local school/education centre of choice by writing or telephoning the school principal or manager to arrange a meeting.

- At the first meeting, the formal school/education centre policy must be provided, which outlines the ethos, selection criteria and other matters

- The school/education centre will require basic information on the student.

- An informal education and linguistic assessment of the student may take place but there is no State interpretation facility for this process. Schools/education centres cannot refuse access to a student on the basis of their level of English.

- If there are no places, or if the school/education centre is unsuitable for the student, the school/education centre recommends another school/education centre in the locality.

If the student is offered a place in a school, a letter of acceptance from the school/education centre should be obtained stating that the student has been accepted to study in the school, the duration of study, and fees (if applicable). A provisional offer of a place is insufficient.

4.3.2 Applying to third-level colleges

To apply for undergraduate courses, students should contact the Central Applications Office (CAO). The CAO supplies an application pack with a handbook containing details of the courses on offer at Irish universities and institutes of technology.[10]

Post-graduate students should apply directly to the college of their choice.

EU Nationals should submit their application before 1 February of the year they intend to commence study. Applications will be accepted up to 1 May if accompanied by a 'late fee'.[a]

---

a The application fee before 1 February for EU applicants is €25 online and €35 on paper. This fee doubles for late applications.

Non- EU nationals should submit their application before 15 December of the year before they intend to commence study. Applications will be accepted up to 1 May if accompanied by a 'late fee'.[a]

Conditions of entry into third-level vary between educational institutions. For example, proficiency in English may be required, together with specific qualifications.

All students must obtain a formal letter of acceptance from the college where they intend to study and confirmation of fees paid. A provisional letter offering a place is not sufficient.

4.3.3 Applying to English-language schools

Students who want to study the English language should ensure that they only study in a recognised English language school.[b] Persons wishing to study English in Ireland should contact the Marketing English in Ireland ~ Recognised English Language Schools Association (MEI~RELSA). This organisation will provide students with details of recognised English language schools.[11]

Students must obtain a formal letter of acceptance from the language school where they intend to study and confirmation of fees paid. A provisional letter offering a place is not sufficient.

4.4 Applying for Scholarships and Grants

4.4.1 EU nationals

All EU citizens are entitled to equal treatment in the educational sector in Ireland on the same basis as Irish citizens. Thus for example, migrant EU students are entitled to the same fee level (or none as the case may be) and maintenance grants as national students.[12]

4.4.2 EEA and Swiss nationals

EEA nationals (other than those belonging to the EU) and Swiss nationals are not entitled to local authority/VEC education grants. EEA and Swiss nationals in Ireland may be entitled to scholarships from their own government or institutions in their home country. Postgraduate students may also qualify for scholarships granted by the Higher Education Authority in Ireland (HEA).[13] Universities and institutes of technology also offer scholarships to post-graduate students, and students should contact their college for information on these.

4.4.3 Non-EEA and Swiss nationals

Non-EEA and Swiss nationals may qualify for scholarships offered by the Department of Foreign Affairs (Ireland Aid Fellowship), the European Commission and the UN. These scholarships are administered by the Irish Council for International Students (ICOS).[14]

Non-EEA and Swiss are not entitled to higher education grants unless they are already legally resident in Ireland on another basis (for example, having refugee status). Non-EEA and Swiss nationals are charged the full fee rate for third-level education. Third-level education fees vary between educational institutions.

---

a The application fee before 15 December for non-EU applicants is €50 online and €75 on paper. This increases to €75 online and €105 on paper for applications received after 15 December, up to 1 May.

b Students may not be granted a study visa unless the school is recognised by the Department of Education and Science through the Advisory Council for English Language Schools (ACELS).

4.5 *Applying for Visas*

Non-national students from states whose passport holders are required to possess a visa[15] in order to travel to Ireland must obtain a visa.[a] Applications can be made:

- through the Irish Embassy/Consulate in the applicant's country of residence
- through any Irish Embassy or Consulate if there is none in the applicant's country of residence
- by post, directly to the Visa Office, Department of Foreign Affairs, 13/14 Burgh Quay, Dublin 2, if there is no Irish Embassy or Consulate in the applicant's country of residence

Persons wishing to obtain a visa to come to Ireland, as a student must supply the following information/documentation with their application:

- a completed visa application form
- a valid passport (the passport must be valid for at least six months from the date of completion of the course); if applying by post, or directly to the Department of Foreign Affairs, a full copy of the passport must be enclosed; if possible copies of previous passports should also be enclosed
- the date and place of arrival in Ireland and means of travel
- a letter from educational establishment where the applicant has been offered a place confirming that they have been offered a place and have paid the relevant fees (generally evidence that the student has paid a substantial portion of the fees will be accepted)
- a letter stating the sources of funding to cover fees and evidence that the student has sufficient funds to support themselves while in Ireland; such evidence includes bank statements
- the visa application fee[b]
- two passport photographs of the applicant

Students should ensure that the college they have applied to is a recognised college. The college may have to satisfy the Department of Justice, Equality & Law Reform of its credentials.

4.6 *Applying to Extend the Duration of Visas/Residence Permits*

Students who wish to study in Ireland for less than three months should apply for a 'C study visa'. If their course lasts longer than three months they should apply for a 'D study visa'. C-visas are issued to visitors, whereas D-visas are issued to persons who intend to reside in Ireland on a more long-term basis.

Persons who possess a 'C study visa' and who wish to extend the duration of their stay, may be able to extend their residence permit by presenting themselves

---

a Under the provisions of the *Aliens (Visas) Order* 2002,SI No. 178 of 2002, certain non-nationals are not required to possess a visa to travel to Ireland. Persons from states not listed are required to have a visa (see Appendix A).

b Visa application processing fees are currently: €25 for a single journey and €50 for a multiple entry visa. Citizens of the following countries are exempt for the visa application fee: Bosnia, Bulgaria, Ecuador, Indonesia, Ivory Coast, Kirghizstan, Morocco, Peru, Slovak Republic, Sri Lanka, Tanzania, Tunisia, Uganda, Yugoslavia and Zambia (as of 1 January 2002).

to the registration officer in the area where they reside. The local registration officer is a member of the Gardaí. Applicants should inquire at their local Garda station for the location of the registration officer for the area in which they reside. In Dublin, this is the Garda National Immigration Bureau. They may also be requested to apply in writing to the Department of Justice, Equality & Law Reform.[16] In either case, their application should contain the following information:

- details of, and proof of payment of relevant fees

- details of the proposed course

- accommodation details

- evidence of self-sufficiency

- details of attendance at the initial course

- a copy of passport showing the original visa

- visa reference number and nationality

Generally, the duration of a C-visa, and permission to remain granted thereon, is not extended once the person has arrived in Ireland. An extension of a student's temporary permission to remain will be granted in exceptional cases only and students should ensure that they are certain of the duration of their course before making an application for a visa.

4.7 What Rules Govern Entry to the State for International Students?

4.7.1 UK nationals

Ireland and the UK[a] share a Common Travel Area. This means that UK nationals coming to Ireland to study (or for any other purpose) are not subject to immigration controls at Irish airports and ports. Since June 1997, as a result of an order made under the *Aliens Act*, 1935,[17] Immigration Officers may carry out checks on persons arriving from the UK. UK nationals should carry their passport or some other form of identification to satisfy Immigration Officers that they are in fact UK nationals.

4.7.2 EEA and Swiss nationals

EEA and Swiss nationals are not required to possess a visa to travel to Ireland. They must possess a passport or national identity card, which should be shown to Immigration Officers at the port or airport of entry.

In accordance with the *European Communities (Aliens) Regulations,* 1977, EEA and Swiss nationals may only be refused leave to land if: "...his or her personal conduct has been such that it would be contrary to public policy or would endanger public security",[18] or if the person is suffering from a scheduled disease.[b]

4.7.3 Non-EEA and Swiss nationals

Non-EEA and Swiss nationals coming to Ireland for study purposes should possess a valid passport and visa (if required). They should also be able to

a This includes the Isle of Man and the Channel Islands.
b See Appendix B for details.

satisfy Immigration Officers that they can support themselves for the duration of their course and carry evidence that they have enrolled in a school or third-level institution.

4.7.3.1 Refusal of leave to land

Persons who arrive in Ireland must fulfil certain criteria before they are allowed to enter the country, otherwise they may be refused leave to land.[a] The Aliens Order, 1946 (as amended) lists the grounds on which a non-national may be refused leave to land.[b]

A person who is refused leave to land must be informed of the reasons for refusal. They may be arrested and detained until such time as they may be removed from the State.[19] A deportation order may be made in respect of them by the Minister for Justice, Equality & Law Reform.[20] The person will be notified of the Minister's intention to make such an order and informed that they must either:

● make representations to the Minister within 15 working days, setting out the reasons why they should not be deported

● leave Ireland voluntarily within 15 working days (if the person agrees to leave, they must inform the Minister of their arrangements)

● consent to the making of the deportation order within 15 working days

4.8 Registering with the (Garda) Registration Officer [21]

4.8.1 EEA and Swiss nationals

The *European Communities (Right of Residence for Non-Economically Active Persons) Regulations* 1997[22] apply to students coming to Ireland to engage in a course of study. The regulations oblige students who are EEA and Swiss nationals[c] to apply for a residence permit within three months of arrival in Ireland if they intend to remain in Ireland for more than three months.

An application for a residence permit should be made to the registration officer in the area where the person resides. The local registration officer is a member of the Gardaí. Applicants should inquire at their local Garda station for the location of the registration officer for the area in which they reside. In Dublin this is the Garda National Immigration Bureau. Students will be required to produce their passport and documentation relating to the purpose of their arrival in Ireland. The duration of the residence permit is five years and it is renewable.

The residence permit will be granted where the student has 'sufficient resources to support himself, his spouse and any accompanying dependants'.[23]

A valid residence permit may be withdrawn in certain circumstances:[24]

● if the conduct of the permit holder has been such that it would be 'contrary to public policy or would endanger public security to allow them to remain in the State'

---

a To 'land' means "to arrive or enter by any means including over a land frontier" (from Northern Ireland). *Aliens Order* 1946 Section 3.

b See Appendix C for details.

c These regulations apply to nationals of the other EEA States and Switzerland.

- if the residence permit holder no longer has adequate resources to support themselves and their spouse and accompanying dependants

- if the student no longer has full medical insurance for themselves, their spouse and any accompanying dependants

- if the regulations no longer apply to them

4.8.2 Non-EEA and Swiss nationals

Non-EEA and Swiss nationals who come to Ireland to engage in a course of study must report to the registration officer in the area where the person resides. The local registration officer is a member of the Gardaí. Applicants should inquire at their local Garda station for the location of the registration officer for the area in which they reside. In Dublin, this is the Garda National Immigration Bureau. They will be required to produce their passport and documentation relating to the purpose of their arrival in Ireland. In the case of students, this is a letter of acceptance from the school or college where they intend to study, evidence of payment of fees and other documentation relating to their study and their financial circumstances.

The person is then issued with a Certificate of Registration by the registration officer. The Certificate of Registration contains a photograph of the holder and states the duration of their permission to remain in Ireland. It also contains a stamp,[a] the number of which indicates the basis on which the Certificate of Registration was provided.

4.9 What Rights and Entitlements Do International Students Have?

4.9.1 What are the rights of international students in the work place?

Students who are EEA or Swiss nationals are entitled to work in the same manner as any other EEA or Swiss national resident here. Non-EEA nationals may work part time while pursuing their studies and full time during holiday periods.

The rights of part-time workers are protected under the *Protection of Employees (Part-time work) Act*, 2001. According to the Act:

- a part-time worker may not be treated in a less favourable manner than a full-time worker[b]

- an employee (or the trade union of which the employee is a member) if they consider that their rights as a part-time worker were infringed, can make a complaint to a Rights Commissioner[25]

- employee protection legislation now applies to part-time employees in the same way that it applies to full-time employees.

Therefore, the rights and entitlements afforded to full-time workers may also be enjoyed by students who are employed on a part-time basis during term. These are described below.

---

a Stamp No. 2 refers to students who are entitled to work 20 hours per week part time (see Appendix D).

b *Protection of Employees (Part-Time Work) Act*, 2001, Section 9 (1). There are some exceptions to this: Section 9 (2), if the less favourable treatment can be justified on 'objective grounds'; Section 9(4), in relation to pension schemes; or Section 11, in relation to casual workers. With regard to casual workers, they may, if such less favourable treatment can be justified on 'objective grounds', be treated, in respect of a particular condition of employment, in a less favourable manner than a comparable full-time employee'.

4.9.1.1 What taxes and social contributions do international students pay?

All employees must pay tax on their earnings, known as 'pay as you earn' or PAYE and PRSI 'pay-related social insurance'.[a] These are deducted from employees' salaries each week or month. All employees are required to have a Personal Public Service Number (PPS No.), and persons who do not have a PPS No.[b] should contact the Department of Social Community and Family Affairs.[26] This number should be quoted in all contact with the Tax Office and the Department.

In addition, persons who are commencing their first employment in Ireland should complete a Certificate of Tax Credits and Standard Rate Cut-Off Point (Form 12A).[27] The Revenue Commissioners usually grant married tax credits even if the worker's spouse is not resident in the State.

4.9.1.2 What details of employment are international students entitled to receive?

Within two months of starting employment, the employer is required to provide the employee[c] with a written statement of certain details of the terms of employment.[28]

These include:

- name and address of employer
- place of work
- job title and nature of work
- date of commencement of employment
- nature of contract (temporary or fixed term)
- rate of pay
- pay intervals
- hours of work (including overtime)
- paid leave
- arrangements for when the employee is unable to work due to sickness or injury
- pensions and pension schemes
- notice entitlements
- collective agreement/s, and the parties to the agreement/s

If the particulars contained in the statement change, the employer must notify the employee within one week.

If an employer has either failed to provide a written statement, or failed to notify the employee of changes that have taken place regarding the particulars

---

a There are some exceptions to this, for example, low-paid workers.

b This replaces the old RSI Number.

c The term 'employee' covers those working under contract of employment or apprenticeship; those employed through an employment agency and those employed in the service of the State.

contained in the statement, the employee may complain to a Rights Commissioner. If either party is dissatisfied with the recommendation of the Rights Commissioner, they may appeal to the Employment Appeals Tribunal.[a]

4.9.1.3 *What is the minimum rate of pay for international students?*

- All employees over the age of 18 who have worked for at least two years since turning 18 are entitled to a minimum rate of pay. This is currently €6.35 per hour since 1 October 2002.[29] Persons who have not worked for two years must generally be paid 80 per cent of the minimum wage in the first year, and 90 per cent in the second year.[30]

- With their wages, employees must receive a written statement of the gross pay and deductions made.[31]

- Employees have the right to a readily negotiable mode of wage payment such as by cheque, credit transfer, cash, postal order or bank draft.

- Employers may only make deductions in certain circumstances[b] that are agreed with the employee.[c]

4.9.1.4 *What are the rules governing working hours?*

- Employees must not be required to work in excess of the maximum hours permitted each week. This is an average of 48 hours per week averaged over four, six or 12 months depending on the nature of the employment.[d]

- Employees are entitled to breaks and rest time as follows:

  - 11 hours rest per 24 hour period

  - one period of 24 hours rest per week preceded by a daily rest period (11 hours)

  - 15 minutes break after working four-and-a-half hours and another break of 15 minutes after six hours, or 30 minutes after six hours if the 15 minutes break was not taken after four-and-a-half hours[e]

4.9.1.5 *What holidays are international students entitled to?*

Full-time workers are entitled to four working weeks annual leave[32] and nine public holidays per year.[f] These are: 1 January, St Patrick's Day, Easter Monday, First Monday in May, First Monday in June, First Monday in August, Last Monday in October, Christmas Day and St Stephen's Day.

---

a See Section 4.9.1.12 page 93 for details of the procedure for referring a complaint to the Rights Commissioner. In addition, the Rights Commissioner can investigate grievances or claims under most of the legislation dealing with rights in the workplace including: *Payment of Wages Act* 1991; *Terms of Employment Act* 1994; *Organisation of Working Time Act* 1997; *Parental Leave Act* 1998 and *National Minimum Wages Act*, 2000.

b When the deductions are required by law; when they are provided for in the contract of employment and when they are made with the written consent of the employee.

c For example, VHI, BUPA, Union Dues, Pension Plan and so on.

d Four months for employees generally, six months for seasonal workers and workers who are directly involved in ensuring continuity of service or production, and twelve months for employees who have entered a collective agreement with their employer.

e The break cannot be taken at the end of the work period.

f The employer has four alternatives with regard to the public holidays. They may give the employee: the day of the holiday off with pay, a paid day off within a month, an extra day of annual leave or an extra day's pay.

Part-time workers are entitled to annual leave consisting of eight per cent of the hours they work up to a maximum of four weeks and to public holidays if they have worked at least 40 hours in the five weeks preceding the public holiday.

4.9.1.6 What compensation for Sunday work are international students entitled to?

Employees are entitled to be compensated for Sunday work. This can be extra pay[a] or time off in lieu.[33] For persons working in the retail sector, there is a *Code of Practice on Sunday Working in the Retail Trade.*[b]

4.9.1.7 What maternity leave are international students entitled to?

- A pregnant employee is entitled to maternity leave from employment for a period of at least 14 weeks.[34]

- To be entitled to maternity leave, the employee must notify her employer and produce a medical certificate confirming the pregnancy and expected week of confinement. The notice must be given at least four weeks before the commencement of maternity leave and must be in writing.[35]

- An employee can choose the period of maternity leave. However, maternity leave must be taken at least four weeks before the end of the expected week of confinement and shall end not earlier than four weeks after the end of the expected week of confinement.[36]

- The employee has the right to return to work when the period of maternity leave has expired. Employees who have taken maternity leave are entitled to return to the:

  - same employer

  - job the employee held immediately before commencement of leave

  - same contract and conditions of employment[37]

4.9.1.8 What parental leave are international students entitled to?

- Persons who have at least one year's continuous employment and are the parents of children (natural or adopted) may take up to a total of 14 weeks unpaid leave (for each child) to take care of their children who are no older than five years.[38]

- Employees who have taken parental leave are entitled to return to the:

  - same employer

  - job the employee held immediately before commencement of leave

  - same contract and conditions of employment[39]

4.9.1.9 What force majeure *leave are international students entitled to?*

- Employees may also take *force majeure* leave in the case of sudden injury or illness to an immediate family member, where the dependant needs the worker to be present.[40]

a With premium payment (that is, above normal payment).

b This was drawn up by the Labour Relations Commission and is based on the entitlements set out in the *Organisation of Working Time Act* 1997. It is available on the Department of Enterprise, Trade & Employment website *http://www.entemp.ie/*

- An 'immediate family member' of the employee is a child, spouse/partner, person to whom the employee is *in loco parentis,* brother, sister, parent or grandparent.[41]

- An employee may take three days in any consecutive 12 months or five days in any 36 consecutive months[42]

- *Force majeure* leave is paid leave[43]

4.9.1.10 What laws protect international students from unfair dismissal?

Employees who have over 12 months continuous employment,[a] are protected by law from unfair dismissal. Dismissals may be regarded as unfair where they have resulted wholly or mainly from:

- the employee's trade union membership or activities

- the religious or political beliefs of the employee

- the race, skin colour or sexual orientation of the employee

- legal proceedings against the employer if the employee is a party or a witness

- the employee's pregnancy

- the employee taking leave provided for under the *Maternity Protection Act,* 1994

A dismissal will usually be considered fair if it is based wholly or mainly on one of the following:

- the employee's capability, competence or qualifications for the job

- the employee's conduct

- the employee's redundancy

- if continuation of the employment would contravene other legal requirements

Both 'actual' unfair dismissals and 'constructive' dismissals are prohibited by legislation. Constructive dismissal can occur where the employee's conditions of employment are made so difficult that they have no alternative but to leave.

4.9.1.11 What claims for redress[b] exist for international students who consider they have been unfairly dismissed?

An employee who considers that they have been unfairly dismissed (this includes 'actual' and 'constructive' dismissal) and who wishes to make a claim for redress must do so within six months.[c]

The employee must give formal notice of his/her claim in writing to a Rights Commissioner or to the Employment Appeals Tribunal. The claim is considered by the Employment Appeals Tribunal where the employee or the employer have

a Two fixed terms of six months would qualify.

b Redress in the case of unfair dismissal can be any of the following:

- re-instatement in the employee's old job

- re-engagement in the old job or a suitable alternative

- financial compensation

c In exceptional circumstances, this can be twelve months.

notified a Rights Commissioner that they object to the claim being heard by a Rights Commissioner.

Persons who are employed through an employment agency must make their claim against whoever is paying their wages (this could be the actual 'employer' or the agency).

4.9.1.12 How can international students take a claim to the Rights Commissioner?

Rights Commissioners are appointed by the Minister for Enterprise, Trade & Employment on the recommendation of the Labour Relations Commission. They are independent of the Minister in carrying out their functions. The procedure for persons wishing to make an appeal to the Rights Commissioner is described below:

- Persons wishing to make an appeal to a Rights Commissioner must:

  - notify their former employer that they intend to take a case to the Rights Commissioner

  - complete the standard form[44] (full details of the complaint must be given)

- The Rights Commissioner hears the case as soon as possible. The hearing takes place in private.

- Both parties can be represented at the hearing by a lawyer or trade union representative (in the cases of the employee).

- Both parties have the opportunity to present their case.

- The Rights Commissioner makes a recommendation, which may be appealed to the Employment Appeals Tribunal (EAT).

4.9.1.13 What is the minimum notice[45] period for international students?

Employees who are in continuous employment with the same employer for 13 weeks or more and who normally work at least eight hours per week are entitled to a minimum period of notice from their employer if they intend to dismiss them.

The period of notice depends on the length of service. For persons who have served from 13 weeks to two years the minimum notice period is one week.

Employees must also give notice if they intend to leave the job. If the employee is in employment for 13 weeks or over, they must give the employer at least one week's notice. If the contract of employment requires further notice to be given, they must adhere to the terms of the contract.

The Employment Appeals Tribunal considers disputes between employers and workers regarding minimum notice.

4.9.1.14 What redundancy payments[a] are international students entitled to?

Employees are entitled to a lump sum redundancy payment when their employment is ended due to redundancy providing they:

- have 109 weeks continuous service

a Redundancy payments are dealt with under the *Redundancy Payments Acts* 1967 to 1991. Redundancy occurs when the employee's job ceases to exist, there is insufficient work, the firm closes down or the firm re-organises.

- are aged between 16 and 66

- are normally expected to work at least eight hours per week

The redundancy pay is calculated in the following manner:

- a half week's pay for each year of employment up to 41 years' service

- one week's pay for each year over 41 years' service

- one week's pay irrespective of the length of service

4.9.1.15 *What rules govern discrimination in employment?*

Discrimination against employees on grounds of age, gender, marital status,[46] family status,[47] race,[48] religion,[49] sexual orientation,[50] disability[51] and membership of the Travelling Community is prohibited under the *Employment Equality Act, 1998*.[a] The Act prohibits:

- direct and indirect discrimination

- discrimination in access to employment, conditions of employment, promotion, training and classification of posts[52]

The Equality Authority may provide legal advice, assistance and representation to persons who consider that they have a complaint under the legislation.[53]

A person who considers that they have been discriminated against on any of the nine grounds listed above can refer their complaint to:

Authority	Employees refer to this body if they...
the ODEI - the equality tribunal	are still in employment
the Labour Court	have already been dismissed (including 'actual' and 'constructive' dismissal)

4.9.1.16 *How can international students bring a claim to the equality tribunal?*

The ODEI - the equality tribunal (referred to as the equality tribunal in this handbook) is an independent body established to investigate claims of discrimination under the *Employment Equality Act, 1998* and the *Equal Status Act, 2000*. The equality tribunal also offers a mediation service.

Persons wishing to refer their complaint to the equality tribunal must complete the complaint form (Form ODEI 1).[b] Persons who have difficulty in completing the form due to disability, language or other difficulties, should contact the equality tribunal immediately, and if appropriate, other arrangements will be made to enable the person to refer their complaint.

a The *Employment Equality Authority Act* 1998 came into force 18 October 1999, and only incidents of discrimination occurring on, or after that date can be dealt with under the Act. Incidents of discrimination on grounds of sex or marital status can be investigated by the ODEI - the equality tribunal under earlier legislation.

b The forms, and all the other form to be used in this process, may be downloaded from the ODEI - the equality tribunal website *http://www.odei.ie/* or from the ODEI - the equality tribunal, 3 Clonmel Street, Dublin 2, telephone (01) 477 4100.

The person making the complaint (the complainant) may write to the person they believe has discriminated against them (the respondent), to request information in order to ascertain more fully, what actually took place. The complainant must use the standard form provided by the equality tribunal (Form ODEI 3).[54]

If the respondent does not reply promptly, the complainant may refer their complaint to the equality tribunal.

When the complaint is received, the Director of Equality Investigations will refer it to an Equality Officer within the equality tribunal.

4.9.1.17 How can international students bring a claim to the Labour Court?

Persons who have been dismissed from their employment on grounds of discrimination or victimisation, may bring their claim to the Labour Court.

- The person can send a questionnaire to the former employer to obtain information. The employer can also give their version of what occurred through this procedure. The Questionnaire Form may be downloaded from the Labour Court website.[55]

- The application must be made within six months from the incident of discrimination or victimisation taking place. If there were a series of incidents, the application must be made six months from the last one taking place.

- The application may be made by completing the application form, which can be downloaded from the Labour Court website.

4.9.1.18 What are the rules governing the victimisation of international students who bring claims?

If a person making a complaint to the equality tribunal is penalised in any manner by the person against whom they made the complaint or another person because they made the complaint, this is regarded as victimisation. Victimisation also occurs if the person in good faith lawfully opposed any act of discrimination or victimisation or gave evidence in any proceedings under the Act.

Victimisation is also prohibited under the *Employment Equality Act* and a person who considers that they were victimised may make a complaint to the equality tribunal in the manner described above for other types of discrimination.

4.9.2 What types of accommodation can international students access?

Some primary and secondary students coming to Ireland will attend boarding school, and will live in the school. Other students will attend day school. In this case, schools sometimes provide a list of accommodation provided by families in the area. Students and parents should enquire about accommodation when applying to the school.

Most of the universities and some institutes of technology offer on-campus accommodation. Some universities also provide hostels for students, and may provide lists of persons offering accommodation to students. Students should contact the Accommodation Officer in their college or the Students Union.

However, there is a shortage of such accommodation and most students will have to find their own, usually in the private rented sector. Students may also apply for local authority housing.

4.9.2.1 Private rented accommodation

Persons wishing to rent a house or apartment from a private landlord can do so directly themselves by replying to advertisements in newspapers or seek the assistance of a letting agency. Finding accommodation can be expensive and time-consuming, particularly in big cities. Prospective tenants should:

- Inspect the property before agreeing to move in and record the condition of the property and its contents in writing. Houses and apartments to let should comply with certain minimum standards.[56]

- Agree the amount of deposit and rent to be paid and the time of payment. A receipt should be obtained for all money paid to the landlord. The deposit should be returned to the tenant when s/he leaves the accommodation. However, the landlord may retain some or all of the deposit if: the tenant gives insufficient notice, damages the property or leaves without paying bills or rent.

- Find out whether the rent covers such items as electricity, gas and bin charges (where relevant).

- Agree on who is responsible for any repairs that need to be carried out in the future.

Tenants should be aware of their rights and duties as a tenant. The most important of these are:

- The landlord must provide a rent book. The rent book should contain the name and address of the landlord, amount of deposit paid, the amount of rent and the time and method of payment. All rent payments should be entered in the rent book. The rent book should also include the terms of the tenancy.

- The landlord is not permitted (except in cases of emergency) to enter the accommodation without making an appointment with the tenant.

- The landlord must give a minimum of four weeks notice in writing if they require the tenant to leave the accommodation. This is referred to as a 'notice to quit'. If the tenant does not leave by the end of the four-week period, the landlord can go to court to apply for an eviction order.

- The tenant must also provide notice to the landlord if they decide to move out.

4.9.2.2 Local authority (council or corporation) Housing

Local authority housing is available, generally for persons who do not have sufficient resources to provide their own accommodation. Practice with regard to eligibility for local authority housing varies. Priority is usually given to low-income families with children and to older persons. However, there is usually a long waiting list of people for local authority housing.

Persons who are interested in being considered for local authority housing should:

- Contact their nearest local authority (see Appendix E for a full list of local authorities in Ireland), and obtain a copy of the authority's scheme of letting priorities. This sets out the rules for the allocation of accommodation including such matters as how applicants are prioritised and what type of accommodation may be provided to different categories of applicants.

- If the person is still interested in local authority accommodation, they should complete the application form, which is provided by the local authority.

- There is no requirement to live in the area for a certain time in order to qualify for local authority housing. It is possible to apply to more than one local authority, but not all local authorities accept applications from outside their area.

- Non-nationals who wish to apply for local authority accommodation may be required to provide evidence that they intend, and are entitled, to live in Ireland permanently. The practice varies with regard to this requirement and persons should contact their local authority.

- When the application has been received, an official from the local authority or health board will usually visit the applicant. (However, practice varies between local authorities and they may visit the applicant only when suitable accommodation is available.)

- As most local authorities have insufficient accommodation to meet the demand, they will put the applicant's name on a list. Some local authorities have a 'points system' to assist them in determining the greatest need for accommodation among applicants. An applicant will be awarded points for issues such as overcrowding.

4.9.2.2.1 *Offer of accommodation:*

If the person is offered a house or flat by the local authority and decides to take it, they must sign a tenancy agreement.

- The tenancy agreement is legal document and both the tenant and the local authority must adhere to the terms of the agreement.

- In the case of a married couple or partners, the tenancy is usually in joint names.

- The amount of rent to be paid per week is based on the income of the household.

- It is important to ensure that rent is paid up to date as the tenant may be issued with a notice to quit if arrears of rent have built up.

- Tenants can apply to transfer to another area.

4.9.2.3 *What laws govern discrimination in the provision of accommodation?*

The *Equal Status Act*, 2000, prohibits discrimination on the grounds of gender, marital status, family status, sexual orientation, religious belief, age, disability, "race" and membership of the Traveller Community in the provision of goods and services, the disposal of property and access to education. Discrimination on the nine grounds listed in the Act is prohibited in both the public and private sectors. The process for referring complaints is similar to that under the *Employment Equality Act*, 1998. Further information is available from the equality tribunal.[57]

4.9.3 What medical services are international students entitled to?

Students coming to Ireland have three options with regard to medical care:

- public health care
- private health care
- on-campus medical facilities

4.9.3.1 Public health care

The public health care system, including primary and hospital services, can be accessed by any person resident in Ireland including students.

Generally, to get free medical care in Ireland a person needs a medical card. However, EEA and Swiss students (and accompanying family members) are covered for free medical care if they present Form E128 at the time of treatment. If their course is of one year's duration or longer they can apply for a medical card as a person who is 'ordinarily resident' here.

4.9.3.1.1 Who is entitled to a medical card?

Entitlement to a medical card in Ireland is based on a person's residence and means. To be fully eligible for a medical card a person must:

- be 'ordinarily resident' in Ireland; this means that they must intend to live in Ireland for at least one year and be permitted to do so; this includes all students who are pursuing a course of study of one year's duration or longer.

- satisfy the means test; a person will only be eligible for free medical care (Category A entitlement, that is medical card holders) if their gross income, less PRSI contributions is less than €138 and in the case of a married couple or single parent €200.[a]

4.9.3.1.2 What does a medical card entitle you to?

A medical card entitles you to the following free medical services:

- General Practitioner (GP) services (but you must register with a GP (see Section 4.9.3.1.3 page 99))
- prescribed medicines

---

a A married couple or a single parent must earn less than €200. These rates apply to persons under 66 years of age. Persons applying for the medical card are permitted to have the following amounts over the income level and still qualify for the medical card, as of 1 January 2003:

- €25 for each child under 16 years of age
- €26 for each child over 16 years of age with no income maintained by applicant
- the amount by which the rent or mortgage paid each week exceeds €25
- the amount by which the costs of travelling to and from work each week exceeds €22
- weekly expenditure on medicines

- in-patient hospital treatment in a public ward

- out-patient hospital treatment

- dental, ophthalmic and aural services

- community care services

4.9.3.1.3 *Registering with a General Practitioner (GP)*

Persons who qualify for the medical card must register with a General Practitioner (family doctor). Not all GPs accept medical card patients, so the medical card holder should obtain a list of doctors in their area who accept medical card patients:

- They can obtain this list from the local health board offices and health centre together with a registration form, which the doctor will be required to sign.

- GPs are only permitted to accept a certain number of medical card patients. Therefore, they will sometimes refuse to accept any further patients.

- If a person is unable to find a doctor who will accept them as a patient under the medical card scheme, one will be assigned to them by the health board office or health centre.

4.9.3.1.4 *Applying for a medical card*

Persons who wish to apply for a medical card should submit a completed application form, together with evidence that they are 'ordinarily resident' in Ireland and that they satisfy the means test, to their local health board offices or health centre.

4.9.3.1.5 *What should you do if you are not entitled to a medical card?*

Persons who are not entitled to a medical card are entitled to a range of services including the following:

- in-patient hospital treatment in a public ward subject to a daily charge of €40[a]

- all other out-patient services including consultants

- visits to hospital Accident and Emergency Departments subject to a charge of €40 (persons who are referred by their GP will not be charged)

- maternity and infant care

4.9.3.2 *Private health care*

Persons can also take out private health insurance.[b] Non-EEA nationals whose course of study is for less than one year are required to take out full private medical insurance before travelling to Ireland to commence study, and must possess evidence (such as a Certificate of Private Insurance) that they have done so. This insurance will cover private care in public or private hospitals. There are two private health insurers in Ireland, VHI and BUPA.[58] Medical insurance will not

---

a Up to a maximum of €400 in any twelve-month period (as of 1 January 2003).

b Persons who wish to avail of private health care and who have not taken out private health insurance will be required to pay for hospital treatment.

cover pre-existing medical conditions and the cover may not, in any event, take effect for an initial period.

4.9.3.3 Who can use on-campus medical facilities?

Most of the universities and larger colleges (but not the institutes of technology or the private colleges) have medical facilities, which all registered students may use free or for a nominal charge. They can avail of a consultation with a nurse or doctor, but must pay for any medicines prescribed.

4.9.4 What social welfare entitlements do international students have?

Irish social welfare legislation does not distinguish between nationals and non-nationals. Essentially, any person from outside the State who complies with the relevant laws covering entry, living and working here is entitled to seek social welfare payments in compliance with the normal conditions. For further information, contact the Information Service of the Department of Social and Family Affairs on (01) 704 3000.

4.9.5 What family reunification rights do international students have?

4.9.5.1 EEA and Swiss nationals

EEA and Swiss nationals studying in Ireland on a full-time basis are permitted to have their spouse and dependent family members with them in Ireland. In the case of students, 'dependent' family members means "the person's spouse, children under 18 years of age of the person and his spouse".[59]

4.9.5.1.1 Entry to the State

EEA and Swiss nationals who are coming to Ireland to pursue a course of study, and their accompanying dependants, must produce passports or national identity cards. Immigration Officers will only refuse leave to land when: "his or her personal conduct has been such that it would be contrary to public policy or would endanger public security". They may also be refused leave to land if they are suffering from a scheduled disease.[a]

4.9.5.1.2 Residence permits

Family members of EEA and Swiss nationals may apply for a residence permit.[60] If the family members are not EEA or Swiss nationals, they may apply to the registration officer[61] for a residence permit. The local registration officer is a member of the Gardaí. Applicants should inquire at their local Garda station for the location of the registration officer for the area in which they reside. In Dublin, this is the Garda National Immigration Bureau. Family members may remain in the State for three months without applying for a residence permit.[62]

4.9.5.2 Non-EEA nationals

Non-EEA nationals who are full-time students in Ireland, do not have a statutory entitlement to family reunification. However, they may apply for family reunification, if they are in a position to support their family members for the duration of their stay in Ireland.

a See Appendix B for details.

4.9.6 How can international students acquire Irish citizenship?

Since 30 November 2002, the time a person spends in Ireland as a student will no longer be counted when calculating the period of residence in relation to an application for naturalisation.[63] This does not apply to EEA national students. However, any period of time an EEA national spends in Ireland without a residence permit will not be counted as part of the period of residence required for an application for naturalisation.[64]

If during, or upon completion of, their studies, a former student changes their immigration status and is granted permission to remain on other grounds, the time from the granting of the residence permit is counted.

International students in Ireland can become Irish citizens in three ways:

- naturalisation
- post-nuptial citizenship
- by descent

The *Irish Nationality and Citizenship Acts* 1956, 1986, 1994 and 2001 set out the criteria under which Irish citizenship is granted.

4.9.6.1 Acquiring citizenship by naturalisation

A person wishing to apply for a certificate of naturalisation must fulfil certain conditions including having legally resided in Ireland for five years out of the previous nine-year period. The Minister for Justice, Equality & Law Reform may grant an application for a certificate of naturalisation at their discretion if they are satisfied that the applicant:

- is of full age
- is of good character
- has had a period of one year's continuous residence in Ireland immediately prior to their application, and in the eight years immediately preceding that period has had a total residence of four years in Ireland
- intends in good faith to continue to reside in Ireland after naturalisation
- has made a declaration of fidelity to the nation and loyalty to the State, either before a District Court Justice or in such other manner permitted by the Minister

The Minister for Justice, Equality & Law Reform may waive these conditions in certain circumstances specified in the Acts. The number of circumstances in which the Minister may waive the conditions, has been reduced by the 2001, Act. [a]

4.9.6.2 Acquiring post-nuptial citizenship

A non-national who married an Irish national on or before 29 November 2002, and has been in a subsisting marriage with that person for a minimum of three years, may become an Irish citizen by making a post-nuptial declaration of citizenship. However, this is not possible if the Irish spouse has acquired

---

a *Irish Nationality and Citizenship Act* 1956, Section 16 (as amended by *Irish Nationality and Citizenship Act,* 1986, Section 5). Since the coming into force of the 2001 Act, this no longer applies to persons married to a naturalised Irish citizen or persons married to a person who is an Irish citizen otherwise than by naturalisation.

citizenship by naturalisation, post-nuptial declaration, or was granted citizenship as a token of honour. Any such declarations will have to be made before 30 November 2005.

In the case of spouses of Irish nationals who got married on or after 30 November, 2002, the Minister may at his 'absolute discretion' grant an application for a certificate of naturalisation to the spouse of an Irish citizen if the applicant:

- is of full age

- is of good character

- is married to an Irish citizen for at least three years

- is in a subsisting marriage, recognised as being in accordance with Irish legislation

- is living together with the Irish citizen as husband and wife (the applicant must submit an affidavit to that effect to the Minister)

- has lived in Ireland for at least one year continuously prior to the application

- has been resident in Ireland for at least two years of the four years immediately preceding that period

- intends in good faith to continue to reside in Ireland after naturalisation

- has made a declaration of 'fidelity to the nation and loyalty to the State' in whatever manner may be prescribed[65]

The Minister for Justice, Equality & Law Reform may waive certain of the above conditions if satisfied that the applicant would suffer serious consequences in respect of his or her bodily integrity or liberty if not granted Irish citizenship.[66]

4.9.6.3 Acquiring citizenship by descent

Persons whose father or mother was an Irish Citizen at the time of their birth are automatically Irish citizens. However, if a person is born outside Ireland, and the parent through whom they are claiming citizenship was also born outside Ireland, they will not be entitled to citizenship except in certain limited circumstances.[67] Persons whose grandparents were Irish citizens can become Irish citizens by registering in the Foreign Births Register in the Department of Foreign Affairs or, if residing outside Ireland, at the nearest Irish Embassy or Consulate.

4.9.6.4 Acquiring permission to remain without condition as to time

Persons who have been legally resident in Ireland for ten years and who have not applied for naturalisation may obtain a residence stamp giving them 'permission to remain without condition as to time'.[68]

4.9.7 What do international students need to open a bank account?

Banks require new customers to produce the following documents when opening a bank account:

- photo identification (a passport satisfies this requirement)

- proof of address in Ireland, for example a utility bill (electricity, gas or other utility) or lease agreement

- letter from the educational institution confirming the person's registration and the expected duration of the course

- although not officially documented as a requirement, banks often request applicants to provide a personal introduction from an existing customer

4.9.8 Can international students vote in elections?

Non-national residents in Ireland over 18 years of age may vote in some elections:

Citizens of...	Permitted to vote at...
The UK	Dáil, European and local elections
EU states apart from the UK	European and local elections
Non-EU states	Local elections only

Those permitted to vote must have their name included in the Electoral Register if they want to vote. Application forms are available in post offices, libraries and council and corporation offices.

Endnotes

1 Council Directive 90/336 (later replaced by Council Directive 93/96) on *Migrant Students* [1993] OJ L317/59; Council Directive 90/365 *Employed and Self-employed People who have Ceased to Work* [1990] OJ L180/28; Directive 90/364 [1990] OJ L180/26.

2 Case C-413/99 *Baumbast*, 17 September 2002.

3 Proposal for a European Parliament and Council Directive 29 June 2001on the *Right of Citizens of the Union and their Family Members to Move and Reside Freely within the Territory of the Member States* COM(2001) 257 final[2001] OJ C270 E/23.

4 Case C-184/99 *Grzelczyk v CPAS* [2001] ECR I-6193.

5 Case C-85/96 *Maria Martinez Sala v Freistaat Bayern* [1998] ECR I-2691.

6 Council Directive 93/96/EEC, 29 October 1993, on the *Right of Residence for Students*, Article 1.

7 *European Communities (Right of Residence for Non-Economically Active Persons), Regulations*,1997 SI No. 57/1997:

8 Department of Education and Science, Marlborough Street, Dublin 1, telephone (01) 873 4700, website *http://www.education.ie/*

9 Details are available from the International Education Board of Ireland (IEBI), IPC House, 35-39 Shelbourne Road, Dublin 4, telephone (01) 614 4836.

10 Central Applications Office, Tower House, Eglington Street, Galway, telephone (091) 509 800, website *http://www.cao.ie/*

11 MEI~RELSA Ireland, 107 South Circular Road, Dublin 8, telephone (01) 475 3122.

12 Case C-184/99 *Grzelczyk v CPAS* [2001] ECR I-6193.

13 Interested persons should consult the HEA website *http://www.hea.ie/*

14 ICOS Advisory Service, 41 Morehampton Road, Dublin 4, telephone (01) 660 5233, website *http://www.icosirl.ie/*

15 For further information, see the Department of Justice, Equality & Law Reform information leaflet *Student Visa Requirements*. This leaflet is available on the Department's website *http://www.justice.ie/*

16 Immigration Division, Department of Justice, Equality & Law Reform, 13/14 Burgh Quay, Dublin 2. Further information is available on the Department of Justice, Equality & Law Reform website *http://www.justice.ie/*

17 *Aliens (Amendment) (No.3) Order* 1997, SI No. 277.

18 *European Communities (Aliens) Regulations* 1977, Regulations 4 (i) and 4 (ii), SI No. 393.

19 The *Aliens Order* 1946 (as amended), Section 5.

20 The *Immigration Act* 1999,Section 3 (1)(g).

21 This is provided for in the *Aliens Order* 1946, Section 11.

22 SI No. 57 of 1997.

23 The *European Communities (Right of Residence for Non-Economically Active Persons) Regulations* 1997 Regulation 7 (1)(a).

24 *Ibid,* Regulation1

25 The procedure for making a complaint to a Rights Commissioner is described in Section 4.9.1.12 page 93 and further information is available on the Labour Relations Commission website *http://www.irc.ie/*

26 Department of Social and Family Affairs, Gandon House, Amiens Street, Dublin 1, telephone (01) 8748444, website *http://www.welfare.ie/* The Department's leaflet SW100 *Personal Public Service Number* provides additional information on obtaining a PPS.

27 Further information may be obtained on Revenue Publication RES 2 *Coming to Live in Ireland* *http://www.revenue.ie/*

28 *Terms of Employment (Information) Act* 1994.

29 *National Minimum Wages Act* 2000.

30 This is provided for in the *National Minimum Wages Act* 2000, Section 15(1):

"Subject to subsection (2) and Sections 16, 17 and 18, a person who:

(a) enters employment for the first time after attaining the age of 18 years or

(b) having entered into employment before attaining the age of 18 years, continues in employment on attaining that age

shall be remunerated by his or her employer in respect of his or her working hours in any pay reference period at an hourly rate of pay that on average is not less than :

(i) in the case of an employee commencing employment for the first time after attaining the age of 18 years:

(I) in his or her first year after commenced employment, 80% and

(II) in his or her second year after having commenced employment, 90%

(ii) in the case if an employee having entered into employment before attaining the age of 18 years and continuing in employment on attaining that age

(I) in his or her first year after having attained the age of 18 years, 80%

(II) in his or her second year after having attained that age, 90%

of the national minimum hourly rate of pay, notwithstanding that the employee, if he or she has changed his or her employer during the relevant period, may have been remunerated at a higher rate by the previous employer."

31 *Payment of Wages Act* 1991

32 *Organisation of Working Time Act* 1997, Section 19.

33 *Ibid,* Section 14(1).

34 *Ibid,* Section 8.

35 *Ibid,* Section 9(1)(a) and (b.

36 *Ibid,* Section 10.

37 *Ibid,* Section 26.

38 *Parental Leave Act* 1998 Section 7 (1).

39 *Ibid,* Section 19 (3)(c).

40 *Ibid,* Section 13 (1).

41 *Ibid,* Section 13 (2).

42 *Ibid,* Section 13 (4).

43 *Ibid,* Section 13 (1).

44 This form may be downloaded from the Labour Relations Commission website *www.lrc.ie/lrc_services/rights_commissioner.htm* or can be obtained from the Secretariat, Rights Commissioner Service, Labour Relations Commission, Tom Johnson House, Haddington Road, Dublin 4, telephone: (01) 613 6700.

45 Minimum notice is provided for in the *Minimum Notice and Terms of Employment Act* 1973, as amended by the *Work Protection (Regular Part-Time Employees) Act* 1991.

46 According to the *Employment Equality Act* 1998,Section 2(1), (dealing with interpretation), 'marital status' means

"single, married, separated, divorced and widowed".

47 'Family status' is described in Section 2(1) of the Act as "responsibility

(a) as a parent or as a person in loco parentis in relation to a person who has not attained the age of 18 years, or

(b) as a parent or the resident primary carer in relation to a person of or over that age with a disability which is of such a nature as to give rise to the need for care or support on a continuing, regular or frequent basis".

48 Discrimination on the basis of 'race' is described in the *Employment Equality Act* 1998, Section 6 (2)(h) as "between any two persons that are of a different 'race', 'colour', nationality or ethnic or national origins".

49 'Religious belief' as defined in the *Employment Equality Act* 1998, includes religious background or outlook.

50 The *Employment Equality Act* 1998, Section 2(1) defines 'sexual orientation' as meaning "heterosexual, homosexual or bisexual orientation".

51 'Disability' is defined in the *Employment Equality Act* 1998, Section 2(1) as:

"(a) the total or partial absence of a person's bodily or mental functions, including the absence of a part of the person's body,

(b) the presence in the body of organisms causing, or likely to cause, chronic disease or illness,

(c) the malfunction, malformation or disfigurement of a part of a person's body,

(d) a condition or malfunction which results in a person learning differently from a person without the condition or malfunction, or

(e) a condition, illness or disease which affects a person's thought processes, perception of reality, emotions or judgement which results in disturbed behaviour,

and shall be taken to include a disability which exists at present, or which previously existed but no longer exists, or which may exist in the future or which is imputed to a person".

52 *Employment Equality Act* 1998,Section 8(1).

53 The Equality Authority may be contacted at 2, Clonmel Street, Dublin 2, telephone (01) 417 3333, fax (01) 417 3366, email *info@equality.ie*

54 The respondent must also use the form provided by the ODEI - the equality tribunal to reply (Form ODEI 4). If the correct forms are not used, the provisions in the *Employment Equality Act* 1998, permitting the director to draw inferences from failure to supply information, do not apply.

55 *http://www.labourcourt.ie/labour/labour.nsf/LookupPageLink/formsDownload*

56 Details of these can be obtained from Threshold, 21 Stoneybatter, Dublin 7, email *advice@threshold.ie*

57 Further information is available from the ODEI - the equality tribunal, 3 Clonmel Street, Dublin 2, telephone (01) 477 4100, website *http://www.odei.ie/*

58 Voluntary Health Insurance (VHI), VHI House, Lower Abbey Street, Dublin 1, telephone (01) 874 4499, Lo-call 1850 444 444.

BUPA Ireland, Mill Island, Fermoy, Co. Cork, telephone (021) 42121, or 12 Fitzwilliam Square, Dublin 2, telephone (01) 6627 662, Lo-call 1890 700 890.

59 *European Communities (Right of Residence for non-Economically Active Persons) Regulations* 1997, Sections 2(1) and 3(1), SI No. 57 of 1997.

60 *European Communities (Aliens) Regulations* 1977, Regulation 5(1) SI No. 393 of 1977.

61 *Ibid,* Regulation 5(2).

62 *Ibid,* Regulation 5(4).

63 *Irish Nationality and Citizenship Act* 1956, Section 16A(b)(ii)(I), (as amended by the *Irish Nationality and Immigration Act* 2001, Section 6).

64 *Ibid,* Section 16A (1)(a).

65 *Irish Nationality and Citizenship Act* 1956, Section 15A (1), as amended by the *Irish Nationality and Citizenship Act* 2001, Section 5.

66 *Irish Nationality and Citizenship Act* 1956, Section 15A (2), as amended by the *Irish Nationality and Citizenship Act* 2001, Section 5.

67 *Irish Nationality and Citizenship Act* 1956, Section 7 (3), as amended by the *Irish Nationality and Citizenship Act* 2001, Section 5.

68 Further information available on the Department of Justice, Equality & Law Reform website *http://www.justice.ie/*

CHAPTER *5*

Non-Economically Active Persons

NON-ECONOMICALLY ACTIVE PERSONS

The rights and entitlements of non-economically active persons in Ireland are dependent on whether they are EEA and Swiss or non-EEA nationals.

5.1 EEA and Swiss Nationals

5.1.1 EU nationals

The status of Citizenship of the Union was introduced by the Treaty of Maastricht (1992). Article 17 of the *EC Treaty*[a] states:

> *Citizenship of the Union is hereby established. Every person holding the nationality of a Member State shall be a citizen of the Union. Citizenship of the Union shall complement and not replace national citizenship.*
>
> *Citizens of the Union shall enjoy the rights conferred by this Treaty and shall be subject to the duties imposed thereby.*

Article 18(1) of the *EC Treaty* states:

> *Every Citizen of the Union shall have the right to move and reside freely within the territory of the Member States, subject to the limitations and conditions laid down by this Treaty and by the measures adopted to give it effect.*

The right to move and reside referred to in Article 18(1) may be subject to limits and conditions. For non-economically active migrants, these conditions include various financial conditions set out in a series of Community Directives.[1] However, the competent authorities and, where necessary, the national courts must ensure that these limitations and conditions are applied in compliance with the general principles of Community law and, in particular, the principle of proportionality.[2]

The Commission has proposed replacing these Directives with a general all-embracing Directive to deal with Citizens' migration rights, but this has not been adopted yet.[3] However, it is clear that the effect of Article 18(1) is such that once a Citizen of the Union is lawfully resident in the territory of another Member State, they are entitled to equal treatment with nationals of that State in most circumstances. For example, regarding welfare rights equal treatment extends to all EU migrants, regardless of whether they are workers, service providers or simply visitors, provided they are lawfully resident.[4] Regarding political rights, Citizens of the Union have the right to vote and stand in both municipal and European elections, when resident in another Member State.

Other rights for nationals of EU Member States are set out in the *European Communities (Right of Residence for Non-Economically Active Persons) Regulations*, 1997.

---

a Unless otherwise stated, all references to the *EC Treaty* refer to the *EC Treaty* as amended by the Treaties of Amsterdam and Nice.

5.1.2 EEA nationals

In 1994, the European Economic Area Agreement (EEA) was signed between the European Union and Norway, Iceland and Liechtenstein. Nationals of these states enjoy rights within the EU that are similar to those of nationals of EU Member States and include those set out in the *European Communities (Right of Residence for Non-Economically Active Persons) Regulations*, 1997.

5.1.3 Swiss nationals

The *European Communities and Swiss Confederation Act*, 2001, came into force in June 2002. As a result, Swiss nationals now have the same rights as EEA nationals in Ireland. EEA and Swiss Nationals do not need a visa to enter Ireland to take up employment or for any other purpose.

5.1.4 EEA and Swiss nationals who have ceased employment or self-employment

EEA and Swiss nationals who have been in employment or self-employment in Ireland may remain permanently when they cease work if the following criteria apply:

- They have been in employment or self-employed for at least the previous twelve months and have resided in Ireland for at least three years at the time they have reached pensionable age.[a]

- They have resided in Ireland for at least two years and have ceased employment or self-employment as a result of 'permanent incapacity for work'.[b]

- They have become incapacitated for work due to an accident at work or an occupational illness which entitles them to a pension payable by the Irish Government in whole or in part.[5]

Dependent family members of an EEA or Swiss national, who was in employment or was self-employed for at least two years in Ireland, may remain here permanently. Dependent family members of a person who died as a result of an accident, or from an occupational illness, are also entitled to remain in Ireland permanently.[6]

5.2 Non-EEA and Swiss Nationals

Non-EEA and Swiss nationals, who are not economically active (with the exception of international students who are dealt with separately, see Chapter 4) have no statutory rights to come to Ireland and reside here. However, they may be permitted to reside here if they fulfil certain criteria, in particular, they must be in a position to maintain themselves without recourse to public funds. They are not permitted to engage in employment or self-employment and they must have full medical insurance. They must possess a valid passport and a visa (if required) before coming here.

5.3 Applying for Visas

Non-economically active persons coming to Ireland, who are nationals of a state whose passport holders require a visa in order to travel to Ireland, must obtain a visa[c]

---

a *Social Welfare Consolidation Act,* 1993, Section 2(1).

b *Social Welfare Consolidation Act,* 1993, Section 2(1).

c Under the provisions of the *Aliens (Visas) Order,* 2002, SI No. 178/2002: certain non-nationals are not required to possess a visa to travel to Ireland. Persons from states not listed are required to have a visa (see Appendix A).

Applicants must include the following documentation with their application:

- a completed visa application form
- evidence regarding their stay in Ireland (in particular their ability to support themselves without recourse to public funds, and have adequate health insurance)
- a valid passport (or copy of the passport if the application is being made to the Department of Foreign Affairs)
- two passport photographs
- the appropriate visa application fee[a]

Applications can be made:

- through the Irish Embassy/Consulate in the applicant's country of residence
- through any Irish Embassy or Consulate if there is none in the applicant's country of residence
- by post, directly to the Visa Office, Department of Foreign Affairs, 13/14 Burgh Quay, Dublin 2, if there is no Irish Embassy or Consulate in the applicant's country of residence

If insufficient information is provided, the applicant may be asked to furnish the required information. However, it is important to note that applications may be refused without any further information being sought.

In some circumstances the applicant will be asked to provide the name of a person in Ireland, who may be asked to supply further information.

5.4 Appealing Visa Applications that Have Been Refused

A person whose application for a visa has been refused may apply to the Visa Section of the Department of Justice, Equality and Law Reform to have the application reviewed by a more senior official. Before doing so, they should request the reasons for the initial refusal of the visa application; these are not automatically provided but in most cases contain important information relevant to the appeal.

5.5 What Rules Govern Entry to the State for Non-economically Active Persons?

5.5.1 EEA and Swiss nationals

5.5.1.1 UK nationals

Ireland and the UK[b] share a Common Travel Area. This means that UK nationals coming to Ireland to retire (or for any other purpose) are not subject to immigration controls at Irish airports and ports. Since June 1997, as a result of an order made under the *Aliens Act, 1935,*[7] Immigration Officers may carry out checks on persons arriving from the UK. UK nationals should carry their passport or some other form of identification to satisfy Immigration Officers that they are in fact UK nationals.

---

a The visa application fee is €25 for a single journey and €50 for a multiple journey visa. Citizens of the following countries are exempt from the visa application fee: Bosnia, Bulgaria, Ecuador, Indonesia, Ivory Coast, Kirghizstan, Morocco, Peru, Slovak Republic, Sri Lanka, Tanzania, Tunisia, Uganda, Yugoslavia and Zambia (as of 1 January 2002, Visa Section, Department of Justice, Equality & Law Reform)

b This includes the Isle of Man and the Channel Islands.

5.5.1.2 EEA and Swiss nationals

EEA and Swiss nationals are not required to possess a visa to travel to Ireland. They must possess a passport or national identity card, which should be shown to Immigration Officers at the port or airport of entry.

In accordance with the *European Communities (Aliens) Regulations*, 1977, EEA and Swiss nationals may only be refused leave to land if: "... his or her personal conduct has been such that it would be contrary to public policy or would endanger public security",[8] or if the person is suffering from a scheduled disease.[a]

5.5.2 Non-EEA and Swiss nationals

Non-economically active persons coming to Ireland from outside the EEA and Switzerland to take up employment, must possess a valid passport, and a visa (if required).[b] However, a visa is not an entitlement to enter and remain in Ireland.[c]

5.5.2.1 Refusal of leave to land

Persons who arrive in Ireland must fulfil certain criteria before they are allowed to enter the country, otherwise they may be refused leave to land.[d] The *Aliens Order*, 1946 (as amended) lists the grounds on which a non-national may be refused leave to land.[e]

A person who is refused leave to land must be informed of the reasons for refusal. They may be arrested and detained until such time as they may be removed from the State. [9] A deportation order may be made in respect of them by the Minister for Justice, Equality & Law Reform. [10] The person will be notified of the Minister's intention to make such an order and informed that they must either:

- make representations to the Minister within 15 working days, setting out the reasons why they should not be deported

- leave Ireland voluntarily within 15 working days (if the person agrees to leave, they must inform the Minister of their arrangements)

- consent to the making of the deportation order within 15 working days

5.6 Registering with the (Garda) Registration Officer

5.6.1 EEA and Swiss nationals

The *European Communities (Right of Residence for Non-economically Active Persons) Regulations*, 1997, 11 oblige retired or other non-economically active persons who are EEA or Swiss nationals to apply for a residence permit within three months of arrival in Ireland if they intend to remain in Ireland for more than three months.

---

a See Appendix B for details.

b See Appendix A for details.

c The *Aliens Order* 1946 Section 5(1) (as amended by the *Aliens Amendment Order* 1975, Section 3) states that: "An alien coming from any place outside the State other than Great Britain shall on arrival in the State, present himself to an Immigration Officer for leave to land."

d To 'land' means "to arrive or enter by any means including over a land frontier" (from Northern Ireland). *Aliens Order* 1946 Section 3.

e See Appendix C for details.

An application for a residence permit should be made to the registration officer in the area where the person resides. The local registration officer is a member of the Gardaí. Applicants should inquire at their local Garda station for the location of the registration officer for the area in which they reside. In Dublin, this is the Garda National Immigration Bureau.

A residence permit is issued in the case of retired persons if the Minister is satisfied that the retired person is in receipt of certain benefits or is in a position to support themselves and their spouse and dependants.[a] In the case of other non-economically active persons, the Minister must be satisfied that the person has sufficient resources to support themselves, their spouse and dependants.

5.6.2 *Non-EEA and Swiss nationals*

Non-EEA and Swiss nationals who are not economically active are required to register with the registration office in the area where they reside, if they intend to remain in Ireland for more than three months. The local Registration Office in Dublin is the Garda National Immigration Bureau; outside the Dublin area, applicants should inquire at their local Garda station for the location of the registration officer for the area in which they reside. They are required to bring their passport and evidence that they can support themselves while in Ireland without recourse to public funds.

They are normally regarded as visitors. If a non-economically active person who is not a national of the EEA or Switzerland wishes to remain in Ireland on a more permanent basis, they need to make an application in writing to the Immigration Division of the Department of Justice, Equality & Law Reform outlining the reasons why they wish to remain and submitting evidence showing that they are able to maintain themselves without recourse to public funds and that they have adequate health insurance.

A person granted permission to remain is then issued with a Certificate of Registration by the registration officer. The Certificate of Registration contains a photograph of the holder and states the duration of their permission to remain in Ireland. It also contains a stamp,[b] the number of which indicates the basis on which the Certificate of Registration was provided.

5.7 *What Rights and Entitlements Do Non-economically Active Persons Have?*

5.7.1 *What types of accommodation can non-economically active persons access?*

Non-economically active persons have the following options with regard to accommodation:

- private rented accommodation
- purchase

a Regulation 7 (1)(b)ii *EC Right of Residence for Non-Economically Active Persons* 1997 provides that the Minister will issue a residence permit if s/he is satisfied the applicant (retired person) "is in receipt of an invalidity or early retirement pension or old age benefits or of a pension in respect of an industrial accident or disease of an amount sufficient to support himself, his spouse and accompanying dependants".

b Stamp 3 refers to visitors who are not entitled to work (see Appendix D).

5.7.1.1 Private rented accommodation

Persons wishing to rent a house or apartment from a private landlord can do so directly themselves by replying to advertisements in newspapers or seek the assistance of a letting agency. Finding accommodation can be expensive and time-consuming, particularly in big cities. Prospective tenants should:

- Inspect the property before agreeing to move in and record the condition of the property and its contents in writing. Houses and apartments to let should comply with certain minimum standards.[12]

- Agree the amount of deposit and rent to be paid and the time of payment. A receipt should be obtained for all money paid to the landlord. The deposit should be returned to the tenant when s/he leaves the accommodation. However, the landlord may retain some or all of the deposit if: the tenant gives insufficient notice, damages the property or leaves without paying bills or rent.

- Find out whether the rent covers such items as electricity, gas and bin charges (where relevant).

- Agree on who is responsible for any repairs that need to be carried out in the future.

Tenants should be aware of their rights and duties as a tenant. The most important of these are:

- The landlord must provide a rent book. The rent book should contain the name and address of the landlord, amount of deposit paid, the amount of rent and the time and method of payment. All rent payments should be entered in the rent book. The rent book should also include the terms of the tenancy.

- The landlord is not permitted (except in cases of emergency) to enter the accommodation without making an appointment with the tenant.

- The landlord must give a minimum of four weeks notice in writing if they require the tenant to leave the accommodation. This is referred to as a 'notice to quit'. If the tenant does not leave by the end of the four-week period, the landlord can go to court to apply for an eviction order.

- The tenant must also provide notice to the landlord if they decide to move out.

5.7.1.2 Purchase

There are no restrictions on non-nationals buying private residential property in Ireland.[a] However, there are requirements under the Land Acts and additional documents may be required. There are some restrictions with regard to farmland.[b]

---

a The *Aliens Act*, 1935 states that "Real and personal property of every description in Saorstat Eireann or subject to the law of Saorstat Eireann may be taken, acquired, held and disposed of by an alien in like manner and to the like extend as such property may be taken, acquired, held or disposed of by a citizen of Saorstat Eireann".

b These restrictions apply to non-EU nationals wishing to buy land over five acres in size. They should contact the Department of Agriculture, Food and Rural Development, Agriculture House, Kildare Street, Dublin 2, telephone (01) 607 2000, Lo-call 1890 200 510.

However, persons should be aware that house purchase can be a lengthy and costly process, therefore, for some, renting a property may be a better option. It is important to note that a person's Certificate of Registration will not be extended simply because the person has bought property in Ireland, or is in the process of purchasing property.

Persons interested in buying a private house or apartment may find a suitable property through an auctioneer/estate agent or through advertisements in local and national newspapers.

- Persons who cannot afford to buy a property from their own resources need to get a mortgage from a building society or bank.

- Houses/apartments should be viewed and in the case of a second-hand house or apartment, a survey should be carried out to ensure that it is structurally sound.

- If the person is satisfied that they have found a property they wish to buy, they should make an offer, if the property is for sale by private treaty. If the property is for sale by auction, they must attend the auction and the highest bidder purchases the property.

- Generally, estate agents do not charge a fee to purchasers of property.

- The purchase of property can be complicated, and prospective buyers should always engage a solicitor to act for them.

5.7.1.2.1 What laws govern discrimination in the provision of accommodation?

The *Equal Status Act*, 2000, prohibits discrimination on the grounds of gender, marital status, family status, sexual orientation, religious belief, age, disability, "race" and membership of the Traveller Community in the provision of goods and services, the disposal of property and access to education. Discrimination on the nine grounds listed in the Act is prohibited in both the public and private sectors. The process for referring complaints is similar to that under the *Employment Equality Act*, 1998. Further information is available from the equality tribunal.[13]

5.7.2 What medical services are non-economically active persons entitled to?

Non-economically active persons legally resident in Ireland have two options with regard to medical care:

- public health care
- private health care

5.7.2.1 Public health care

The public health care system, including primary and hospital services, can be accessed by any person resident in Ireland including those who are non-economically active. This system can be accessed for a nominal charge, or free of charge for medical card holders. Generally, to get free medical care in Ireland a person needs a medical card.

5.7.2.1.1 What services can be accessed for a nominal charge?

A range of services are available including:

- General Practitioner (GP) services (family doctor) with a charge of between €30 and €50 per consultation

- in-patient hospital treatment in a public ward subject to a daily charge of €40[a]

- all other out-patient services including consultants

- visits to hospital Accident and Emergency Departments subject to a charge of €40 (persons who are referred by their GP will not be charged)

- maternity and infant care

5.7.2.1.2 Who is entitled to a medical card?

Entitlement to a medical card in Ireland is based on a person's residence and means. In order to be fully eligible for a medical card a person must:

- be 'ordinarily resident' in Ireland; this means that they must intend to live in Ireland for at least one year and be permitted to do so

- satisfy the means test; a person will only be eligible for free medical care (Category A entitlement, that is medical card holders) if their gross income, less PRSI contributions is less than €138 (or €151 for persons aged between 66 and 69 years) and in the case of a married couple or single parent €200,[b](or €224 for couples aged between 66 and 69 years)

EU nationals who are resident in Ireland and in receipt of a social security pension from another EU State may get a medical card regardless of their income. Persons in receipt of an Irish social welfare pension will be subject to a means test.

Other non-EU nationals resident in the State are required to take out medical insurance.

5.7.2.1.3 What does a medical card entitle you to?

A medical card entitles you to the following free medical services:

- General Practitioner (GP) services (but you must register with a GP (see Section 5.7.2.1.4 page 117))

- prescribed medicines

- in-patient hospital treatment in a public ward

- out-patient hospital treatment

- dental, ophthalmic and aural services

- community care services

---

a Up to a maximum of €400 in any twelve-month period (as of 1 January 2003).

b A married couple or a single parent must earn less than €200. These rates apply to persons under 66 years of age. Persons applying for the medical card are permitted to have the following amounts over the income level and still qualify for the medical card, as of 1 January 2003:

- €25 for each child under 16 years of age

- €26 for each child over 16 years of age with no income maintained by applicant

- the amount by which the rent or mortgage paid each week exceeds €25

- the amount by which the costs of travelling to and from work each week exceeds €22

- weekly expenditure on medicines

5.7.2.1.4 Registering with a General Practitioner (GP)

Persons who qualify for the medical card must register with a General Practitioner (family doctor). Not all GPs accept medical card patients, so the medical card holder should obtain a list of doctors in their area who accept medical card patients:

- They can obtain this list from the local health board offices and health centre together with a registration form, which the doctor will be required to sign.

- GPs are only permitted to accept a certain number of medical card patients. Therefore, they will sometimes refuse to accept any further patients.

- If a person is unable to find a doctor who will accept them as a patient under the medical card scheme, one will be assigned to them by the health board office or health centre.

5.7.2.1.5 Applying for a medical card

Persons who wish to apply for a medical card should submit a completed application form, together with evidence that they are 'ordinarily resident' in Ireland and that they satisfy the means test, to their local health board offices or health centre.

5.7.2.2 Private health care

Persons can also take out private health insurance.[a] This insurance covers private care in public or private hospitals. There are two private health insurers in Ireland, VHI and BUPA.[14] Medical insurance will not cover pre-existing medical conditions and the cover may not, in any event, take effect for an initial period.

5.7.3 What social welfare entitlements do non-economically active persons have?

Irish social welfare legislation does not distinguish between nationals and non-nationals. Essentially, any person from outside the State who complies with the relevant laws covering entry, living and working here is entitled to seek social welfare payments in compliance with the normal conditions. For further information, contact the Information Service of the Department of Social and Family Affairs on (01) 704 3000.

5.7.4 What education can non-economically active persons access?

5.7.4.1 EEA and Swiss nationals

All EU citizens are entitled to equal treatment in the educational sector in Ireland on the same basis as Irish citizens. Thus for example, migrant EU students are entitled to the same fee level (or none as the case may be) and maintenance grants as national students.[15] However, EEA nationals (other than those belonging to the EU) and Swiss nationals are not entitled to local authority/VEC education grants. Third-level education fees vary between educational institutions.

If they choose to commence full-time study while in Ireland as non-economically active persons, the *European Communities (Right of Residence for non-Economically Active Persons) Regulations*, 1997 will still apply to them, but the regulations differ in some circumstances. In particular, students may only be accompanied by their spouse and minor children.[16] Non-economically active persons may enrol in part-time studies without their status changing to that of a student, within the meaning of the 1997 Regulations.

---

a Persons who wish to avail of private health care and who have not taken out private health insurance will be required to pay for hospital treatment.

Non-EEA and Swiss national family members of EEA and Swiss nationals who are non-economically active, are entitled to education on the same basis as their partner so long as the relationship is valid.

5.7.4.2 *Non-EEA and Swiss nationals*

Non-economically active persons from outside the EEA and Switzerland, living in Ireland are not entitled to change their status and enter full-time study. If they are interested in full-time study in Ireland, they must generally return to their country and make the necessary applications from there.[a]

5.7.4.3 *Children of non-economically active persons*

All children and young people under the age of 18 in Ireland have the same rights irrespective of the child's or parent's/parents' or legal caregivers' race, colour, sex, language, religion, political or other opinion, national, ethnic or social origin, property, disability, birth or other status.[17] Children of non-EEA nationals can therefore access services on the same basis as an Irish child. Children of non-EEA nationals are registered on their parent's/parents' or legal caregivers' Certificate of Registration until the age of 16. However, children's birth certificates are usually required for identification and other purposes. Thereafter, they must register themselves, in their own name, with the registration officer in the area where reside. The local registration officer is a member of the Gardaí. Applicants should inquire at their local Garda station for the location of the registration officer for the area in which they reside. In Dublin, this is the Garda National Immigration Bureau.

All children and young people in Ireland must engage in full-time education until they are 16 years old. At first and second level, there are two main education sectors: primary school (first level), and post-primary and vocational training (second level).

Schools are managed by the State (Comprehensive, Vocational Education Committees [VECs]) and religious bodies (Catholic, Protestant, Muslim, Jewish) and governed by their own ethos/philosophy. Lists of schools are available from the Department of Education and Science.[18]

Children with language needs are generally placed in classes with other children/young people of a similar age. Government support is provided to allow schools to offer limited language support programmes for bilingual and multilingual children.

To apply to a school or education centre parents or legal caregivers should follow the process below:

- The parents/legal caregivers contact the local school/education centre of choice by writing or telephoning the school principal or manager to arrange a meeting.

- At the first meeting, the parents/legal caregivers are provided with the formal school/education centre policy which outlines the ethos, selection criteria and other matters.

a For further information see Chapter 4 on International Students.

- The parents/legal caregivers are required to provide the school/education centre with basic information on the student.

- An informal education and linguistic assessment of the student may take place but there is no State interpretation facility for this process. Schools/education centres cannot refuse access to a student on the basis of their level of English.

- If there are no places, or if the school/education centre is unsuitable for the student, the school/education centre recommends another school/education centre in the locality.

- If the student is offered a place in a school, the parents/legal caregivers should obtain a letter of acceptance from the school/education centre.

5.7.5 What family reunification rights do non-economically active persons have?

5.7.5.1 EEA and Swiss nationals

EEA and Swiss nationals who are non-economically active are entitled to be accompanied by: their spouse; children under 18 years of age; other dependent children; grandchildren and dependent parents and grandparents. They must be in a position to support their dependent family members.[a]

5.7.5.2 Non-EEA and Swiss nationals

Persons from outside the EEA and Switzerland do not have a statutory right to family reunification. However, they may be permitted to be accompanied, or joined, by immediate family members provided they can support these family members without recourse to public funds.

5.7.6 How can non-economically active persons acquire Irish citizenship?

Non-economically active persons in Ireland can become Irish citizens in three ways:

- naturalisation
- post-nuptial citizenship
- by descent

The *Irish Nationality and Citizenship Acts* 1956, 1986, 1994 and 2001 set out the criteria under which Irish citizenship is granted.

5.7.6.1 Acquiring citizenship by naturalisation

A person wishing to apply for a certificate of naturalisation must fulfil certain conditions including having legally resided in Ireland for five years out of the previous nine-year period. The Minister for Justice, Equality & Law Reform may grant an application for a certificate of naturalisation at their discretion if they are satisfied that the applicant:

- is of full age
- is of good character

---

a A residence permit will only be issued if the person can satisfy the Minister that they are in a position to support dependent family members and to provide health insurance for them, *European Communities (Rights of Residence for Non-economically Active Persons) Regulations*, 1997, Regulation 7.

- has had a period of one year's continuous residence in Ireland immediately prior to their application, and in the eight years immediately preceding that period has had a total residence of four years in Ireland

- intends in good faith to continue to reside in Ireland after naturalisation

- has made a declaration of fidelity to the nation and loyalty to the State, either before a District Court Justice or in such other manner permitted by the Minister

The Minister for Justice, Equality & Law Reform may waive these conditions in certain circumstances specified in the Acts. The number of circumstances in which the Minister may waive the conditions, has been reduced by the 2001, Act.[a]

5.7.6.2 Acquiring post-nuptial citizenship

A non-national who married an Irish national on or before 29 November 2002, and has been in a subsisting marriage with that person for a minimum of three years, may become an Irish citizen by making a post-nuptial declaration of citizenship. However, this is not possible if the Irish spouse has acquired citizenship by naturalisation, post-nuptial declaration, or was granted citizenship as a token of honour. Any such declarations will have to be made before 30 November 2005.

In the case of spouses of Irish nationals who got married on or after 30 November 2002, the Minister may at his/her 'absolute discretion' grant an application for a certificate of naturalisation to the spouse of an Irish citizen if the applicant:

- is of full age

- is of good character

- is married to an Irish citizen for at least three years

- is in a subsisting marriage, recognised as being in accordance with Irish legislation

- is living together with the Irish citizen as husband and wife (the applicant must submit an affidavit to that effect to the Minister)

- has lived in Ireland for at least one year continuously prior to the application

- has been resident in Ireland for at least two years of the four years immediately preceding that period

- intends in good faith to continue to reside in Ireland after naturalisation

- has made a declaration of 'fidelity to the nation and loyalty to the State' in whatever manner may be prescribed[19]

The Minister for Justice, Equality & Law Reform may waive certain of the above conditions if satisfied that the applicant would suffer serious consequences in respect of his or her bodily integrity or liberty if not granted Irish citizenship.[20]

a *Irish Nationality and Citizenship Act* 1956, Section 16 (as amended by *Irish Nationality and Citizenship Act*, 1986, Section 5). Since the coming into force of the 2001 Act, this no longer applies to persons married to a naturalised Irish citizen or persons married to a person who is an Irish citizen otherwise than by naturalisation.

5.7.6.3 *Acquiring citizenship by descent*

Persons whose father or mother was an Irish Citizen at the time of their birth are automatically Irish citizens. However, if a person is born outside Ireland, and the parent through whom they are claiming citizenship was also born outside Ireland, they will not be entitled to citizenship except in certain limited circumstances.[21] Persons whose grandparents were Irish citizens can become Irish citizens by registering in the Foreign Births Register in the Department of Foreign Affairs or, if residing outside Ireland, at the nearest Irish Embassy or Consulate.

5.7.6.4 *Permission to remain without condition as to time*

Persons who have been legally resident in Ireland for ten years and who have not applied for naturalisation may obtain a residence stamp giving them 'permission to remain without condition as to time'.[22]

5.7.7 What do non-economically active persons need to open a bank account?

Banks require new customers to produce the following documents when opening a bank account:

- photo identification (a passport satisfies this requirement)
- proof of address in Ireland, for example a utility bill (electricity, gas or other utility) or lease agreement
- although not officially documented as a requirement, banks often request applicants to provide a personal introduction from an existing customer

5.7.8 *Can non-economically active persons vote in elections?*

Non-national residents in Ireland over eighteen years of age may vote in some elections:

Citizens of...	Permitted to vote at...
The UK	Dáil, European and local elections
EU states apart from the UK	European and local elections
Non-EU states	Local elections only

Those permitted to vote must have their name included in the Electoral Register if they want to vote. Application forms are available in post offices, libraries and council and corporation offices.

Endnotes

1   Council Directive 90/336 (later replaced by Council Directive 93/96) on *Migrant Students* [1993] OJ L317/59; Council Directive 90/365 *Employed and Self-employed people who have Ceased to Work* [1990] OJ L180/28; Directive 90/364 [1990] OJ L180/26.

2   Case C-413/99 *Baumbast*, 17 September 2002.

3   Proposal for a European Parliament and Council Directive 29 June 2001 on the *Right of Citizens of the Union and their Family Members to Move and Reside Freely within the Territory of the Member States* COM(2001) 257 final [2001] OJ C270 E/23.

4   Case C-85/96 *Maria Martinez Sala v Freistaat Bayern* [1998] ECR I-2691.

5   *European Communities (Aliens) Regulations* 1977, Regulation 8 (1), SI No. 393/1977.

6   *Ibid*, Regulation 8 (7), SI No. 393/1977.

7   *Aliens (Amendment)* (No.3) Order 1997, SI No. 277.

8   *European Communities (Aliens) Regulations* 1977, Regulations 4 (i) and 4 (ii), SI No. 393.

9   The *Aliens Order* 1946 (as amended), Section 5.

10 The *Immigration Act* 1999, Section 3 (1)(g).

11 *European Communities (Right of Residence for Non-economically Active Persons) Regulations* 1997, Section 6 (1).

12 Details of these can be obtained from Threshold, 21 Stoneybatter, Dublin 7, email *advice@threshold.ie*

13 Further information is available from the ODEI - the equality tribunal, 3 Clonmel Street, Dublin 2, telephone (01) 477 4100, website *http://www.odei.ie/*

14 Voluntary Health Insurance (VHI), VHI House, Lower Abbey Street, Dublin 1, telephone (01) 874 4499, Lo-call 1850 444 444.

    BUPA Ireland, Mill Island, Fermoy, Co. Cork, telephone (021) 42121, or 12 Fitzwilliam Square, Dublin 2, telephone (01) 6627 662, Lo-call 1890 700 890.

15 Case C-184/99 *Grzelczyk v CPAS* [2001] ECR I-6193.

16 The *European Communities (Right of Residence for Non-Economically Active Persons) Regulations* 1997 Regulation 2.

17 Refer to the *International Convention on the Rights of the Child* 1989, Article 2(1), signed by Ireland, 30 September 1990 and ratified 28 September 1992.

18 Department of Education and Science, Marlborough Street, Dublin 1, telephone (01) 873 4700, website *http://www.education.ie/*

19 *Irish Nationality and Citizenship Act* 1956, Section 15A (1), as amended by the *Irish Nationality and Citizenship Act* 2001, Section 5.

20 *Irish Nationality and Citizenship Act* 1956, Section 15A (2), as amended by the *Irish Nationality and Citizenship Act* 2001, Section 5.

21 *Irish Nationality and Citizenship Act* 1956, Section 7 (3), as amended by the *Irish Nationality and Citizenship Act* 2001, Section 5.

22 Further information available on the Department of Justice, Equality & Law Reform website *http://www.justice.ie/*

Parents and Siblings of Irish Citizen Children

6.1 *Making Representations for Leave to Remain*

6.2 *What Rights and Entitlements do Parents and Siblings of Irish Citizen Children Have?*

PARENTS AND SIBLINGS OF IRISH CITIZEN CHILDREN

Every person born in Ireland (including Northern Ireland) is entitled to be an Irish citizen. According to Article 2 of the Constitution

It is the entitlement and birthright of every person born in the island of Ireland, which includes its islands and seas, to be part of the Irish nation. This is also the entitlement of all persons qualified in accordance with law to be citizens of Ireland. Furthermore, the Irish nation cherishes its special affinity with people of Irish ancestry living abroad who share its cultural identity and heritage.

Section 3(2)(a) of the *Irish Nationality and Citizenship Act*, 2001 states that:

Subject to subsections (4) and (5), a person born in the island of Ireland is an Irish citizen from birth if he or she does, or if not of full age, has done on his or her behalf, any act which only an Irish Citizen is entitled to do.[a]

The Act does not specify what such an act should entail, but it is understood by some lawyers that an application for a passport would be regarded as such an act.

This entitlement at present, applies to persons born in Ireland, irrespective of the nationality of their parents.

Since the 1990 Supreme Court judgment in the *Fajujonu* case,[b] which held that the non-national parents of Irish children in that case had a strong claim to reside in Ireland because they had been living in Ireland for 'an appreciable time' and had three Irish children who were entitled to their 'company',[c] non-national parents and siblings of Irish children have been entitled to apply for permission to reside in Ireland.

From 1996 to 2001, 4,859 persons were granted permission to remain in Ireland on that basis, including 2,747 in 2001.[1] The Government is concerned that the present system is open to abuse by persons who have children in Ireland in order to be granted permission to remain here.

This practice is now in question. The government has announced that it will no longer accept applications from persons for residency based on their parentage to an Irish citizen child[2] and there will no longer be a separate application procedure for parents of Irish citizens applying for leave to remain. This announcement follows an unsuccessful Supreme Court challenge by a Nigerian father and a Czech family,[d] who challenged the validity of the deportation orders issued in respect of them, despite an Irish citizen child having been born into the family.

---

a Subsection 4 refers to persons born in Ireland to a non-national who is entitled to diplomatic immunity or a non-national on a foreign ship or aircraft. Subsection 5 deals with persons born in Ireland who have made a declaration of alienage.

b This case involved the Fajujonu family, who were living in Ireland illegally since 1983 and had three children born in Ireland and therefore, Irish citizens. The Minister for Justice had requested Mr Fajujonu to make arrangements for his departure and this request together with the fear that the Minister would issue a deportation order in respect of him, led to proceedings being taken first to the High Court and later appealed to the Supreme Court. It was argued that the Fajujonu children as Irish citizens were entitled to be raised by their parents in Ireland and to enjoy their company and society within the State.

c The Court held that only the interests of 'the common good' and 'the protection of the State and society' justified any interference with the Constitutional rights of the child as an Irish citizen.

d *L. & O. v. The Minister for Justice, Equality & Law Reform* [2002] IESC 109/02 & 108/02, 23 January 2003. These cases concern the transfer under the Dublin Convention of two families, with Irish citizen children, to the EU State responsible for their applications for refugee status.

As of 20 February 2003, parents of Irish citizen children cannot make an application for residency based on their parentage to their child and the child's right to their care and company in the State, until the Minister for Justice, Equality & Law Reform proposes to actually deport them.

Once any person receives notification of the Minister's intention to deport them, they can make representations pursuant to Section 3 (6) of the *Immigration Act, 1999* as amended, setting out the reasons why they should not be deported.[a] The Minister considers all factors relevant to the determination, including the family and domestic circumstances of the person.[3]

In January 2003, the Supreme Court had confirmed that "every citizen, including the minor applicants in the case they were considering, enjoys, in general terms, the right not to be expelled from the State". However, this was held **not** to be an **absolute right.** "Irish citizens, as a matter of law, may be extradited to other countries to undergo trials on criminal charges". According to the Court, it is clear and again accepted on behalf of the Minister that **"the State has no right to deport any Irish citizen, including the minor applicants in the present case"**.[4]

However, according to the majority of the Court:

> the State may, for reasons associated with the interests of the common good, deport non-nationals who are the parents of a child who is a citizen of Ireland even if that means, de facto, that the child is compelled to leave and reside out side the State with its parents. [5]

In distinguishing the Fajujonu case, the Court held that the **Minister was obliged to give consideration to whether there were grave and substantial reasons associated with the common good which required the deportation of the non-national members of the family,** having as its inevitable consequence, either the departure of the entire family from the State or its break-up by the departure of the non-nationals alone with the consequent infringement of the constitutional rights of the Irish citizens who were members of the family.[6]

In his judgment, Chief Justice Keane held that:

> it can reasonably be inferred from the judgments in Fajujonu that there were specific circumstances to which the court thought the Minister should have regard together with the constitutional rights of the family and any other matters relevant to their continued stay in the State which might come to the Minister's attention, that is
>
> 1) the **'appreciable time'** (approximately eight years at the date of the hearing in this court) for which they had resided as a family in Ireland;
>
> 2) the fact that the family had made its 'home and residence' in Ireland; and
>
> 3) the fact that the first plaintiff had been **offered employment**, that the relevant authority was prepared to issue him with a work permit and that the only ground on which a permit would not be issued was that the Minister in that case had refused to grant him permission to stay in Ireland.[7]

a See Chapter 7 for information on making an application for permission to remain in the State.

Effectively, the judgment will mean that some non-EEA and Swiss national parents and siblings of Irish citizens will still be permitted to remain in the State. The Minister for Justice, Equality & Law Reform has ruled out 'mass deportations' and indicated that people who have already been granted permission to remain in the State would probably not be subjected to deportation orders.

Furthermore, the Court confirmed that the Minister **must consider each case involving deportation on its individual merits**. However, it also held that the Minister is entitled to take into account the policy considerations that would arise from allowing a particular applicant to remain "where that would inevitably lead to similar decisions in other cases, again undermining the orderly administration of the immigration and asylum system".[8]

6.1 Making Representations for Leave to Remain

Once threatened with deportation, non EEA and Swiss nationals who are the parents of Irish citizen children may apply for permission to remain in Ireland for themselves and any of their other dependent children.

The parent or parents must make representations in writing to the Immigration and Citizenship Division of the Department of Justice, Equality and Law Reform setting out the reasons why they should not be deported. As part of their considerations, the Minister for Justice, Equality & Law Reform must take into account the family and domestic circumstances of the person. As outlined above, the Minister must consider each case involving deportation on its individual merits and should have regard to the constitutional rights of the family and any other matters relevant to their continued stay in the State.

The documents that should be enclosed with representations made to the Minister setting out the reasons why a person should not be deported will depend on the circumstances of the case. However, where a person wants the Minister to consider the fact that they are the parent of an Irish citizen child, the following documents should be included in the submission to the Minister:

- the birth certificate of the child
- evidence that the applicant is providing care and company to the child
- evidence of the fact that the applicant resides together with the child
- evidence, in the case of parents who are separated, of joint guardianship and/or a binding maintenance agreement

Applicants may be requested to submit further documentation in support of their claim. If the paternity of the child is disputed, a DNA test may be requested.

If a parent or sibling of an Irish citizen is subsequently refused permission to remain, a deportation order will be issued without further notice being given. There is no administrative appeal mechanism even though the decision to refuse a residence permit following submissions made pursuant to Section 3 (6) of the *Immigration Act*, 1999 as amended may be judicially reviewable in the High Court.

Persons, who are granted leave to remain on the basis of their parentage to an Irish child, are required to register with the registration officer in the area in which they reside. If the child's siblings are over the age of 16, they will also be required to register with their Garda registration officer. The local registration officer is a member of the Gardaí. Applicants should inquire at their local Garda station for the location of the registration officer for the area in which they reside. In Dublin, this is the Garda National Immigration Bureau.

They will generally be required to produce their passports or national identity cards, which may cause difficulties for asylum seekers or persons who were in the asylum process and may not have a passport, and are unable to approach the authorities of their country of origin in order to obtain one.

Once the requirements are met, the person is issued with a Certificate of Registration by the registration officer. The Certificate of Registration contains a photograph of the holder and states the duration of their permission to remain in Ireland. It also contains a stamp, the number of which indicates the basis on which the Certificate of Registration was provided.[a]

6.2 What Rights and Entitlements do Parents and Siblings of Irish Citizen Children Have?

Persons granted leave to remain on the basis of being the parents/siblings of an Irish citizen child are generally entitled to the same rights as Irish nationals.[b] They are permitted to work without an employment permit, are entitled to social welfare if they satisfy the means test and will qualify for local authority housing if they are otherwise eligible for it.

6.2.1 What rights in the work place do parents of Irish citizen children have?

Non-national employees are entitled to the same rights in the work place as Irish employees.[9]

6.2.1.1 What taxes and social contributions do parents of Irish citizen children pay?

All employees must pay tax on their earnings, known as 'pay as you earn' or PAYE and PRSI 'pay-related social insurance'.[c] These are deducted from employees' salaries each week or month. All employees are required to have a Personal Public Service Number (PPS No.), and persons who do not have a PPS No.[d] should contact the Department of Social Community and Family Affairs.[10] This number should be quoted in all contact with the Tax Office and the Department.

In addition, persons who are commencing their first employment in Ireland should complete a Certificate of Tax Credits and Standard Rate Cut-Off Point (Form 12A).[11] The Revenue Commissioners usually grant married tax credits even if the worker's spouse is not resident in the State.

6.2.1.2 What details of employment are parents of Irish citizen children entitled to receive?

Within two months of starting employment, the employer is required to provide the employee[e] with a written statement of certain details of the terms of employment.[12]

---

a Stamp 4 in this case (see Appendix D).

b However, parents are only afforded these rights by virtue of the fact that they are parents or siblings of an Irish citizen and should the child die or no longer reside in the state, the parents may no longer be able to avail of them.

c There are some exceptions to this, for example, low-paid workers.

d This replaces the old RSI Number.

e The term 'employee' covers those working under contract of employment or apprenticeship; those employed through an employment agency and those employed in the service of the State.

These include:

- name and address of employer
- place of work
- job title and nature of work
- date of commencement of employment
- nature of contract (temporary or fixed term)
- rate of pay
- pay intervals
- hours of work (including overtime)
- paid leave
- arrangements for when the employee is unable to work due to sickness or injury
- pensions and pension schemes
- notice entitlements
- collective agreement/s, and the parties to the agreement/s

If the particulars contained in the statement change, the employer must notify the employee within one week.

If an employer has either failed to provide a written statement, or failed to notify the employee of changes that have taken place regarding the particulars contained in the statement, the employee may complain to a Rights Commissioner. If either party is dissatisfied with the recommendation of the Rights Commissioner, they may appeal to the Employment Appeals Tribunal.[a]

6.2.1.3 What is the minimum rate of pay for parents of Irish citizen children?

All employees over the age of 18 who have worked for at least two years since turning 18 are entitled to a minimum rate of pay. This is currently €6.35 per hour since 1 October 2002.[13] Persons who have not worked for two years must generally be paid 80 per cent of the minimum wage in the first year, and 90 per cent in the second year.[14]

- With their wages, employees must receive a written statement of the gross pay and deductions made.[15]

- Employees have the right to a readily negotiable mode of wage payment such as by cheque, credit transfer, cash, postal order or bank draft.

- Employers may only make deductions in certain circumstances[b] that are agreed with the employee.[c]

---

a See Section 6.2.1.12, page 132 for details of the procedure for referring a complaint to the Rights Commissioner. In addition, the Rights Commissioner can investigate grievances or claims under most of the legislation dealing with rights in the workplace including: *Payment of Wages Act* 1991; *Terms of Employment Act* 1994; *Organisation of Working Time Act* 1997; *Parental Leave Act* 1998 and *National Minimum Wages Act,* 2000.

b When the deductions are required by law; when they are provided for in the contract of employment and when they are made with the written consent of the employee.

c For example, VHI, BUPA, Union Dues, Pension Plan and so on.

6.2.1.4 What are the rules governing working hours?

- Employees must not be required to work in excess of the maximum hours permitted each week. This is an average of 48 hours per week averaged over four, six or 12 months depending on the nature of the employment.[a]

- Employees are entitled to breaks and rest time as follows:

  - 11 hours rest per 24 hour period

  - one period of 24 hours rest per week preceded by a daily rest period (11 hours)

  - 15 minutes break after working four-and-a-half hours and another break of 15 minutes after six hours, or 30 minutes after six hours if the 15 minutes break was not taken after four-and-a-half hours[b]

6.2.1.5 What holidays are parents of Irish citizen children entitled to?

Full-time workers are entitled to four working weeks annual leave[16] and nine public holidays per year.[c] These are: 1 January, St Patrick's Day, Easter Monday, First Monday in May, First Monday in June, First Monday in August, Last Monday in October, Christmas Day and St Stephen's Day.

Part-time workers are entitled to annual leave consisting of eight per cent of the hours they work up to a maximum of four weeks and to public holidays if they have worked at least 40 hours in the five weeks preceding the public holiday.

6.2.1.6 What compensation for Sunday work are parents of Irish citizen children entitled to?

Employees are entitled to be compensated for Sunday work. This can be extra pay[d] or time off in lieu.[17] For persons working in the retail sector, there is a *Code of Practice on Sunday Working in the Retail Trade*.[e]

6.2.1.7 What maternity leave are parents of Irish citizen children entitled to?

- A pregnant employee is entitled to maternity leave from employment for a period of at least 14 weeks.[18]

- To be entitled to maternity leave, the employee must notify her employer and produce a medical certificate confirming the pregnancy and expected week of confinement. The notice must be given at least four weeks before the commencement of maternity leave and must be in writing.[19]

- An employee can choose the period of maternity leave. However, maternity leave must be taken at least four weeks before the end of the expected week of confinement and shall end not earlier than four weeks after the end of the expected week of confinement.[20]

a Four months for employees generally, six months for seasonal workers and workers who are directly involved in ensuring continuity of service or production, and twelve months for employees who have entered a collective agreement with their employer.

b The break cannot be taken at the end of the work period.

c The employer has four alternatives with regard to the public holidays. They may give the employee: the day of the holiday off with pay, a paid day off within a month, an extra day of annual leave or an extra day's pay.

d With premium payment (that is, above normal payment).

e This was drawn up by the Labour Relations Commission and is based on the entitlements set out in the *Organisation of Working Time Act* 1997. It is available on the Department of Enterprise, Trade & Employment website http://www.entemp.ie/

- The employee has the right to return to work when the period of maternity leave has expired. Employees who have taken maternity leave are entitled to return to the:

  - same employer

  - job the employee held immediately before commencement of leave

  - same contract and conditions of employment[21]

6.2.1.8 What parental leave are parents of Irish citizen children entitled to?

- Persons who have at least one year's continuous employment and are the parents of children (natural or adopted) may take up to a total of 14 weeks unpaid leave (for each child) to take care of their children who are no older than five years.[22]

- Employees who have taken parental leave are entitled to return to the:

  - same employer

  - job the employee held immediately before commencement of leave

  - same contract and conditions of employment[23]

6.2.1.9 What force majeure leave are parents of Irish citizen children entitled to?

- Employees may also take *force majeure* leave in the case of sudden injury or illness to an immediate family member, where the dependant needs the worker to be present.[24]

- An 'immediate family member' of the employee is a child, spouse/partner, person to whom the employee is *in loco parentis,* brother, sister, parent or grandparent.[25]

- An employee may take three days in any consecutive 12 months or five days in any 36 consecutive months[26]

- *Force majeure* leave is paid leave[27]

6.2.1.10 What laws protect parents of Irish citizen children from unfair dismissal?

Employees who have over 12 months continuous employment,[a] are protected by law from unfair dismissal. Dismissals may be regarded as unfair where they have resulted wholly or mainly from:

- the employee's trade union membership or activities

- the religious or political beliefs of the employee

- the race, skin colour or sexual orientation of the employee

- legal proceedings against the employer if the employee is a party or a witness

- the employee's pregnancy

- the employee taking leave provided for under the *Maternity Protection Act*, 1994

a Two fixed terms of six months would qualify.

CHAPTER 6

A dismissal will usually be considered fair if it is based wholly or mainly on one of the following:

- the employee's capability, competence or qualifications for the job
- the employee's conduct
- the employee's redundancy
- if continuation of the employment would contravene other legal requirements

Both 'actual' unfair dismissals and 'constructive' dismissals are prohibited by legislation. Constructive dismissal can occur where the employee's conditions of employment are made so difficult that they have no alternative but to leave.

6.2.1.11 What claims for redress[a] exist for parents of Irish citizen children who consider they have been unfairly dismissed?

An employee who considers that they have been unfairly dismissed (this includes 'actual' and 'constructive' dismissal) and who wishes to make a claim for redress must do so within six months.[b]

The employee must give formal notice of his/her claim in writing to a Rights Commissioner or to the Employment Appeals Tribunal. The claim is considered by the Employment Appeals Tribunal where the employee or the employer have notified a Rights Commissioner that they object to the claim being heard by a Rights Commissioner.

Persons who are employed through an employment agency must make their claim against whoever is paying their wages (this could be the actual 'employer' or the agency).

6.2.1.12 How can parents of Irish citizen children take a claim to the Rights Commissioner?

Rights Commissioners are appointed by the Minister for Enterprise, Trade & Employment on the recommendation of the Labour Relations Commission. They are independent of the Minister in carrying out their functions. The procedure for persons wishing to make an appeal to the Rights Commissioner is described below:

- Persons wishing to make an appeal to a Rights Commissioner must:
  - notify their former employer that they intend to take a case to the Rights Commissioner
  - complete the standard form[28] (full details of the complaint must be given)
- The Rights Commissioner hears the case as soon as possible. The hearing takes place in private.
- Both parties can be represented at the hearing by a lawyer or trade union representative (in the cases of the employee).
- Both parties have the opportunity to present their case.
- The Rights Commissioner makes a recommendation, which may be appealed to the Employment Appeals Tribunal (EAT).

a Redress in the case of unfair dismissal can be any of the following:
  - re-instatement in the employee's old job
  - re-engagement in the old job or a suitable alternative
  - financial compensation

b In exceptional circumstances, this can be twelve months.

6.2.1.13 What is the minimum notice[29]period for employees?

Employees who are in continuous employment with the same employer for 13 weeks or more and who normally work at least eight hours per week are entitled to a minimum period of notice from their employer if they intend to dismiss them.

The period of notice depends on the length of service. For persons who have served from 13 weeks to two years the minimum notice period is one week.

Employees must also give notice if they intend to leave the job. If the employee is in employment for 13 weeks or over, they must give the employer at least one week's notice. If the contract of employment requires further notice to be given, they must adhere to the terms of the contract.

The Employment Appeals Tribunal considers disputes between employers and workers regarding minimum notice.

6.2.1.14 What redundancy payments[a]are parents of Irish citizen children entitled to?

Employees are entitled to a lump sum redundancy payment when their employment is ended due to redundancy providing they:

- have 109 weeks continuous service
- are aged between 16 and 66
- are normally expected to work at least eight hours per week

The redundancy pay is calculated in the following manner:

- a half week's pay for each year of employment up to 41 years' service
- one week's pay for each year over 41 years' service
- one week's pay irrespective of the length of service

6.2.1.15 What rules govern discrimination in employment?

Discrimination against employees on grounds of age, gender, marital status,[30] family status,[31] race,[32] religion,[33] sexual orientation,[34] disability[35] and membership of the Travelling Community is prohibited under the *Employment Equality Act, 1998*.[b] The Act prohibits:

- direct and indirect discrimination
- discrimination in access to employment, conditions of employment, promotion, training and classification of posts[36]

The Equality Authority may provide legal advice, assistance and representation to persons who consider that they have a complaint under the legislation.[37]

---

a Redundancy payments are dealt with under the *Redundancy Payments Acts 1967 -1991*. Redundancy occurs when the employee's job ceases to exist, there is insufficient work, the firm closes down or the firm re-organises.

b The *Employment Equality Authority Act 1998* came into force 18 October 1999, and only incidents of discrimination occurring on, or after that date can be dealt with under the Act. Incidents of discrimination on grounds of sex or marital status can be investigated by the ODEI - the equality tribunal under earlier legislation.

A person who considers that they have been discriminated against on any of the nine grounds listed above can refer their complaint to:

Authority	Employees refer to this body if they...
the ODEI - the equality tribunal	are still in employment
the Labour Court	have already been dismissed (including 'actual' and 'constructive' dismissal)

6.2.1.16 How can parents and siblings of Irish citizen children bring a claim to the equality tribunal?

The ODEI - the equality tribunal (referred to as the equality tribunal in this handbook), is an independent body established to investigate claims of discrimination under the *Employment Equality Act*, 1998 and the *Equal Status Act*, 2000. The equality tribunal also offers a mediation service.

Persons wishing to refer their complaint to the equality tribunal must complete the complaint form (Form ODEI 1).[a] Persons who have difficulty in completing the form due to disability, language or other difficulties, should contact the equality tribunal immediately, and if appropriate, other arrangements will be made to enable the person to refer their complaint.

The person making the complaint (the complainant) may write to the person they believe has discriminated against them (the respondent), to request information in order to ascertain more fully, what actually took place. The complainant must use the standard form provided by the equality tribunal (Form ODEI 3).[38]

If the respondent does not reply promptly, the complainant may refer their complaint to the equality tribunal.

When the complaint is received, the Director of Equality Investigations will refer it to an Equality Officer within the equality tribunal.

6.2.1.17 How can parents of Irish citizen children bring a claim to the Labour Court?

Persons who have been dismissed from their employment on grounds of discrimination or victimisation, may bring their claim to the Labour Court.

- The person can send a questionnaire to the former employer to obtain information. The employer can also give their version of what occurred through this procedure. The Questionnaire Form may be downloaded from the Labour Court website.[39]

- The application must be made within six months from the incident of discrimination or victimisation taking place. If there were a series of incidents, the application must be made six months from the last one taking place.

- The application may be made by completing the application form, which can be downloaded from the Labour Court website.

a The forms, and all the other form to be used in this process, may be downloaded from the ODEI - the equality tribunal website *http://www.odei.ie/* or from the Office of Director of Equality Investigations, 3 Clonmel Street, Dublin 2, telephone (01) 477 4100.

6.2.1.18 *What are the rules governing the victimisation of parents of Irish citizen children who bring claims?*

If a person making a complaint to the equality tribunal is penalised in any manner by the person against whom they made the complaint or another person because they made the complaint, this is regarded as victimisation. Victimisation also occurs if the person in good faith lawfully opposed any act of discrimination or victimisation or gave evidence in any proceedings under the Act.

Victimisation is also prohibited under the *Employment Equality Act* and a person who considers that they were victimised may make a complaint to the equality tribunal in the manner described above for other types of discrimination.

6.2.2 *What types of accommodation can parents and siblings of Irish citizen children access?*

The accommodation alternatives for parents and siblings of Irish citizen children who have to find their own accommodation are:

- private rented accommodation
- local authority accommodation
- purchase

6.2.2.1 *Private rented accommodation*

Persons wishing to rent a house or apartment from a private landlord can do so directly themselves by replying to advertisements in newspapers or seek the assistance of a letting agency. Finding accommodation can be expensive and time-consuming, particularly in big cities. Prospective tenants should:

- Inspect the property before agreeing to move in and record the condition of the property and its contents in writing. Houses and apartments to let should comply with certain minimum standards.[40]

- Agree the amount of deposit and rent to be paid and the time of payment. A receipt should be obtained for all money paid to the landlord. The deposit should be returned to the tenant when s/he leaves the accommodation. However, the landlord may retain some or all of the deposit if: the tenant gives insufficient notice, damages the property or leaves without paying bills or rent.

- Find out whether the rent covers such items as electricity, gas and bin charges (where relevant).

- Agree on who is responsible for any repairs that need to be carried out in the future.

Tenants should be aware of their rights and duties as a tenant. The most important of these are:

- The landlord must provide a rent book. The rent book should contain the name and address of the landlord, amount of deposit paid, the amount of rent and the time and method of payment. All rent payments should be entered in the rent book. The rent book should also include the terms of the tenancy.

- The landlord is not permitted (except in cases of emergency) to enter the accommodation without making an appointment with the tenant.

- The landlord must give a minimum of four weeks notice in writing if they require the tenant to leave the accommodation. This is referred to as a 'notice to quit'. If the tenant does not leave by the end of the four-week period, the landlord can go to court to apply for an eviction order.

- The tenant must also provide notice to the landlord if they decide to move out.

6.2.2.2 Local authority (council or corporation) Housing

Local authority housing is available, generally for persons who do not have sufficient resources to provide their own accommodation. Practice with regard to eligibility for local authority housing varies. Priority is usually given to low-income families with children and to older persons. However, there is usually a long waiting list of people for local authority housing.

Persons who are interested in being considered for local authority housing should:

- Contact their nearest local authority (see Appendix E for a full list of local authorities in Ireland), and obtain a copy of the authority's scheme of letting priorities. This sets out the rules for the allocation of accommodation including such matters as how applicants are prioritised and what type of accommodation may be provided to different categories of applicants.

- If the person is still interested in local authority accommodation, they should complete the application form, which is provided by the local authority.

- There is no requirement to live in the area for a certain time in order to qualify for local authority housing. It is possible to apply to more than one local authority, but not all local authorities accept applications from outside their area.

- Non-nationals who wish to apply for local authority accommodation may be required to provide evidence that they intend, and are entitled, to live in Ireland permanently. The practice varies with regard to this requirement and persons should contact their local authority.

- When the application has been received, an official from the local authority or health board will usually visit the applicant. (However, practice varies between local authorities and they may visit the applicant only when suitable accommodation is available.)

- As most local authorities have insufficient accommodation to meet the demand, they will put the applicant's name on a list. Some local authorities have a 'points system' to assist them in determining the greatest need for accommodation among applicants. An applicant will be awarded points for issues such as overcrowding.

6.2.2.2.1 Offer of accommodation:

If the person is offered a house or flat by the local authority and decides to take it, they must sign a tenancy agreement.

- The tenancy agreement is legal document and both the tenant and the local authority must adhere to the terms of the agreement.

- In the case of a married couple or partners, the tenancy is usually in joint names.

- The amount of rent to be paid per week is based on the income of the household.

- It is important to ensure that rent is paid up to date as the tenant may be issued with a notice to quit if arrears of rent have built up.

- Tenants can apply to transfer to another area.

6.2.2.3 Purchase

There are no restrictions on non-nationals buying private residential property in Ireland.[a] However, there are requirements under the Land Acts and additional documents may be required. There are some restrictions with regard to farmland.[b]

However, persons should be aware that house purchase can be a lengthy and costly process, therefore, for some, renting a property may be a better option. It is important to note that a person's Certificate of Registration will not be extended simply because the person has bought property in Ireland, or is in the process of purchasing property.

Persons interested in buying a private house or apartment may find a suitable property through an auctioneer/estate agent or through advertisements in local and national newspapers.

- Persons who cannot afford to buy a property from their own resources need to get a mortgage from a building society or bank.

- Houses/apartments should be viewed and in the case of a second-hand house or apartment, a survey should be carried out to ensure that it is structurally sound.

- If the person is satisfied that they have found a property they wish to buy, they should make an offer, if the property is for sale by private treaty. If the property is for sale by auction, they must attend the auction and the highest bidder purchases the property.

- Generally, estate agents do not charge a fee to purchasers of property.

- The purchase of property can be complicated, and prospective buyers should always engage a solicitor to act for them.

6.2.2.4 What laws govern discrimination in the provision of accommodation?

The *Equal Status Act*, 2000, prohibits discrimination on the grounds of gender, marital status, family status, sexual orientation, religious belief, age, disability, "race" and membership of the Traveller Community in the provision of goods and

---

a The *Aliens Act*, 1935 states that "Real and personal property of every description in Saorstat Eireann or subject to the law of Saorstat Eireann may be taken, acquired, held and disposed of by an alien in like manner and to the like extend as such property may be taken, acquired, held or disposed of by a citizen of Saorstat Eireann".

b These restrictions apply to non-EU nationals wishing to buy land over five acres in size. They should contact the Department of Agriculture, Food and Rural Development, Agriculture House, Kildare Street, Dublin 2, telephone (01) 607 2000, Lo-call 1890 200 510.

services, the disposal of property and access to education. Discrimination on the nine grounds listed in the Act is prohibited in both the public and private sectors. The process for referring complaints is similar to that under the *Employment Equality Act*, 1998. Further information is available from the equality tribunal.[41]

6.2.3 What medical services are parents and siblings of Irish citizen children entitled to?

Parents and siblings of Irish citizen children legally resident in Ireland have two options with regard to medical care:

- public health care

- private health care

6.2.3.1 Public health care

The public health care system, including primary and hospital services, can be accessed by any person resident in Ireland including those who are the parents and siblings of Irish citizen children. This system can be accessed for a nominal charge, or free of charge for medical card holders.

6.2.3.1.1 What services can be accessed for a nominal charge?

A range of services are available including:

- General Practitioner (GP) services (family doctor) with a charge of between €30 and €50 per consultation

- in-patient hospital treatment in a public ward subject to a daily charge of €40[a]

- all other out-patient services including consultants

- visits to hospital Accident and Emergency Departments subject to a charge of €40 (persons who are referred by their GP will not be charged)

- maternity and infant care

Generally, to get free medical care in Ireland a person needs a medical card.

6.2.3.1.2 Who is entitled to a medical card?

Entitlement to a medical card in Ireland is based on a person's residence and means. To be fully eligible for a medical card a person must:

- be 'ordinarily resident' in Ireland; this means that they must intend to live in Ireland for at least one year and be permitted to do so

- satisfy the means test; a person will only be eligible for free medical care (Category A entitlement, that is medical card holders) if their gross income, less PRSI contributions is less than €138 and in the case of a married couple or single parent €200.[b]

---

a Up to a maximum of €400 in any twelve-month period (as of 1 January 2003).

b A married couple or a single parent must earn less than ¤200. These rates apply to persons under 66 years of age. Persons applying for the medical card are permitted to have the following amounts over the income level and still qualify for the medical card, as of 1 January 2003:
  - €25 for each child under 16 years of age
  - €26 for each child over 16 years of age with no income maintained by applicant
  - the amount by which the rent or mortgage paid each week exceeds €25
  - the amount by which the costs of travelling to and from work each week exceeds €22
  - weekly expenditure on medicines

6.2.3.1.3 *What does a medical card entitle you to?*

A medical card entitles you to the following free medical services:

- General Practitioner (GP) services (but you must register with a GP (see Section 6.2.3.1.4))

- prescribed medicines

- in-patient hospital treatment in a public ward

- out-patient hospital treatment

- dental, ophthalmic and aural services

- community care services

6.2.3.1.4 *Registering with a General Practitioner (GP)*

Persons who qualify for the medical card must register with a General Practitioner (family doctor). Not all GPs accept medical card patients, so the medical card holder should obtain a list of doctors in their area who accept medical card patients:

- They can obtain this list from the local health board offices and health centre together with a registration form, which the doctor will be required to sign.

- General practitioners are only permitted to accept a certain number of medical card patients. Therefore, they will sometimes refuse to accept any further patients.

- If a person is unable to find a doctor who will accept them as a patient under the medical card scheme, one will be assigned to them by the health board office or health centre.

6.2.3.1.5 *Applying for a medical card*

Persons who wish to apply for a medical card should submit a completed application form, together with evidence that they are 'ordinarily resident' in Ireland and that they satisfy the means test, to their local health board offices or health centre.

6.2.3.2 *Private health care*

Persons can also take out private health insurance.[a] This insurance covers private care in public or private hospitals. There are two private health insurers in Ireland, VHI and BUPA.[42] Medical insurance will not cover pre-existing medical conditions and the cover may not, in any event, take effect for an initial period.

6.2.4 *What social welfare entitlements do parents and siblings of Irish citizen children have?*

Irish social welfare legislation does not distinguish between nationals and non-nationals. Essentially, any person from outside the State who complies with the relevant laws covering entry, living and working here is entitled to seek social welfare payments in compliance with the normal conditions. For further information, contact the Information Service of the Department of Social and Family Affairs on (01) 704 3000.

---

a Persons who wish to avail of private health care and who have not taken out private health insurance will be required to pay for hospital treatment.

6.2.5 What education are parents and siblings of Irish citizen children entitled to?

6.2.5.1 Parents of Irish citizen children

Non-EEA parents of Irish citizen children who have been granted leave to remain have limited education entitlements.

Non-EEA parents of Irish citizen children, who have been granted leave to remain, are not entitled to third-level education on the same basis as an EU national. They are unable to obtain a local authority/VEC grant, and may also be charged the international economic fee rate. Third-level fees vary between educational institutions.

Conditions of entry into third-level institutions vary between educational institutions. For example, proficiency in English may be required, together with specific qualifications.

Non-National parents of Irish citizens may attend part-time courses, some of which require a fee. However, basic education (literacy) is free of charge from the Adult Literacy Service.

Persons granted leave to remain in the State are also entitled to enrol in FÁS courses[a] and the Vocational Training Opportunities Scheme (VTOS) in the VEC.

6.2.5.2 Siblings of Irish citizen children

All children and young people under the age of 18 in Ireland have the same rights irrespective of the child's or parent's/parents' or legal caregivers' race, colour, sex, language, religion, political or other opinion, national, ethnic or social origin, property, disability, birth or other status.[43] Children of non-EEA nationals can therefore access services on the same basis as an Irish child. However, after they reach the age of eighteen, siblings lose these rights unless they have secured their own right of residence. Children of non-EEA nationals are registered on their parent's/parents' or legal caregivers' Certificate of Registration until the age of 16. However, children's birth certificates are usually required for identification and other purposes. Thereafter, they must register themselves, in their own name, with the registration officer in the area where reside. The local registration officer is a member of the Gardaí. Applicants should inquire at their local Garda station for the location of the registration officer for the area in which they reside. In Dublin, this is the Garda National Immigration Bureau.

All children and young people in Ireland must engage in full-time education until they are 16 years old. At first and second level, there are two main education sectors: primary school (first level), and post-primary and vocational training (second level).

Schools are managed by the State (Comprehensive, Vocational Education Committees [VECs]) and religious bodies (Catholic, Protestant, Muslim, Jewish) and governed by their own ethos/philosophy. Lists of schools are available from the Department of Education and Science.[44]

---

a FÁS is the Irish Training and Employment Authority. Interested persons should contact their local FÁS office or the FÁS website *http://www.fas.ie/*

Children with language needs are generally placed in classes with other children/young people of a similar age. Government support is provided to allow schools to offer limited language support programmes for bilingual and multilingual children.

To apply to a school or education centre parents or legal caregivers should follow the process below:

- The parents/legal caregivers contact the local school/education centre of choice by writing or telephoning the school principal or manager to arrange a meeting.

- At the first meeting, the parents/legal caregivers are provided with the formal school/education centre policy which outlines the ethos, selection criteria and other matters.

- The parents/legal caregivers are required to provide the school/education centre with basic information on the student.

- An informal education and linguistic assessment of the student may take place but there is no State interpretation facility for this process. Schools/education centres cannot refuse access to a student on the basis of their level of English.

- If there are no places, or if the school/education centre is unsuitable for the student, the school/education centre recommends another school/education centre in the locality.

- If the student is offered a place in a school, the parents/legal caregivers should obtain a letter of acceptance from the school/education centre.

6.2.6 What family reunification rights do parents and siblings of Irish citizen children have?

There are no statutory provisions for family reunification of an Irish citizen child with family members who are outside the State. However, as a result of the *Fajujonu* judgement, applications for family reunification of parents and minor siblings of Irish children are usually granted.

- In the case of a parent of an Irish citizen, they should apply to the nearest Irish Embassy or Consulate for a D-reside visa (if there is no Irish Embassy or Consulate in the country the person currently resides in, the application can be made to the Visa Office of the Department of Foreign Affairs in Dublin).

- The application for a D-reside family reunification visa should contain all relevant documentation including evidence that the person is the parent of the Irish citizen child.

- In the case of a sibling of an Irish citizen child who is under eighteen years of age, the application must be signed by either of their parents. The application must be lodged in the same way as that of an adult visa applicant, that is at the nearest Irish Embassy or Consulate or, if there is not an Irish Embassy or Consulate in the country the person currently resides in, the application can be made to the Visa Office of the Department of Foreign Affairs in Dublin.

- The application for a D-reside family reunification visa for a minor must contain evidence that the child is related to the Irish citizen child through the same parent or parents. In the case of a child whose second parent does not reside in Ireland, the second parent has to consent to the child being brought to Ireland to be cared for by the parent resident here.

Once a family member who is over 16 years of age has arrived in Ireland, they should apply in writing to the Immigration Section of the Department of Justice, Equality & Law Reform for a residence permit, on foot of which, the Garda National Immigration Bureau, or local registration officer, will issue a Certificate of Registration.

6.2.7 How can parents and siblings of Irish citizen children acquire Irish citizenship?

Parents and siblings of Irish citizen children can become Irish citizens in three ways:

- naturalisation
- post-nuptial citizenship
- by descent

The *Irish Nationality and Citizenship Acts* 1956, 1986, 1994 and 2001 set out the criteria under which Irish citizenship is granted.

6.2.7.1 Acquiring citizenship by naturalisation

A person wishing to apply for a certificate of naturalisation must fulfil certain conditions including having legally resided in Ireland for five years out of the previous nine-year period. The Minister for Justice, Equality & Law Reform may grant an application for a certificate of naturalisation at their discretion if they are satisfied that the applicant:

- is of full age
- is of good character
- has had a period of one year's continuous residence in Ireland immediately prior to their application, and in the eight years immediately preceding that period has had a total residence of four years in Ireland
- intends in good faith to continue to reside in Ireland after naturalisation
- has made a declaration of fidelity to the nation and loyalty to the State, either before a District Court Justice or in such other manner permitted by the Minister

The Minister for Justice, Equality & Law Reform may waive these conditions in certain circumstances specified in the Acts. The number of circumstances in which the Minister may waive the conditions, has been reduced by the 2001, Act.[a]

6.2.7.2 Acquiring post-nuptial citizenship

A non-national who married an Irish national on or before 29 November 2002, and has been in a subsisting marriage with that person for a minimum of three years, may become an Irish citizen by making a post-nuptial declaration of citizenship. However, this is not possible if the Irish spouse has acquired

---

a *Irish Nationality and Citizenship Act* 1956, Section 16 (as amended by *Irish Nationality and Citizenship Act*, 1986, Section 5). Since the coming into force of the 2001 Act, this no longer applies to persons married to a naturalised Irish citizen or persons married to a person who is an Irish citizen otherwise than by naturalisation.

citizenship by naturalisation, post-nuptial declaration, or was granted citizenship as a token of honour. Any such declarations will have to be made before 30 November 2005.

In the case of spouses of Irish nationals who got married on or after 30 November, 2002, the Minister may at his 'absolute discretion' grant an application for a certificate of naturalisation to the spouse of an Irish citizen if the applicant:

- is of full age
- is of good character
- is married to an Irish citizen for at least three years
- is in a subsisting marriage, recognised as being in accordance with Irish legislation
- is living together with the Irish citizen as husband and wife (the applicant must submit an affidavit to that effect to the Minister)
- has lived in Ireland for at least one year continuously prior to the application
- has been resident in Ireland for at least two years of the four years immediately preceding that period
- intends in good faith to continue to reside in Ireland after naturalisation
- has made a declaration of 'fidelity to the nation and loyalty to the State' in whatever manner may be prescribed [45]

The Minister for Justice, Equality & Law Reform may waive certain of the above conditions if satisfied that the applicant would suffer serious consequences in respect of his or her bodily integrity or liberty if not granted Irish citizenship. [46]

6.2.7.3 Acquiring citizenship by descent

Persons whose father or mother was an Irish Citizen at the time of their birth are automatically Irish citizens. However, if a person is born outside Ireland, and the parent through whom they are claiming citizenship was also born outside Ireland, they will not be entitled to citizenship except in certain limited circumstances. [47] Persons whose grandparents were Irish citizens can become Irish citizens by registering in the Foreign Births Register in the Department of Foreign Affairs or, if residing outside Ireland, at the nearest Irish Embassy or Consulate.

6.2.7.4 Acquiring permission to remain without condition as to time

Persons who have been legally resident in Ireland for ten years and who have not applied for naturalisation may obtain a residence stamp giving them 'permission to remain without condition as to time'. [48]

6.2.8 What do parents and siblings of Irish citizen children need to open a bank account?

Banks require new customers to produce the following documents when opening a bank account:

- photo identification (a passport satisfies this requirement)
- proof of address in Ireland, for example a utility bill (electricity, gas or other utility) or lease agreement

- although not officially documented as a requirement, banks often request applicants to provide a personal introduction from an existing customer

6.2.9 Can parents and siblings of Irish citizen children vote in elections?

Non-national residents in Ireland over 18 years of age may vote in some elections:

Citizens of...	Permitted to vote at...
The UK	Dáil, European and local elections
EU states apart from the UK	European and local elections
Non-EU states	Local elections only

Those permitted to vote must have their name included in the Electoral Register if they want to vote. Application forms are available in post offices, libraries and council and corporation cffices.

Endnotes

1   *Irish Times* 9 January 2002.

2   Department of Justice, Equality & Law Reform, *Immigration Division Applications for Residency Based on Parentage of an Irish-born Child* 19 February 2003.

3   *Immigration Act* 1999 as amended, Section 3 (6)(c).

4   *L. & O. v. The Minister for Justice, Equality & Law Reform* [2002] IESC 109/02 & 108/02, 23 January 2003, Keane CJ, p.18.

5   *Ibid* p. 1.

6   *Ibid* p. 61.

7   *Ibid* pp. 61-62.

8   *Ibid* p. 6.

9   The Department of Enterprise, Trade & Employment have produced a *Guide to Labour Law* which may be downloaded from their website http://www.entemp.ie/. The Department also provide an information service, the Employment Rights Information Unit, which is contactable at Room G05, Davitt House, 65a Adelaide Road, Dublin 2, telephone (01) 631 3131, Lo-call 1890 201 615, or e-mail *erinfo@entemp.ie* All employees are entitled to join a trade union and they are often a useful source of information on employee rights.

10 Department of Social, Community and Family Affairs, Gandon House, Amiens Street, Dublin 1, telephone (01) 874 8444, website http://www.welfare.ie/. The Department's leaflet SW100 *Personal Public Service Number* provides additional information on obtaining a PPS.

11 Further information may be obtained on Revenue Publication RES 2 *Coming to Live in Ireland* http://www.revenue.ie/

12 *Terms of Employment (Information) Act* 1994.

13 *National Minimum Wages Act* 2000.

14 This is provided for in the *National Minimum Wages Act* 2000, Section 15(1):
"Subject to subsection (2) and Sections 16, 17 and 18, a person who:

(a) enters employment for the first time after attaining the age of 18 years or

(b) having entered into employment before attaining the age of 18 years, continues in employment on attaining that age

shall be remunerated by his or her employer in respect of his or her working hours in any pay reference period at an hourly rate of pay that on average is not less than:

(i) in the case of an employee commencing employment for the first time after attaining the age of 18 years:

(I) in his or her first year after commenced employment, 80% and

(II) in his or her second year after having commenced employment, 90%

(ii) in the case if an employee having entered into employment before attaining the age of 18 years and continuing in employment on attaining that age

    (I) in his or her first year after having attained the age of 18 years, 80%

    (II) in his or her second year after having attained that age, 90%

of the national minimum hourly rate of pay, notwithstanding that the employee, if he or she has changed his or her employer during the relevant period, may have been remunerated at a higher rate by the previous employer."

15 *Payment of Wages Act* 1991

16 *Organisation of Working Time Act* 1997, Section 19.

17 *Ibid,* Section 14(1).

18 *Ibid,* Section 8.

19 *Ibid,* Section 9(1)(a) and (b.

20 *Ibid,* Section 10.

21 *Ibid,* Section 26.

22 *Parental Leave Act* 1998 Section 7 (1).

23 *Ibid,* Section 19 (3)(c).

24 *Ibid,* Section 13 (1).

25 *Ibid,* Section 13 (2).

26 *Ibid,* Section 13 (4).

27 *Ibid,* Section 13 (1).

28 This form may be downloaded from the Labour Relations Commission website *www.lrc.ie/lrc_services/rights_commissioner.htm* or can be obtained from the Secretariat, Rights Commissioner Service, Labour Relations Commission, Tom Johnson House, Haddington Road, Dublin 4, telephone: (01) 613 6700.

29 Minimum notice is provided for in the *Minimum Notice and Terms of Employment Act* 1973, as amended by the *Work Protection (Regular Part-Time Employees) Act* 1991.

30 According to the *Employment Equality Act* 1998,Section 2(1), (dealing with interpretation), 'marital status' means "single, married, separated, divorced and widowed".

31 'Family status' is described in Section 2(1) of the Act as "responsibility

(a) as a parent or as a person in loco parentis in relation to a person who has not attained the age of 18 years, or

(b) as a parent or the resident primary carer in relation to a person of or over that age with a disability which is of such a nature as to give rise to the need for care or support on a continuing, regular or frequent basis".

32 Discrimination on the basis of 'race' is described in the *Employment Equality Act* 1998, Section 6 (2)(h) as "between any two persons that are of a different 'race', 'colour', nationality or ethnic or national origins".

33 'Religious belief' as defined in the *Employment Equality Act* 1998, includes religious background or outlook.

34 The *Employment Equality Act* 1998, Section 2(1) defines 'sexual orientation' as meaning "heterosexual, homosexual or bisexual orientation".

35 'Disability' is defined in the *Employment Equality Act* 1998, Section 2(1) as:

"(a) the total or partial absence of a person's bodily or mental functions, including the absence of a part of the person's body,

(b) the presence in the body of organisms causing, or likely to cause, chronic disease or illness,

(c) the malfunction, malformation or disfigurement of a part of a person's body,

(d) a condition or malfunction which results in a person learning differently from a person without the condition or malfunction, or

(e) a condition, illness or disease which affects a person's thought processes, perception of reality, emotions or judgement which results in disturbed behaviour,

and shall be taken to include a disability which exists at present, or which previously existed but no longer exists, or which may exist in the future or which is imputed to a person".

36 *Employment Equality Act* 1998,Section 8(1).

37 The Equality Authority may be contacted at 2, Clonmel Street, Dublin 2, telephone (01) 417 3333, fax (01) 417 3366, email info@equality.ie.

38 The respondent must also use the form provided by the ODEI - the equality tribunal to reply (Form ODEI 4). If the correct forms are not used, the provisions in the *Employment Equality Act* 1998, permitting the director to draw inferences from failure to supply information, do not apply.

39 *http://www.labourcourt.ie/labour/labour.nsf/LookupPageLink/formsDownload*

40 Details of these can be obtained from Threshold, 21 Stoneybatter, Dublin 7, email advice@threshold.ie.

41 Further information is available from the ODEI - the equality tribunal, 3 Clonmel Street, Dublin 2,
    telephone (01) 477 4100, website *http://www.odei.ie/*

42 Voluntary Health Insurance (VHI), VHI House, Lower Abbey Street, Dublin 1, telephone (01) 874 4499,
    Lo-call 1850 444 444.

    BUPA Ireland, Mill Island, Fermoy, Co. Cork, telephone (021) 42121, or 12 Fitzwilliam Square, Dublin 2,
    telephone (01) 6627 662, Lo-call 1890 700 890.

43 Refer to the *International Convention on the Rights of the Child* 1989, Article 2(1), signed by Ireland,
    30 September 1990 and ratified 28 September 1992.

44 Department of Education and Science, Marlborough Street, Dublin 1, telephone (01) 873 4700,
    website *http://www.education.ie/*

45 *Irish Nationality and Citizenship Act* 1956, Section 15A (1), as amended by the *Irish Nationality and Citizenship Act*
    2001, Section 5.

46 *Irish Nationality and Citizenship Act* 1956, Section 15A (2), as amended by the *Irish Nationality and Citizenship Act*
    2001, Section 5.

47 *Irish Nationality and Citizenship Act* 1956, Section 7 (3), as amended by the *Irish Nationality and Citizenship Act*
    2001, Section 5.

48 Further information available on the Department of Justice, Equality & Law Reform
    website *http://www.justice.ie/*

Persons Granted Leave to Remain

PERSONS GRANTED LEAVE TO REMAIN

While no formal system of subsidiary or complementary protection currently exists in Ireland, under the provisions of the *Immigration Act,* 1999, persons who fear being returned to a country where they may suffer torture or other ill-treatment, and in respect of whom the Minister is considering making a deportation order, may make representations to the Minister setting out reasons why they should be permitted to remain in Ireland. The Minister may, at his/her discretion, grant such persons leave to remain.

Although a substantial number of representations to the Minister are made by persons who have applied for refugee status and have been refused, but still fear to return to their country, leave to remain may be granted for other reasons. Therefore, this avenue is also open to other persons in respect of whom the Minister is considering making a deportation order, after they have unsuccessfully applied for permission to remain in the State outside the refugee protection system.

There is no separate application procedure for persons who wish to remain in Ireland on any of the grounds outlined above without previously applying for either refugee status or a residence permit on the basis of various grounds, such as being married to an Irish or EEA or Swiss national.

The rights and entitlements afforded to persons granted leave to remain are not defined in law. However, persons granted leave to remain may generally be afforded many of the same rights as Irish nationals, while remaining in Ireland.

7.1 Applying for Leave to Remain

There is no separate application procedure for leave to remain. Instead, any person who has received a notification under the provisions of the *Immigration Act,* 1999 that the Minister intends to make a deportation order, may make representations setting out the reasons why they should be allowed to remain in the State[1] and the Minister will consider these representations.[2] The Act, sets out the issues to be considered by the Minister before s/he makes a deportation order.[a]

If the Minister, after considering the matters raised, decides that the person should not be deported s/he will grant the person leave to remain in Ireland. Should the Minister decide to issue a deportation order in respect of the person, they will be notified in writing of the decision to make a deportation order[b] and of the reasons for the decision. They will also receive a copy of the deportation order.

7.1.1 On what grounds may the Minister propose to make a deportation order?

Section 3 of the *Immigration Act,* 1999, permits the Minister for Justice, Equality and Law Reform to order certain non-nationals to leave the State. The Minister may make a deportation order in respect of the following:

- a person who has served or is serving a term of imprisonment imposed by a court of the State

---

a For details see Section 7.1.2.1 page 150.

b According to Section 3 (3)(b)(ii) and (9) (a)(iii), this should be done in a language that the person understands, where necessary and possible.

- a person whose deportation was recommended by a court in the State before which a person was indicted for or charged with any crime or offence

- a person who has been required to leave the State under Regulation 14 of the *European Communities (Aliens) Regulations, 1977*

- a person to whom Regulation 19 of the *European Communities (Right of Residence for Non-Economically Active Persons) Regulations 1997* applies

- a person whose application for refugee status has been transferred to another country under the Dublin Convention

- a person whose application for asylum has been refused by the Minister

- a person to whom leave to land in the State has been refused

- a person who has contravened a restriction imposed on him/her in respect of landing in or entering into or leave to stay in the State

- a person whose deportation would be conducive to the common good in the opinion of the Minister

7.1.2 Responding to notification that the Minister proposes to make a deportation order

Persons who are notified in writing that the Minister proposes to make a deportation order may:

- make representations in writing to the Minister within 15 working days (from the date of the letter) setting out the reasons why they should be allowed to remain in the State

- leave Ireland voluntarily (if the person agrees to leave voluntarily, they must inform the Minister of their travel arrangements)

- consent to the making of a deportation order

7.1.2.1 Making representations to the Minister

Before deciding the matter, the Minister will take into consideration any representations duly made to him/her under Section 3 (6) of the *Immigration Act, 1999* as amended in relation to the proposal to make a deportation order.[3]

- Persons should make representations in writing to the Minister.

- It is advisable to avail of legal advice and representation, particularly in cases where the person may fear torture, inhuman or degrading treatment if returned to his/her country of origin. In such cases, Ireland's commitments under international law, in particular the European Convention on Human Rights and the International Covenant on Civil and Political Rights may be relevant.

- The person's reasons for wishing to remain in the State should be set out fully and any supporting evidence should be included.

- Representations on behalf of the person may be made by others who wish to support the person's application for permission to remain.

Section 3 (6)(a) of the *Immigration Act, 1999* lists certain matters to which the Minister for Justice, Equality & Law Reform shall have regard in determining whether to make a deportation order. These are as follows:

- the age of the person
- the duration of residence in the State of the person
- the family and domestic circumstances of the person
- the nature of the person's connection with the State, if any
- the employment (including self-employment) record of the person
- the employment (including self-employment) prospects of the person
- the character and conduct of the person both within and (where relevant and ascertainable) outside the State (including any criminal convictions)
- humanitarian considerations
- any representations made by or on behalf of the person
- the common good
- considerations of national security and public policy

If the Minister considers that the person should not be deported, the person will be granted leave to remain in Ireland usually for a period of one year, which may be renewed.

Persons who have been granted leave to remain in Ireland must obtain a Certificate of Registration from their local Garda registration officer. The local registration officer is a member of the Gardaí. Applicants should inquire at their local Garda station for the location of the registration officer for the area in which they reside. In Dublin, this is the Garda National Immigration Bureau. They must bring with them the letter informing them that they have been granted leave to remain. In addition, they should also bring a passport or other identity document.

Persons granted leave to remain will have to apply for the renewal of their Certificate of Registration thirty days in advance of the expiry date of their current one. They should report to their local Garda registration officer to apply for the renewal. The local registration officer is a member of the Gardaí. Applicants should inquire at their local Garda station for the location of the registration officer for the area in which they reside. In Dublin, this is the Garda National Immigration Bureau. They may be required to make representations to the Minister for Justice, Equality & Law Reform providing details of their current situation in the State. Documentation that is normally required is evidence of employment/college attendance and evidence of financial circumstances. It is also recommended that information regarding the reasons for the person's unwillingness to return to their country of origin be updated at this point.

7.1.2.2 Leaving Ireland voluntarily

A person who decides to return to their country of origin or former habitual residence should inform the Repatriation Unit of the Immigration Division of the Department of Justice, Equality & Law Reform[a] of their intention. The Department will then seek to facilitate the person's departure from the State and make a record of their departure. Doing this ensures that if the person makes an

a The phone number for the Repatriation Unit of the Immigration Division of the Department of Justice, Equality & Law Reform is (01) 616 7700#5#1.

application to come to Ireland at any time in the future, their prior presence in the State will not negatively affect the assessment of their visa application and/or application for leave to enter the State.

Generally, an appointment with a Department official will be made for the necessary arrangements to be put in place. The Department of Justice, Equality & Law Reform requires persons arranging their own voluntary departure to:

- withdraw any pending applications for residency before beginning the voluntary procedure
- journey by air
- buy a one-way ticket to their country of return (should a return ticket be bought, the Department of Justice, Equality & Law Reform will retain the return stubs)
- avoid transiting via the UK or any other country for which they do not have transit permission; they must verify that any State through which they intend to transit will allow them to embark for their connecting flight (this can be verified by enquiring at the relevant Embassy in Dublin/London); the obligation is on the returnee to confirm and conform with such requirements
- give the Department of Justice, Equality & Law Reform at least five days notice of their flight
- show their tickets, or travel agent's receipt of payment with the flight details to the Department of Justice, Equality & Law Reform
- allow their passport to be retained by the Department of Justice, Equality & Law Reform until the day of their flight; the passport will be transmitted to the airport before the flight
- arrive at the airport at least two hours before check-in time and go to the information desk on the ground floor and ask for an information officer; this officer will return their passport before they board the flight and will supervise their departure
- ensure the journey is finalised within a 24-hour period

The International Organisation for Migration (IOM) is an inter-governmental, yet independent organisation, with offices in over 120 countries worldwide. IOM works with governments and project partners to uphold the rights of migrants. The IOM Dublin office currently provides Voluntary Assisted Return Programmes, which aim to assist asylum seekers and irregular migrants who wish to return home but may not have the means or the necessary documentation to do so. IOM has, to date, assisted people to return to almost thirty countries of origin. For nationals of the CIS countries (these include all the former Soviet States, with the exception of the Baltic States), IOM's Voluntary Assisted Return and Reintegration Programme can additionally provide reintegration assistance for returnees in their home country, facilitating sustainable return.[4]

7.1.2.3 Consenting to deportation

A person who consents to the making of a deportation order must to do so in writing by signing a consent form. If the Minister for Justice, Equality & Law Reform is satisfied that the person understands the consequences of their consent, s/he will issue a deportation order in respect of the person without further notice being required.[5] The Minister for Justice, Equality & Law Reform in co-operation with the person and the Garda National Immigration Bureau will then proceed to arrange for the removal of the person as soon as practicable.

A person in respect of whom a deportation order has been issued, will generally not be permitted to return to Ireland once they have been deported unless the deportation order is revoked prior to the person's application for permission to return (visa application/application for leave to enter the State).[a]

Where a person who has consented in writing to the making of a deportation order is not deported within three months from the making of the order, the order shall cease to have effect.

Persons in respect of whom a deportation order has been made, by the Minister, may be detained in order to ensure their deportation.[6]

Persons who are the subject of a deportation order may be required to comply with the following in order to ensure their deportation:[7]

- present themselves to a Garda, or Immigration Officer, at a date, time and place specified in the notice informing the person of the decision to issue a deportation order

- produce any travel document, passport, travel ticket or other document which may be required for the purpose of his/her deportation

- co-operate with Gardaí, or Immigration Officers, in order to obtain a travel document, passport, travel ticket or other document required for the purpose of the deportation

- reside, or remain, in a particular district or place in the State pending removal from the State

- report to a specified Garda Station, or Immigration Officer, at specified intervals pending deportation

- notify the Gardaí, or Immigration Officers, of any change of address

If a Garda, or Immigration Officer, 'with reasonable cause suspects' that a person who is the subject of a deportation order:

- has failed to comply with any provisions of the deportation order, or with a requirement in a notice informing the person of the decision to issue a deportation order;

- intends to leave the State and enter another State without permission;

- has destroyed their identity documents;

- is in possession of forged identity documents; or

- intends to avoid removal from the State;[8]

---

a *The Immigration Act,* 1999 (as amended), Section 3 (1) provides that "the Minister may by order require any non-national specified in the order to leave the State within such period as may be specified in the order and to remain thereafter out of the State".

they may arrest the person without warrant and detain them in a prescribed place.[a]

If the Minister decides not to make a deportation order, the person will be granted leave to remain usually for a period of one year initially.

7.2 What Rights and Entitlements Do Persons Granted Leave to Remain Have?

Generally, persons are granted leave to remain in the State for a set period of time (usually one year) after which persons apply for a renewal of the permission to remain. The rights and entitlements afforded to persons granted leave to remain are not defined in law. However, persons granted leave to remain may generally be afforded many of the same rights as Irish nationals, while remaining in Ireland.

7.2.1 What rights in the work place do persons granted leave to remain have?

Persons who have been granted leave to remain are entitled to enter employment in Ireland without a employment permit. They have the same rights and entitlements with regard to employment as Irish nationals.

7.2.1.1 What taxes and social contributions do persons granted leave to remain pay?

All employees must pay tax on their earnings, known as 'pay as you earn' or PAYE and PRSI 'pay-related social insurance'.[b] These are deducted from employees' salaries each week or month. All employees are required to have a Personal Public Service Number (PPS No.), and persons who do not have a PPS No.[c] should contact the Department of Social and Family Affairs.[9] This number should be quoted in all contact with the Tax Office and the Department.

In addition, persons who are commencing their first employment in Ireland should complete a Certificate of Tax Credits and Standard Rate Cut-Off Point (Form 12A).[10] The Revenue Commissioners usually grant married tax credits even if the worker's spouse is not resident in the State.

7.2.1.2 What details of employment are persons granted leave to remain entitled to receive?

Within two months of starting employment, the employer is required to provide the employee[d] with a written statement of certain details of the terms of employment.[11]

---

a The 'prescribed places' for the detention of persons awaiting deportation are as follows: Castlerea Prison; Central Mental Hospital; Cloverhill Prison; Cork Prison; Limerick Prison; Midland Prison; Mountjoy Prison; St Patrick's Institution; The Training Unit, Glengarriff Parade; and Wheatfield Prison. *Immigration Act 1999 (Deportation) Regulations*, 2000 SI No. 103 of 2002.

b There are some exceptions to this, for example, low-paid workers.

c This replaces the old RSI Number.

d The term 'employee' covers those working under contract of employment or apprenticeship; those employed through an employment agency and those employed in the service of the State.

These include:

- name and address of employer
- place of work
- job title and nature of work
- date of commencement of employment
- nature of contract (temporary or fixed term)
- rate of pay
- pay intervals
- hours of work (including overtime)
- paid leave
- arrangements for when the employee is unable to work due to sickness or injury
- pensions and pension schemes
- notice entitlements
- collective agreement/s, and the parties to the agreement/s

If the particulars contained in the statement change, the employer must notify the employee within one week.

If an employer has either failed to provide a written statement, or failed to notify the employee of changes that have taken place regarding the particulars contained in the statement, the employee may complain to a Rights Commissioner. If either party is dissatisfied with the recommendation of the Rights Commissioner, they may appeal to the Employment Appeals Tribunal.[a]

7.2.1.3 What is the minimum rate of pay for persons granted leave to remain?

- All employees over the age of 18 who have worked for at least two years since turning 18 are entitled to a minimum rate of pay. This is currently €6.35 per hour since 1 October 2002.[12] Persons who have not worked for two years must generally be paid 80 per cent of the minimum wage in the first year, and 90 per cent in the second year.[13]

- With their wages, employees must receive a written statement of the gross pay and deductions made.[14]

- Employees have the right to a readily negotiable mode of wage payment such as by cheque, credit transfer, cash, postal order or bank draft.

- Employers may only make deductions in certain circumstances[b] that are agreed with the employee.[c]

---

a See Section 7.2.1.12 page 146for details of the procedure for referring a complaint to the Rights Commissioner. In addition, the Rights Commissioner can investigate grievances or claims under most of the legislation dealing with rights in the workplace including: Payment of Wages Act 1991; Terms of Employment Act 1994; Organisation of Working Time Act 1997; Parental Leave Act 1998 and National Minimum Wages Act, 2000.

b When the deductions are required by law; when they are provided for in the contract of employment and when they are made with the written consent of the employee.

c For example, VHI, BUPA, Union Dues, Pension Plan and so on.

7.2.1.4 What are the rules governing working hours?

- Employees must not be required to work in excess of the maximum hours permitted each week. This is an average of 48 hours per week averaged over four, six or 12 months depending on the nature of the employment.[a]

- Employees are entitled to breaks and rest time as follows:

  - 11 hours rest per 24 hour period

  - one period of 24 hours rest per week preceded by a daily rest period (11 hours)

  - 15 minutes break after working four-and-a-half hours and another break of 15 minutes after six hours, or 30 minutes after six hours if the 15 minutes break was not taken after four-and-a-half hours[b]

7.2.1.5 What holidays are persons granted leave to remain entitled to?

Full-time workers are entitled to four working weeks annual leave[15] and nine public holidays per year.[c] These are: 1 January, St Patrick's Day, Easter Monday, First Monday in May, First Monday in June, First Monday in August, Last Monday in October, Christmas Day and St Stephen's Day.

Part-time workers are entitled to annual leave consisting of eight per cent of the hours they work up to a maximum of four weeks and to public holidays if they have worked at least 40 hours in the five weeks preceding the public holiday

7.2.1.6 What compensation for Sunday work are persons granted leave to remain entitled to?

Employees are entitled to be compensated for Sunday work. This can be extra pay[d] or time off in lieu.[16] For persons working in the retail sector, there is a Code of Practice on Sunday Working in the Retail Trade.[e]

7.2.1.7 What maternity leave are persons granted leave to remain entitled to?

- A pregnant employee is entitled to maternity leave from employment for a period of at least 14 weeks.[17]

- To be entitled to maternity leave, the employee must notify her employer and produce a medical certificate confirming the pregnancy and expected week of confinement. The notice must be given at least four weeks before the commencement of maternity leave and must be in writing.[18]

---

a Four months for employees generally, six months for seasonal workers and workers who are directly involved in ensuring continuity of service or production, and twelve months for employees who have entered a collective agreement with their employer.

b The break cannot be taken at the end of the work period.

c The employer has four alternatives with regard to the public holidays. They may give the employee: the day of the holiday off with pay, a paid day off within a month, an extra day of annual leave or an extra day's pay.

d With premium payment (that is, above normal payment).

e This was drawn up by the Labour Relations Commission and is based on the entitlements set out in the *Organisation of Working Time Act, 1997*. It is available on the Department of Enterprise, Trade & Employment website *http://www.entemp.ie/*

- An employee can choose the period of maternity leave. However, maternity leave must be taken at least four weeks before the end of the expected week of confinement and shall end not earlier than four weeks after the end of the expected week of confinement.[19]

- The employee has the right to return to work when the period of maternity leave has expired. Employees who have taken maternity leave are entitled to return to the:

  - same employer

  - job the employee held immediately before commencement of leave

  - same contract and conditions of employment[20]

7.2.1.8 *What parental leave are persons granted leave to remain entitled to?*

- Persons who have at least one year's continuous employment and are the parents of children (natural or adopted) may take up to a total of 14 weeks unpaid leave (for each child) to take care of their children who are no older than five years.[21]

- Employees who have taken parental leave are entitled to return to the:

  - same employer

  - job the employee held immediately before commencement of leave

  - same contract and conditions of employment[22]

7.2.1.9 *What* force majeure *leave are persons granted leave to remain entitled to?*

- Employees may also take *force majeure* leave in the case of sudden injury or illness to an immediate family member, where the dependant needs the worker to be present.[23]

- An 'immediate family member' of the employee is a child, spouse/partner, person to whom the employee is *in loco parentis*, brother, sister, parent or grandparent.[24]

- An employee may take three days in any consecutive 12 months or five days in any 36 consecutive months[25]

- *Force majeure* leave is paid leave[26]

7.2.1.10 *What laws protect persons granted leave to remain from unfair dismissal?*

Employees who have over 12 months continuous employment,[a] are protected by law from unfair dismissal. Dismissals may be regarded as unfair where they have resulted wholly or mainly from:

- the employee's trade union membership or activities

- the religious or political beliefs of the employee

- the race, skin colour or sexual orientation of the employee

a Two fixed terms of six months would qualify.

- legal proceedings against the employer if the employee is a party or a witness
- the employee's pregnancy
- the employee taking leave provided for under the *Maternity Protection Act*, 1994

A dismissal will usually be considered fair if it is based wholly or mainly on one of the following:

- the employee's capability, competence or qualifications for the job
- the employee's conduct
- the employee's redundancy
- if continuation of the employment would contravene other legal requirements

Both 'actual' unfair dismissals and 'constructive' dismissals are prohibited by legislation. Constructive dismissal can occur where the employee's conditions of employment are made so difficult that they have no alternative but to leave.

7.2.1.11 What claims for redress[a] exist for persons granted leave to remain who consider they have been unfairly dismissed?

An employee who considers that they have been unfairly dismissed (this includes 'actual' and 'constructive' dismissal) and who wishes to make a claim for redress must do so within six months.[b]

The employee must give formal notice of his/her claim in writing to a Rights Commissioner or to the Employment Appeals Tribunal. The claim is considered by the Employment Appeals Tribunal where the employee or the employer have notified a Rights Commissioner that they object to the claim being heard by a Rights Commissioner.

Persons who are employed through an employment agency must make their claim against whoever is paying their wages (this could be the actual 'employer' or the agency).

7.2.1.12 How can persons granted leave to remain take a claim to the Rights Commissioner?

Rights Commissioners are appointed by the Minister for Enterprise, Trade & Employment on the recommendation of the Labour Relations Commission. They are independent of the Minister in carrying out their functions. The procedure for persons wishing to make an appeal to the Rights Commissioner is described below:

- Persons wishing to make an appeal to a Rights Commissioner must:
  - notify their former employer that they intend to take a case to the Rights Commissioner
  - complete the standard form[27] (full details of the complaint must be given)

---

a Redress in the case of unfair dismissal can be any of the following:
- re-instatement in the employee's old job
- re-engagement in the old job or a suitable alternative
- financial compensation

b In exceptional circumstances, this can be twelve months.

- The Rights Commissioner hears the case as soon as possible. The hearing takes place in private.

- Both parties can be represented at the hearing by a lawyer or trade union representative (in the cases of the employee).

- Both parties have the opportunity to present their case.

- The Rights Commissioner makes a recommendation, which may be appealed to the Employment Appeals Tribunal (EAT).

7.2.1.13 What is the minimum notice[28]period for persons granted leave to remain?

Employees who are in continuous employment with the same employer for 13 weeks or more and who normally work at least eight hours per week are entitled to a minimum period of notice from their employer if they intend to dismiss them.

The period of notice depends on the length of service. For persons who have served from 13 weeks to two years the minimum notice period is one week.

Employees must also give notice if they intend to leave the job. If the employee is in employment for 13 weeks or over, they must give the employer at least one week's notice. If the contract of employment requires further notice to be given, they must adhere to the terms of the contract.

The Employment Appeals Tribunal considers disputes between employers and workers regarding minimum notice.

7.2.1.14 What redundancy payments[a]are persons granted leave to remain entitled to?

Employees are entitled to a lump sum redundancy payment when their employment is ended due to redundancy providing they:

- have 109 weeks continuous service

- are aged between 16 and 66

- are normally expected to work at least eight hours per week

The redundancy pay is calculated in the following manner:

- a half week's pay for each year of employment up to 41 years' service

- one week's pay for each year over 41 years' service

- one week's pay irrespective of the length of service

7.2.1.15 What rules govern discrimination in employment?

Discrimination against employees on grounds of age, gender, marital status,[29] family status,[30] race,[31] religion,[32] sexual orientation,[33] disability[34] and membership of the Travelling Community is prohibited under the *Employment Equality Act, 1998*.[b] The Act prohibits:

---

a Redundancy payments are dealt with under the *Redundancy Payments Acts* 1967 -1991. Redundancy occurs when the employee's job ceases to exist, there is insufficient work, the firm closes down or the firm re-organises.

b The *Employment Equality Authority Act* 1998 came into force 18 October 1999, and only incidents of discrimination occurring on, or after that date can be dealt with under the Act. Incidents of discrimination on grounds of sex or marital status can be investigated by the ODEI - the equality tribunal under earlier legislation.

- direct and indirect discrimination
- discrimination in access to employment, conditions of employment, promotion, training and classification of posts[35]

The Equality Authority may provide legal advice, assistance and representation to persons who consider that they have a complaint under the legislation.[36]

A person who considers that they have been discriminated against on any of the nine grounds listed above can refer their complaint to:

Authority	Employees refer to this body if they...
the ODEI - the equality tribunal	are still in employment
the Labour Court	have already been dismissed (including 'actual' and 'constructive' dismissal)

7.2.1.16 How can persons granted leave to remain bring a claim to the equality tribunal?

The ODEI - the equality tribunal (referred to as the equality tribunal in this handbook) is an independent body established to investigate claims of discrimination under the *Employment Equality Act*, 1998 and the *Equal Status Act*, 2000. The equality tribunal also offers a mediation service.

Persons wishing to refer their complaint to the equality tribunal must complete the complaint form (Form ODEI 1).[a] Persons who have difficulty in completing the form due to disability, language or other difficulties, should contact the equality tribunal immediately, and if appropriate, other arrangements will be made to enable the person to refer their complaint.

The person making the complaint (the complainant) may write to the person they believe has discriminated against them (the respondent), to request information in order to ascertain more fully, what actually took place. The complainant must use the standard form provided by the equality tribunal (Form ODEI 3).[37]

If the respondent does not reply promptly, the complainant may refer their complaint to the equality tribunal.

When the complaint is received, the Director of Equality Investigations will refer it to an Equality Officer within the equality tribunal.

7.2.1.17 How can persons granted leave to remain bring a claim to the Labour Court?

Persons who have been dismissed from their employment on grounds of discrimination or victimisation, may bring their claim to the Labour Court.

---

a The forms, and all the other form to be used in this process, may be downloaded from the ODEI - the equality tribunal website *http://www.odei.ie/* or from the Office of Director of Equality Investigations, 3 Clonmel Street, Dublin 2, telephone (01) 477 4100.

- The person can send a questionnaire to the former employer to obtain information. The employer can also give their version of what occurred through this procedure. The Questionnaire Form may be downloaded from the Labour Court website.[38]

- The application must be made within six months from the incident of discrimination or victimisation taking place. If there were a series of incidents, the application must be made six months from the last one taking place.

- The application may be made by completing the application form, which can be downloaded from the Labour Court website.

7.2.1.18 What are the rules governing the victimisation of persons granted leave to remain who bring claims?

If a person making a complaint to the equality tribunal is penalised in any manner by the person against whom they made the complaint or another person because they made the complaint, this is regarded as victimisation. Victimisation also occurs if the person in good faith lawfully opposed any act of discrimination or victimisation or gave evidence in any proceedings under the Act.

Victimisation is also prohibited under the *Employment Equality Act* and a person who considers that they were victimised may make a complaint to the equality tribunal in the manner described above for other types of discrimination.

7.2.2 What types of accommodation can persons granted leave to remain access?

Persons granted leave to remain have the following accommodation options:

- private rented accommodation

- local authority accommodation

- purchase

7.2.2.1 Private rented accommodation

Persons wishing to rent a house or apartment from a private landlord can do so directly themselves by replying to advertisements in newspapers or seek the assistance of a letting agency. Finding accommodation can be expensive and time-consuming, particularly in big cities. Prospective tenants should:

- Inspect the property before agreeing to move in and record the condition of the property and its contents in writing. Houses and apartments to let should comply with certain minimum standards.[39]

- Agree the amount of deposit and rent to be paid and the time of payment. A receipt should be obtained for all money paid to the landlord. The deposit should be returned to the tenant when s/he leaves the accommodation. However, the landlord may retain some or all of the deposit if: the tenant gives insufficient notice, damages the property or leaves without paying bills or rent.

- Find out whether the rent covers such items as electricity, gas and bin charges (where relevant).

- Agree on who is responsible for any repairs that need to be carried out in the future.

Tenants should be aware of their rights and duties as a tenant. The most important of these are:

- The landlord must provide a rent book. The rent book should contain the name and address of the landlord, amount of deposit paid, the amount of rent and the time and method of payment. All rent payments should be entered in the rent book. The rent book should also include the terms of the tenancy.

- The landlord is not permitted (except in cases of emergency) to enter the accommodation without making an appointment with the tenant.

- The landlord must give a minimum of four weeks notice in writing if they require the tenant to leave the accommodation. This is referred to as a 'notice to quit'. If the tenant does not leave by the end of the four-week period, the landlord can go to court to apply for an eviction order.

- The tenant must also provide notice to the landlord if they decide to move out.

7.2.2.2 Local authority (council or corporation) Housing

Local authority housing is available, generally for persons who do not have sufficient resources to provide their own accommodation. Practice with regard to eligibility for local authority housing varies. Priority is usually given to low-income families with children and to older persons. However, there is usually a long waiting list of people for local authority housing.

Persons who are interested in being considered for local authority housing should:

- Contact their nearest local authority (see Appendix E for a full list of local authorities in Ireland), and obtain a copy of the authority's scheme of letting priorities. This sets out the rules for the allocation of accommodation including such matters as how applicants are prioritised and what type of accommodation may be provided to different categories of applicants.

- If the person is still interested in local authority accommodation, they should complete the application form, which is provided by the local authority.

- There is no requirement to live in the area for a certain time in order to qualify for local authority housing. It is possible to apply to more than one local authority, but not all local authorities accept applications from outside their area.

- Non-nationals who wish to apply for local authority accommodation may be required to provide evidence that they intend, and are entitled, to live in Ireland permanently. The practice varies with regard to this requirement and persons should contact their local authority.

- When the application has been received, an official from the local authority or health board will usually visit the applicant. (However, practice varies between local authorities and they may visit the applicant only when suitable accommodation is available.)

- As most local authorities have insufficient accommodation to meet the demand, they will put the applicant's name on a list. Some local authorities have a 'points system' to assist them in determining the greatest need for accommodation among applicants. An applicant will be awarded points for issues such as overcrowding.

7.2.2.2.1 *Offer of accommodation:*

If the person is offered a house or flat by the local authority and decides to take it, they must sign a tenancy agreement.

- The tenancy agreement is legal document and both the tenant and the local authority must adhere to the terms of the agreement.

- In the case of a married couple or partners, the tenancy is usually in joint names.

- The amount of rent to be paid per week is based on the income of the household.

- It is important to ensure that rent is paid up to date as the tenant may be issued with a notice to quit if arrears of rent have built up.

- Tenants can apply to transfer to another area.

7.2.2.3 *Purchase*

There are no restrictions on non-nationals buying private residential property in Ireland.[a] However, there are requirements under the Land Acts and additional documents may be required. There are some restrictions with regard to farmland.[b]

However, persons should be aware that house purchase can be a lengthy and costly process, therefore, for some, renting a property may be a better option. It is important to note that a person's Certificate of Registration will not be extended simply because the person has bought property in Ireland, or is in the process of purchasing property.

Persons interested in buying a private house or apartment may find a suitable property through an auctioneer/estate agent or through advertisements in local and national newspapers.

- Persons who cannot afford to buy a property from their own resources need to get a mortgage from a building society or bank.

- Houses/apartments should be viewed and in the case of a second-hand house or apartment, a survey should be carried out to ensure that it is structurally sound.

- If the person is satisfied that they have found a property they wish to buy, they should make an offer, if the property is for sale by private treaty. If the property is for sale by auction, they must attend the auction and the highest bidder purchases the property.

- Generally, estate agents do not charge a fee to purchasers of property.

- The purchase of property can be complicated, and prospective buyers should always engage a solicitor to act for them.

---

a The *Aliens Act,* 1935 states that "Real and personal property of every description in Saorstat Eireann or subject to the law of Saorstat Eireann may be taken, acquired, held and disposed of by an alien in like manner and to the like extend as such property may be taken, acquired, held or disposed of by a citizen of Saorstat Eireann".

b These restrictions apply to non-EU nationals wishing to buy land over five acres in size. They should contact the Department of Agriculture, Food and Rural Development, Agriculture House, Kildare Street, Dublin 2, telephone (01) 607 2000, Lo-call 1890 200 510.

7.2.2.3.1 What laws govern discrimination in the provision of accommodation?

The *Equal Status Act*, 2000, prohibits discrimination on the grounds of gender, marital status, family status, sexual orientation, religious belief, age, disability, "race" and membership of the Traveller Community in the provision of goods and services, the disposal of property and access to education. Discrimination on the nine grounds listed in the Act is prohibited in both the public and private sectors. The process for referring complaints is similar to that under the *Employment Equality Act*, 1998. Further information is available from the equality tribunal.[40]

7.2.3 What medical services are persons granted leave to remain entitled to?

Persons granted leave to remain, legally resident in Ireland, have two options with regard to medical care:

- public health care
- private health care

7.2.3.1 Public health care

The public health care system, including primary and hospital services, can be accessed by any person resident in Ireland including those who have been granted leave to remain. This system can be accessed for a nominal charge, or free of charge for medical card holders.

7.2.3.1.1 What services can be accessed for a nominal charge?

A range of services are available including:

- General Practitioner (GP) services (family doctor) with a charge of between €30 and €50 per consultation
- in-patient hospital treatment in a public ward subject to a daily charge of €40[a]
- all other out-patient services including consultants
- visits to hospital Accident and Emergency Departments subject to a charge of €40 (persons who are referred by their GP will not be charged)
- maternity and infant care

Generally, to get free medical care in Ireland a person needs a medical card.

7.2.3.1.2 Who is entitled to a medical card?

Entitlement to a medical card in Ireland is based on a person's residence and means. To be fully eligible for a medical card a person must:

- be 'ordinarily resident' in Ireland; this means that they must intend to live in Ireland for at least one year and be permitted to do so
- satisfy the means test; a person will only be eligible for free medical care (Category A entitlement, that is medical card holders) if their gross income, less PRSI contributions is less than €138 and in the case of a married couple or single parent €200.[b]

a Up to a maximum of €400 in any twelve-month period (as of 1 January 2003).

b A married couple or a single parent must earn less than €200. These rates apply to persons under 66 years of age. Persons applying for the medical card are permitted to have the following amounts over the income level and still qualify for the medical card, as of 1 January 2003:
- €25 for each child under 16 years of age
- €26 for each child over 16 years of age with no income maintained by applicant
- the amount by which the rent or mortgage paid each week exceeds €25
- the amount by which the costs of travelling to and from work each week exceeds €22
- weekly expenditure on medicines

7.2.3.1.3 What does a medical card entitle you to?

A medical card entitles you to the following free medical services:

- General Practitioner (GP) services (but you must register with a GP (see Section 7.2.3.1.4))
- prescribed medicines
- in-patient hospital treatment in a public ward
- out-patient hospital treatment
- dental, ophthalmic and aural services
- community care services

7.2.3.1.4 Registering with a General Practitioner (GP)

Persons who qualify for the medical card must register with a General Practitioner (family doctor). Not all GPs accept medical card patients, so the medical card holder should obtain a list of doctors in their area who accept medical card patients:

- They can obtain this list from the local health board offices and health centre together with a registration form, which the doctor will be required to sign.
- General practitioners are only permitted to accept a certain number of medical card patients. Therefore, they will sometimes refuse to accept any further patients.
- If a person is unable to find a doctor who will accept them as a patient under the medical card scheme, one will be assigned to them by the health board office or health centre.

7.2.3.1.5 Applying for a medical card

Persons who wish to apply for a medical card should submit a completed application form, together with evidence that they are 'ordinarily resident' in Ireland and that they satisfy the means test, to their local health board offices or health centre.

7.2.3.2 Private health care

Persons can also take out private health insurance. This insurance covers private care in public or private hospitals. There are two private health insurers in Ireland, VHI and BUPA.[41] Medical insurance will not cover pre-existing medical conditions and the cover may not, in any event, take effect for an initial period.

7.2.4 What social welfare entitlements do persons granted leave to remain have?

Irish social welfare legislation does not distinguish between nationals and non-nationals. Essentially, any person from outside the State who complies with the relevant laws covering entry, living and working here is entitled to seek social welfare payments in compliance with the normal conditions. For further information, contact the Information Service of the Department of Social and Family Affairs on (01) 704 3000.

7.2.5 What education are persons granted leave to remain entitled to?

Persons granted leave to remain at the discretion of the Minister for Justice, Equality & Law Reform are entitled to free first- and second-level education.

7.2.5.1 First- and second-level education

At first and second level, there are two main education sectors: primary school (first level), and post-primary and vocational training (second level). Schools are managed by the State (Comprehensive, Vocational Education Committees [VECs]) and religious bodies (Catholic, Protestant, Muslim, Jewish) and governed by their own ethos/philosophy. Lists of schools are available from the Department of Education and Science.[42]

Government support is provided to allow schools to offer limited language support programmes for bilingual and multilingual persons.

To apply to a school or education centre persons should follow the process below:

- Contact the local school/education centre of choice by writing or telephoning the school principal or manager to arrange a meeting.
- At the first meeting, the formal school/education centre policy, outlining the ethos, selection criteria and other matters, must be provided.
- The school/education centre will require basic information on the student.
- An informal education and linguistic assessment of the student may take place but there is no State interpretation facility for this process. Schools/education centres cannot refuse access to a student on the basis of their level of English.
- If there are no places, or if the school/education centre is unsuitable for the student, the school/education centre recommends another school/education centre in the locality.
- If the student is offered a place in a school, the student should obtain a letter of acceptance from the school/education centre.

7.2.5.2 Third-level education

Persons granted leave to remain at the discretion of the Minister for Justice, Equality & Law Reform cannot access third-level education on the same basis as an EU national. They are unable to obtain a local authority/VEC grant, and may also be charged the international economic fee rate. Third-level fees vary between educational institutions.

Conditions of entry into third level vary between educational institutions. For example, proficiency in English may be required, together with specific qualifications. Places are reserved on some courses for 'mature' applicants who will not be required to have the same qualifications.[a]

Persons granted leave to remain may attend part-time courses, some of which require a fee. However, basic education (literacy) is free of charge from the Adult Literacy Service.

Persons granted leave to remain in the State are also entitled to enrol in FÁS courses[b] and Vocational Training Opportunities Scheme (VTOS) in the VEC.

---

a In the case of mature applicants, generally those persons over the age of twenty-three, other qualifications such as work experience are taken into account, instead of just the school leaving examination.

b FÁS is the Irish Training and Employment Authority. Interested persons should contact their local FÁS office or the FÁS website *http://www.fas.ie/*

7.2.6 What family reunification rights do persons granted leave to remain have?

Although there is no statutory right to family reunification for persons granted leave to remain, generally, they are permitted to be joined by immediate family members, such as spouses and minor children. Persons may also make an application for 'dependant' family members, for example, elderly parents or children over the age of 18 years. The Minister has full discretion in these decisions and the applications often require additional proofs.

7.2.7 How can persons granted leave to remain acquire Irish citizenship?

Persons granted leave to remain in Ireland can become Irish citizens in three ways:

- naturalisation
- post-nuptial citizenship
- by descent

The *Irish Nationality and Citizenship Acts* 1956, 1986, 1994 and 2001 set out the criteria under which Irish citizenship is granted.

7.2.7.1 Acquiring citizenship by naturalisation

A person wishing to apply for a certificate of naturalisation must fulfil certain conditions including having legally resided in Ireland for five years out of the previous nine-year period. The Minister for Justice, Equality & Law Reform may grant an application for a certificate of naturalisation at their discretion if they are satisfied that the applicant:

- is of full age
- is of good character
- has had a period of one year's continuous residence in Ireland immediately prior to their application, and in the eight years immediately preceding that period has had a total residence of four years in Ireland
- intends in good faith to continue to reside in Ireland after naturalisation
- has made a declaration of fidelity to the nation and loyalty to the State, either before a District Court Justice or in such other manner permitted by the Minister

The Minister for Justice, Equality & Law Reform may waive these conditions in certain circumstances specified in the Acts. The number of circumstances in which the Minister may waive the conditions, has been reduced by the 2001, Act.[a]

7.2.7.2 Acquiring post-nuptial citizenship

A non-national who married an Irish national on or before 29 November 2002, and has been in a subsisting marriage with that person for a minimum of three years, may become an Irish citizen by making a post-nuptial declaration of citizenship. However, this is not possible if the Irish spouse has acquired citizenship by naturalisation, post-nuptial declaration, or was granted citizenship as a token of honour.

a *Irish Nationality and Citizenship Act* 1956, Section 16 (as amended by the *Irish Nationality and Citizenship Act*, 1986, Section 5). Since the coming into force of the 2001 Act, this no longer applies to persons married to a naturalised Irish citizen or persons married to a person who is an Irish citizen otherwise than by naturalisation.

Any such declarations will have to be made before 30 November 2005.

In the case of spouses of Irish nationals who got married on or after 30 November, 2002, the Minister may at his 'absolute discretion' grant an application for a certificate of naturalisation to the spouse of an Irish citizen if the applicant:

- is of full age
- is of good character
- is married to an Irish citizen for at least three years
- is in a subsisting marriage, recognised as being in accordance with Irish legislation
- is living together with the Irish citizen as husband and wife (the applicant must submit an affidavit to that effect to the Minister)
- has lived in Ireland for at least one year continuously prior to the application
- has been resident in Ireland for at least two years of the four years immediately preceding that period
- intends in good faith to continue to reside in Ireland after naturalisation
- has made a declaration of 'fidelity to the nation and loyalty to the State' in whatever manner may be prescribed[43]

The Minister for Justice, Equality & Law Reform may waive certain of the above conditions if satisfied that the applicant would suffer serious consequences in respect of his or her bodily integrity or liberty if not granted Irish citizenship.[44]

7.2.7.3 Acquiring citizenship by descent

Persons whose father or mother was an Irish Citizen at the time of their birth are automatically Irish citizens. However, if a person is born outside Ireland, and the parent through whom they are claiming citizenship was also born outside Ireland, they will not be entitled to citizenship except in certain limited circumstances.[45] Persons whose grandparents were Irish citizens can become Irish citizens by registering in the Foreign Births Register in the Department of Foreign Affairs or, if residing outside Ireland, at the nearest Irish Embassy or Consulate.

7.2.7.4 Acquiring permission to remain without condition as to time

Persons who have been legally resident in Ireland for ten years and who have not applied for naturalisation may obtain a residence stamp giving them 'permission to remain without condition as to time'.[46]

7.2.8 What do persons granted leave to remain need to open a bank account?

Banks require new customers to produce the following documents when opening a bank account:

- photo identification (a passport satisfies this requirement)
- proof of address in Ireland, for example a utility bill (electricity, gas or other utility) or lease agreement
- although not officially documented as a requirement, banks often request applicants to provide a personal introduction from an existing customer

7.2.9 Can persons granted leave to remain vote in elections?

Non-national residents in Ireland over 18 years old may vote in some elections:

Citizens of...	Permitted to vote at...
The UK	Dáil, European and local elections
EU states apart from the UK	European and local elections
Non-EU states	Local elections only

Those permitted to vote must have their name included in the Electoral Register if they want to vote. Application forms are available in post offices, libraries and council and corporation offices.

Endnotes

1   *Immigration Act* 1999, Section 3 (3)(b).

2   *Immigration Act* 1999, Section 3 (6) sets out the grounds on the basis of which applications for leave to remain can be granted.

3   *Immigration Act* 1999 (as amended), Section 3 (3)(b)(i).

4   The IOM is located at 9 Marlborough Court, Marlborough Street, Dublin 1 telephone 01-878 7900, e-mail *varp@iomdublin.org*

5   *Immigration Act* 1999 (as amended), Section 3 (5)(a).

6   *Immigration Act* , 1999, Section 3 (1A) (as amended by the *Illegal Immigrants (Trafficking)* Act, 2000), Section 10 (a)(i).

7   *Immigration Act* 1999 Section 3 (9)(a)(i), (as amended by the *Illegal Immigrants (Trafficking)* Act 2000)

8   *Immigration Act* 1999 Section 5 (1) (as amended by the *Illegal Immigrants (Trafficking)* Act 2000)

9   Department of Social, Community and Family Affairs, Gandon House, Amiens Street, Dublin 1, telephone (01) 874 8444, website *http://www.welfare.ie/* The Department's leaflet SW100 Personal Public Service Number provides additional information on obtaining a PPS.

10 Further information may be obtained on Revenue Publication RES 2 *Coming to Live in Ireland* *http://www.revenue.ie/*

11 *Terms of Employment (Information) Act* 1994.

12 *National Minimum Wages Act* 2000.

13 This is provided for in the *National Minimum Wages Act* 2000, Section 15(1):

"Subject to subsection (2) and Sections 16, 17 and 18, a person who:

(a) enters employment for the first time after attaining the age of 18 years or

(b) having entered into employment before attaining the age of 18 years, continues in employment on attaining that age

shall be remunerated by his or her employer in respect of his or her working hours in any pay reference period at an hourly rate of pay that on average is not less than :

(i) in the case of an employee commencing employment for the first time after attaining the age of 18 years:

   (I) in his or her first year after commenced employment, 80% and

   (II) in his or her second year after having commenced employment, 90%

(ii) in the case if an employee having entered into employment before attaining the age of 18 years and continuing in employment on attaining that age

   (I) in his or her first year after having attained the age of 18 years, 80%

   (II) in his or her second year after having attained that age, 90%

of the national minimum hourly rate of pay, notwithstanding that the employee, if he or she has changed his or her employer during the relevant period, may have been remunerated at a higher rate by the previous employer."

14 *Payment of Wages Act* 1991

15 *Organisation of Working Time Act* 1997, Section 19.

16 *Ibid,* Section 14(1).

17 *Ibid,* Section 8.

18 *Ibid,* Section 9(1)(a) and (b).

19 *Ibid,* Section 10.

20 *Ibid,* Section 26.

21 *Parental Leave Act* 1998 Section 7 (1).

22 *Ibid,* Section 19 (3)(c).

23 *Ibid,* Section 13 (1).

24 *Ibid,* Section 13 (2).

25 *Ibid,* Section 13 (4).

26 *Ibid,* Section 13 (1).

27 This form may be downloaded from the Labour Relations Commission
    website *www.lrc.ie/lrc_services/rights_commissioner.htm* or can be obtained from the Secretariat, Rights
    Commissioner Service, Labour Relations Commission, Tom Johnson House, Haddington Road, Dublin 4, telephone: (01) 613 6700.

28 Minimum notice is provided for in the *Minimum Notice and Terms of Employment Act* 1973, as amended by the
    Work Protection (Regular Part-Time Employees) Act 1991.

29 According to the *Employment Equality Act* 1998,Section 2(1), (dealing with interpretation), 'marital status' means
    "single, married, separated, divorced and widowed".

30 'Family status' is described in Section 2(1) of the Act as "responsibility
    (a) as a parent or as a person in loco parentis in relation to a person who has not attained the age of 18 years, or
    (b) as a parent or the resident primary carer in relation to a person of or over that age with a disability which is of
    such a nature as to give rise to the need for care or support on a continuing, regular or frequent basis".

31 Discrimination on the basis of 'race' is described in the *Employment Equality Act* 1998, Section 6 (2)(h) as
    "between any two persons that are of a different 'race', 'colour', nationality or ethnic or national origins".

32 'Religious belief' as defined in the *Employment Equality Act* 1998, includes religious background or outlook.

33 The *Employment Equality Act* 1998, Section 2(1) defines 'sexual orientation' as meaning "heterosexual,
    homosexual or bisexual orientation".

34 'Disability' is defined in the *Employment Equality Act* 1998, Section 2(1) as:
    "(a) the total or partial absence of a person's bodily or mental functions, including the absence of a part of the
    person's body,
    (b) the presence in the body of organisms causing, or likely to cause, chronic disease or illness,
    (c) the malfunction, malformation or disfigurement of a part of a person's body,
    (d) a condition or malfunction which results in a person learning differently from a person without the condition
    or malfunction, or
    (e) a condition, illness or disease which affects a person's thought processes, perception of reality, emotions or
    judgement which results in disturbed behaviour, and shall be taken to include a disability which exists at present,
    or which previously existed but no longer exists, or which may exist in the future or which is imputed to a person".

35 *Employment Equality Act* 1998,Section 8(1).

36 The Equality Authority may be contacted at 2, Clonmel Street, Dublin 2, telephone (01) 417 3333, fax (01) 417 3366,
    email *info@equality.ie*

37 The respondent must also use the form provided by the ODEI - the equality tribunal to reply (Form ODEI 4).
    If the correct forms are not used, the provisions in the *Employment Equality Act* 1998, permitting the director to
    draw inferences from failure to supply information, do not apply.

38 *http://www.labourcourt.ie/labour/labour.nsf/LookupPageLink/formsDownload*

39 Details of these can be obtained from Threshold, 21 Stoneybatter, Dublin 7, email *advice@threshold.ie*

40 Further information is available from the ODEI - the equality tribunal, 3 Clonmel Street, Dublin 2,
    telephone (01) 477 4100, website *http://www.odei.ie/*

41 Voluntary Health Insurance (VHI), VHI House, Lower Abbey Street, Dublin 1, telephone (01) 874 4499,
    Lo-call 1850 444 444.
    BUPA Ireland, Mill Island, Fermoy, Co. Cork, telephone (021) 42121, or 12 Fitzwilliam Square, Dublin 2,
    telephone (01) 6627 662, Lo-call 1890 700 890.

42 Department of Education and Science, Marlborough Street, Dublin 1, telephone (01) 873 4700, website *http://www.education.ie/*

43 *Irish Nationality and Citizenship Act* 1956, Section 15A (1), as amended by the *Irish Nationality and Citizenship Act* 2001, Section 5.

44 *Irish Nationality and Citizenship Act* 1956, Section 15A (2), as amended by the *Irish Nationality and Citizenship Act* 2001, Section 5.

45 *Irish Nationality and Citizenship Act* 1956, Section 7 (3), as amended by the *Irish Nationality and Citizenship Act* 2001, Section 5.

46 Further information available on the Department of Justice, Equality & Law Reform website *http://www.justice.ie/*

Family Members of Migrants and Irish Nationals

8.1 What Are the Categories of Family Members?

8.2 What Rights and Entitlements Do Family Members of Migrants and Irish Nationals Have?

FAMILY MEMBERS OF MIGRANTS AND IRISH NATIONALS

The Constitution recognises the fundamental importance of the family in Irish Society.[a] Article 41 states:

> 1. The State recognises the family are the natural primary and fundamental unit group of society and as a moral institution possessing inalienable and imprescriptible rights, anticendent and superior to all positive law.
>
> 2. The State, therefore, guarantees to protect the family in its constitution and authority as the necessary basis of social order and as indispensable to the welfare of the nation and state.

In general, persons who are in Ireland legally are permitted to apply for family reunification in respect of dependent members of their families. There is no general policy of restriction in operation in relation to family reunion where the family members in question are not subject to a visa requirement, subject to the worker being able to support the family without recourse to public funds. However, restrictions apply in the case of persons who are required to possess a visa to travel to Ireland since, according to the Department of Justice, Equality & Law Reform, "by definition, such countries pose the greater immigration related risks".[1]

8.1 What Are the Categories of Family Members?

8.1.1 Spouses[b] of Irish nationals

Irish nationals are permitted to have their spouse reside in Ireland with them. This applies to both EEA and non-EEA nationals. Irish nationals do not have the right to be joined by their (unmarried) partner even if the relationship is a long-term one.

Spouses of Irish nationals who have been granted residence in Ireland are generally entitled to the same rights as their Irish spouse.[c] The State, recognising the fundamental importance of the family, confers all the rights of the Irish citizen on to their non-EEA spouse. In contrast to EU law, the Irish citizen does not have to be working in order for their spouse to be granted residency.

Non-EEA spouses of Irish nationals do not come within the scope of EU law, except in the following cases:

1. If the Irish citizen was working in another Member State, married their spouse, and then moved back to Ireland to work; this activates the movement clause and the spouse then comes within the scope of EU law

---

a The rights of the family are also protected under international and European law, including the *European Convention on Human Rights and Fundamental Freedoms*, Article 8 which states that "Everyone has the right to respect for his private and family life".

b For information on parents and siblings of Irish citizens, see Chapter 6.

c The rights of the spouse of an Irish national are derived from their Irish spouse and are dependent on the Irish spouse remaining in Ireland and the marriage continuing to subsist.

2. If the Irish citizen goes to another Member State to work with their spouse, the EU law then applies to their spouse. On their return to Ireland, the non-EEA spouse would still be deemed to be a privileged beneficiary of EU law, and would have the same rights as their spouse. The judgement which established this did not clarify[a] how much time the couple would need to spend in another Member State for the non-EEA spouse to benefit from EU law.

8.1.2 *Family members of EEA and Swiss nationals*

8.1.2.1 *EU Nationals*

The status of Citizenship of the Union was introduced by the Treaty of Maastricht (1992). Article 17 of the *EC Treaty*[b] states:

> *Citizenship of the Union is hereby established. Every person holding the nationality of a Member State shall be a citizen of the Union. Citizenship of the Union shall complement and not replace national citizenship.*
>
> *Citizens of the Union shall enjoy the rights conferred by this Treaty and shall be subject to the duties imposed thereby.*

Article 18(1) of the *EC Treaty* states:

> *Every Citizen of the Union shall have the right to move and reside freely within the territory of the Member States, subject to the limitations and conditions laid down by this Treaty and by the measures adopted to give it effect.*

The right to move and reside referred to in Article 18(1) may be subject to limits and conditions. For non-economically active migrants, these conditions include various financial conditions set out in a series of Community Directives.[2] However, the competent authorities and, where necessary, the national courts must ensure that these limitations and conditions are applied in compliance with the general principles of Community law and, in particular, the principle of proportionality.[3]

The Commission has proposed replacing these Directives with a general all-embracing Directive to deal with Citizens' migration rights, but this not been adopted yet.[4] However, it is clear that the effect of Article 18(1) is such that once a Citizen of the Union is lawfully resident in the territory of another Member State, they are entitled to equal treatment with nationals of that State in most circumstances. For example, regarding welfare rights equal treatment extends to all EU migrants, regardless of whether they are workers, service providers or simply visitors, provided they are lawfully resident.[5] Regarding political rights, Citizens of the Union have the right to vote and stand in both municipal and European elections, when resident in another Member State.

EU citizens who have **moved** to another Member State to **work** are the primary beneficiaries of EU law. As a result of case law,[6] it was ruled that spouses of EU citizens who have moved to another Member State to work, come directly within the scope of EU law, and are granted the same rights as their EU spouse. Their rights are referred to as 'derived rights' because they are derived from their spouse.

a *Suriendar Singh ex parte Secretary of State for the Home Department.* For a more detailed discussion of this case, see Barrett, G. *The Rights of Third country Family Members under European Community Law*, available from the Irish Centre for European Law, TCD (2000).

b Unless otherwise stated, all references to the *EC Treaty* refer to the *EC Treaty* as amended by the Treaties of Amsterdam and Nice.

8.1.2.2 Students

EEA or Swiss students may be accompanied to Ireland by:

- their spouse[a]
- children of the student and their spouse who are under 18 years of age[7]

The student must be in a position to support themselves, their spouse and any accompanying dependants and must be able to provide full medical insurance for them.[8]

8.1.2.3 Other non-economically active persons

This category includes retired persons. Non-economically active persons may be accompanied to Ireland by:

- their spouse
- children under 18 years of age
- other dependent children and grandchildren
- dependent parents and grandparents[9]

The non-economically active person must be in receipt of adequate welfare benefits (from their home country),[b] or have sufficient resources to support their spouse and accompanying dependants.[10]

Family members of students and other non-economically active EEA and Swiss nationals (including family members who are not EEA or Swiss nationals) have the following rights and obligations. They:

- are entitled to remain in Ireland while the non-economically active person remains here
- must apply for a residence permit[11]
- are generally not entitled to free medical care
- are entitled to the same housing rights as their EEA/Swiss family member

8.1.2.4 Workers and business persons

An EEA/Swiss national worker or business person (self-employed) may be accompanied to Ireland by:

- their spouse
- their children who are under 18 years of age
- other dependent children
- spouses of the children
- dependent grandchildren
- dependent parents and grandparents[12]

---

a They are not entitled to be joined by an unmarried partner.

b *European Communities (Right of Residence for Non-economically Active Persons) Regulations* 1997, Regulation 7 (1)
(a)(ii) states that such benefits include: "...an invalidity or early retirement pension or old age benefits or of a pension in respect of an industrial accident or disease."

In general, family members of EEA and Swiss national workers or business persons have the same rights as the self-employed or employed person.

EEA and Swiss nationals in employment, and self-employment, in Ireland are not required under the Regulations to be in a position to support their spouse and family members.

8.1.3 Family members of non-EEA migrant workers

8.1.3.1 Family members of migrant workers with work authorisations

A person to whom a work authorisation was issued may be accompanied to Ireland by their spouse and/or minor dependent children provided that they can show that they have sufficient means to support their family members while in Ireland.

8.1.3.2 Family members of migrant workers with working visas

The holder of a working visa may apply to be joined in Ireland by their spouse and/or minor dependent children. They may generally apply after they have been in Ireland three months, in employment and able to support their family.

8.1.3.3 Family members of migrant workers with employment permits

Persons who are employed under the employment permit scheme and whose family members require a visa to travel to Ireland, may generally only apply for family reunification if they have been in the State for at least a year and have been offered a further twelve months contract. Again, this is subject to the worker being able to support the family members without recourse to the public funds.[13]

Spouses and family members who have joined non-EEA workers in Ireland are entitled to reside here as long as the worker is in Ireland and continues to be able to support them. They are entitled to accommodation on the same basis as the worker. They are **not** entitled to:

- work in Ireland (unless they have a work authorisation/working visa in their own right or are permitted to work here under the employment permit scheme)
- establish a business (unless they have been granted a business permission in their own right)
- avail of free medical services (medical card)
- avail of publicly-funded education (with the exception of children who are under eighteen years of age)

8.1.4 Family members of Non-EEA/Swiss persons who are self-employed

The holder of a business permission may apply to be joined in Ireland by their spouse and/or minor dependent children.

Spouses and family members who have joined non-EEA nationals who hold a business permission in Ireland are entitled to reside here as long as the business person is in Ireland and able to support them. They are entitled to accommodation on the same basis as the business person. They are **not** entitled to:

- work in Ireland (unless they have a work authorisation/working visa in their own right or are permitted to work here under the employment permit scheme)

- establish a business (unless they have been granted a business permission in their own right)

- avail of free medical services (medical card)

- avail of publicly-funded education (with the exception of children who are under 18 years of age)

8.1.5 Family members of recognised refugees

A recognised refugee may apply to the Minister for Justice, Equality & Law Reform for permission to be granted to a member or members of their family to enter and reside in the State.[14] If the Minister is satisfied that such persons are members of the refugee's family, they shall grant permission in writing to the person or persons to enter and reside in the State. Such persons will be entitled to the rights and privileges set out in Section 3 of the *Refugee Act, 1996*.

A member of the family means, in the case of a

Category of refugee...	Permission granted to...
refugee who is married	their spouse (the marriage must be subsisting at the time the application for family reunification is made)
refugee who is under 18 and is not married	their parents
refugee who is a parent	child of the refugee who is under eighteen at the time of the application for family reunification

The Minister may, at their discretion, grant permission to dependent members of the refugee's family to enter and reside in the State. A dependent member of the refugee's family is:

...any grandparent, parent, brother, sister, child, grandchild, ward or guardian of the refugee who is dependent on the refugee or is suffering from mental or physical disability to such extent that it not reasonable for him or her to maintain himself or herself fully.[a]

Family members of recognised refugees who have been granted permission to come to Ireland and reside here are entitled to the following rights and entitlements on the same basis as an Irish national:

- to seek and enter employment, carry out any business or trade and have access to the education system

- to avail of the same medical care and services, and social welfare benefits

- to reside in Ireland

- to travel in Ireland and to and from Ireland [b]

- freedom to practice their religion

a *Refugee Act* 1996, Section 18(4)(b). The Minister may refuse permission to members of the refugee's family to enter and reside in the state on grounds of 'national security and public policy'

b They should check with the embassy of the country they intend to visit to ascertain whether they will need a visa to enter that country.

- freedom as regards the religious education of their children
- access to the courts
- to join or establish associations or trade unions
- to acquire, hold, and dispose of real or personal property[15]

8.1.6 Family members of persons granted leave to remain

Persons granted leave to remain on 'humanitarian grounds'[a] have no statutory rights to family reunification. However, such persons may apply to have their immediate family members (spouse and minor children) join them in Ireland and applications are decided on a case-by-case basis.

Family members of persons granted leave to remain who are permitted to reside in Ireland are generally entitled to the same rights as the person granted leave to remain. Although these are not defined in law, they are similar to those accorded to refugees and their family members as outlined above.

8.1.7 Family members of migrants and Irish nationals residing in the State without authorisation.

Persons residing in Ireland without authorisation are not entitled to family reunification.

8.1.8 Visitors

Visitors to Ireland are not entitled to family reunification

8.2 What Rights and Entitlements Do Family Members of Migrants and Irish Nationals Have?

8.2.1 What rights in the work place do family members of migrants and Irish nationals have?

Family members of Irish nationals and migrants, who are permitted to work here,[b] are entitled to the same rights and entitlements with regard to employment as Irish nationals.

8.2.1.1 What taxes and social contributions do family members of migrants and Irish nationals pay?

All employees must pay tax on their earnings, known as 'pay as you earn' or PAYE and PRSI 'pay-related social insurance'.[c] These are deducted from employees' salaries each week or month. All employees are required to have a Personal Public Service Number (PPS No.), and persons who do not have a PPS No.[d] should contact the Department of Social and Family Affairs.[16] This number should be quoted in all contact with the Tax Office and the Department.

---

a This is the term generally used, however, the term used by the Immigration Division of the Department of Justice, Equality & Law Reform is temporary leave to remain on exceptional grounds.

b Several categories of family members of non-EEA nationals are not permitted to work here, in particular family members of migrant employees, business persons, and students.

c There are some exceptions to this, for example, low-paid workers.

d This replaces the old RSI Number.

In addition, persons who are commencing their first employment in Ireland should complete a Certificate of Tax Credits and Standard Rate Cut-Off Point (Form 12A).[17] The Revenue Commissioners usually grant married tax credits even if the worker's spouse is not resident in the State.

8.2.1.2 What details of employment are family members of migrants and Irish nationals entitled to receive?

Within two months of starting employment, the employer is required to provide the employee[a] with a written statement of certain details of the terms of employment.[18]

These include:

- name and address of employer
- place of work
- job title and nature of work
- date of commencement of employment
- nature of contract (temporary or fixed term)
- rate of pay
- pay intervals
- hours of work (including overtime)
- paid leave
- arrangements for when the employee is unable to work due to sickness or injury
- pensions and pension schemes
- notice entitlements
- collective agreement/s, and the parties to the agreement/s

If the particulars contained in the statement change, the employer must notify the employee within one week.

If an employer has either failed to provide a written statement, or failed to notify the employee of changes that have taken place regarding the particulars contained in the statement, the employee may complain to a Rights Commissioner. If either party is dissatisfied with the recommendation of the Rights Commissioner, they may appeal to the Employment Appeals Tribunal.[b]

a The term 'employee' covers those working under contract of employment or apprenticeship; those employed through an employment agency and those employed in the service of the State.

b See Section 8.2.1.12 page 185 for details of the procedure for referring a complaint to the Rights Commissioner. In addition, the Rights Commissioner can investigate grievances or claims under most of the legislation dealing with rights in the workplace including: *Payment of Wages Act* 1991; *Terms of Employment Act* 1994; *Organisation of Working Time Act* 1997; *Parental Leave Act* 1998 and *National Minimum Wages Act*, 2000.

8.2.1.3 What is the minimum rate of pay for family members of migrants and Irish nationals?

- All employees over the age of 18 who have worked for at least two years since turning 18 are entitled to a minimum rate of pay. This is currently €6.35 per hour since 1 October 2002.[19] Persons who have not worked for two years must generally be paid 80 per cent of the minimum wage in the first year, and 90 per cent in the second year.[20]

- With their wages, employees must receive a written statement of the gross pay and deductions made.[21]

- Employees have the right to a readily negotiable mode of wage payment such as by cheque, credit transfer, cash, postal order or bank draft.

- Employers may only make deductions in certain circumstances[a] that are agreed with the employee.[b]

8.2.1.4 What are the rules governing working hours?

- Employees must not be required to work in excess of the maximum hours permitted each week. This is an average of 48 hours per week averaged over four, six or 12 months depending on the nature of the employment.[c]

- Employees are entitled to breaks and rest time as follows:

  - 11 hours rest per 24 hour period

  - one period of 24 hours rest per week preceded by a daily rest period (11 hours)

  - 15 minutes break after working four-and-a-half hours and another break of 15 minutes after six hours, or 30 minutes after six hours if the 15 minutes break was not taken after four-and-a-half hours[d]

8.2.1.5 What holidays are family members of migrants and Irish nationals entitled to?

Full-time workers are entitled to four working weeks annual leave[22] and nine public holidays per year.[e] These are: 1 January, St Patrick's Day, Easter Monday, First Monday in May, First Monday in June, First Monday in August, Last Monday in October, Christmas Day and St Stephen's Day.

Part-time workers are entitled to annual leave consisting of eight per cent of the hours they work up to a maximum of four weeks and to public holidays if they have worked at least 40 hours in the five weeks preceding the public holiday.

---

a When the deductions are required by law; when they are provided for in the contract of employment and when they are made with the written consent of the employee.

b For example, VHI, BUPA, Union Dues, Pension Plan and so on.

c Four months for employees generally, six months for seasonal workers and workers who are directly involved in ensuring continuity of service or production, and twelve months for employees who have entered a collective agreement with their employer.

d The break cannot be taken at the end of the work period.

e The employer has four alternatives with regard to the public holidays. They may give the employee: the day of the holiday off with pay, a paid day off within a month, an extra day of annual leave or an extra day's pay.

8.2.1.6 What compensation for Sunday work are family members of migrants and Irish nationals entitled to?

Employees are entitled to be compensated for Sunday work. This can be extra pay[a] or time off in lieu.[23] For persons working in the retail sector, there is a *Code of Practice on Sunday Working in the Retail Trade.*[b]

8.2.1.7 What maternity leave are family members of migrants and Irish nationals entitled to?

- A pregnant employee is entitled to maternity leave from employment for a period of at least 14 weeks.[24]

- To be entitled to maternity leave, the employee must notify her employer and produce a medical certificate confirming the pregnancy and expected week of confinement. The notice must be given at least four weeks before the commencement of maternity leave and must be in writing.[25]

- An employee can choose the period of maternity leave. However, maternity leave must be taken at least four weeks before the end of the expected week of confinement and shall end not earlier than four weeks after the end of the expected week of confinement.[26]

- The employee has the right to return to work when the period of maternity leave has expired. Employees who have taken maternity leave are entitled to return to the:
  - same employer
  - job the employee held immediately before commencement of leave
  - same contract and conditions of employment[27]

8.2.1.8 What parental leave are family members of migrants and Irish nationals entitled to?

- Persons who have at least one year's continuous employment and are the parents of children (natural or adopted) may take up to a total of 14 weeks unpaid leave (for each child) to take care of their children who are no older than five years.[28]

- Employees who have taken parental leave are entitled to return to the:
  - same employer
  - job the employee held immediately before commencement of leave
  - same contract and conditions of employment[29]

8.2.1.9 What force majeure *leave are family members of migrants and Irish nationals entitled to?*

- Employees may also take *force majeure* leave in the case of sudden injury or illness to an immediate family member, where the dependant needs the worker to be present.[30]

---

a With premium payment (that is, above normal payment).

b This was drawn up by the Labour Relations Commission and is based on the entitlements set out in the *Organisation of Working Time Act* 1997. It is available on the Department of Enterprise, Trade & Employment website *http://www.entemp.ie/*

- An 'immediate family member' of the employee is a child, spouse/partner, person to whom the employee is *in loco parentis*, brother, sister, parent or grandparent.[31]

- An employee may take three days in any consecutive 12 months or five days in any 36 consecutive months[32]

- *Force majeure* leave is paid leave[33]

8.2.1.10 What laws protect family members of migrants and Irish nationals from unfair dismissal?

Employees who have over 12 months continuous employment, a are protected by law from unfair dismissal. Dismissals may be regarded as unfair where they have resulted wholly or mainly from:

- the employee's trade union membership or activities

- the religious or political beliefs of the employee

- the race, skin colour or sexual orientation of the employee

- legal proceedings against the employer if the employee is a party or a witness

- the employee's pregnancy

- the employee taking leave provided for under the *Maternity Protection Act, 1994*

A dismissal will usually be considered fair if it is based wholly or mainly on one of the following:

- the employee's capability, competence or qualifications for the job

- the employee's conduct

- the employee's redundancy

- if continuation of the employment would contravene other legal requirements

Both 'actual' unfair dismissals and 'constructive' dismissals are prohibited by legislation. Constructive dismissal can occur where the employee's conditions of employment are made so difficult that they have no alternative but to leave.

8.2.1.11 What claims for redress[b] exist for family members of migrants and Irish nationals who consider they have been unfairly dismissed?

An employee who considers that they have been unfairly dismissed (this includes 'actual' and 'constructive' dismissal) and who wishes to make a claim for redress must do so within six months.[c]

The employee must give formal notice of his/her claim in writing to a Rights Commissioner or to the Employment Appeals Tribunal. The claim is considered by

a Two fixed terms of six months would qualify.

b Redress in the case of unfair dismissal can be any of the following:
  - re-instatement in the employee's old job
  - re-engagement in the old job or a suitable alternative
  - financial compensation

c In exceptional circumstances, this can be twelve months.

the Employment Appeals Tribunal where the employee or the employer have notified a Rights Commissioner that they object to the claim being heard by a Rights Commissioner.

Persons who are employed through an employment agency must make their claim against whoever is paying their wages (this could be the actual 'employer' or the agency).

8.2.1.12 How can family members of migrants and Irish nationals take a claim to the Rights Commissioner?

Rights Commissioners are appointed by the Minister for Enterprise, Trade & Employment on the recommendation of the Labour Relations Commission. They are independent of the Minister in carrying out their functions. The procedure for persons wishing to make an appeal to the Rights Commissioner is described below:

- Persons wishing to make an appeal to a Rights Commissioner must:
  - notify their former employer that they intend to take a case to the Rights Commissioner
  - complete the standard form[34] (full details of the complaint must be given)
- The Rights Commissioner hears the case as soon as possible. The hearing takes place in private.
- Both parties can be represented at the hearing by a lawyer or trade union representative (in the cases of the employee).
- Both parties have the opportunity to present their case.
- The Rights Commissioner makes a recommendation, which may be appealed to the Employment Appeals Tribunal (EAT).

8.2.1.13 What is the minimum notice[35] period for family members of migrants and Irish nationals?

Employees who are in continuous employment with the same employer for 13 weeks or more and who normally work at least eight hours per week are entitled to a minimum period of notice from their employer if they intend to dismiss them.

The period of notice depends on the length of service. For persons who have served from 13 weeks to two years the minimum notice period is one week.

Employees must also give notice if they intend to leave the job. If the employee is in employment for 13 weeks or over, they must give the employer at least one week's notice. If the contract of employment requires further notice to be given, they must adhere to the terms of the contract.

The Employment Appeals Tribunal considers disputes between employers and workers regarding minimum notice.

8.2.1.14 What redundancy payments[a] are family members of migrants and Irish nationals entitled to?

Employees are entitled to a lump sum redundancy payment when their employment is ended due to redundancy providing they:

- have 109 weeks continuous service
- are aged between 16 and 66
- are normally expected to work at least eight hours per week

The redundancy pay is calculated in the following manner:

- a half week's pay for each year of employment up to 41 years' service
- one week's pay for each year over 41 years' service
- one week's pay irrespective of the length of service

8.2.1.15 What rules govern discrimination in employment?

Discrimination against employees on grounds of age, gender, marital status,[36] family status,[37] race,[38] religion,[39] sexual orientation,[40] disability[41] and membership of the Travelling Community is prohibited under the *Employment Equality Act, 1998*.[b] The Act prohibits:

- direct and indirect discrimination
- discrimination in access to employment, conditions of employment, promotion, training and classification of posts[42]

The Equality Authority may provide legal advice, assistance and representation to persons who consider that they have a complaint under the legislation.[43]

A person who considers that they have been discriminated against on any of the nine grounds listed above can refer their complaint to:

Authority	Employees refer to this body if they...
the ODEI - the equality tribunal	are still in employment
the Labour Court	have already been dismissed (including 'actual' and 'constructive' dismissal)

---

a Redundancy payments are dealt with under the *Redundancy Payments Acts 1967-1991*. Redundancy occurs when the employee's job ceases to exist, there is insufficient work, the firm closes down or the firm re-organises.

b The *Employment Equality Authority Act 1998* came into force 18 October 1999, and only incidents of discrimination occurring on, or after that date can be dealt with under the Act. Incidents of discrimination of grounds of sex or marital status can be investigated by the ODEI - the equality tribunal under earlier legislation.

8.2.1.16 How can family members of migrants and Irish nationals bring a claim to the equality tribunal?

The ODEI - the equality tribunal (referred to as the equality tribunal in this handbook) is an independent body established to investigate claims of discrimination under the *Employment Equality Act*, 1998 and the *Equal Status Act*, 2000. The equality tribunal also offers a mediation service.

Persons wishing to refer their complaint to the equality tribunal must complete the complaint form (Form ODEI 1).[a] Persons who have difficulty in completing the form due to disability, language or other difficulties, should contact the equality tribunal immediately, and if appropriate, other arrangements will be made to enable the person to refer their complaint.

The person making the complaint (the complainant) may write to the person they believe has discriminated against them (the respondent), to request information in order to ascertain more fully, what actually took place. The complainant must use the standard form provided by the equality tribunal (Form ODEI 3).[44]

If the respondent does not reply promptly, the complainant may refer their complaint to the equality tribunal.

When the complaint is received, the Director of Equality Investigations will refer it to an Equality Officer within the equality tribunal.

8.2.1.17 How can family members of migrants and Irish nationals bring a claim to the Labour Court?

Persons who have been dismissed from their employment on grounds of discrimination or victimisation, may bring their claim to the Labour Court.

- The person can send a questionnaire to the former employer to obtain information. The employer can also give their version of what occurred through this procedure. The Questionnaire Form may be downloaded from the Labour Court website.[45]

- The application must be made within six months from the incident of discrimination or victimisation taking place. If there were a series of incidents, the application must be made six months from the last one taking place.

- The application may be made by completing the application form, which can be downloaded from the Labour Court website.

8.2.1.18 What are the rules governing the victimisation of family members of migrants and Irish nationals who bring claims?

If a person making a complaint to the equality tribunal is penalised in any manner by the person against whom they made the complaint or another person because they made the complaint, this is regarded as victimisation. Victimisation also occurs if the person in good faith lawfully opposed any act of discrimination or victimisation or gave evidence in any proceedings under the Act.

Victimisation is also prohibited under the *Employment Equality Act* and a person who considers that they were victimised may make a complaint to the equality tribunal in the manner described above for other types of discrimination.

a The forms, and all the other form to be used in this process, may be downloaded from the ODEI - the equality tribunal website *http://www.odei.ie/* or from the Office of Director of Equality Investigations, 3 Clonmel Street, Dublin 2, telephone (01) 477 4100.

8.2.2 What types of accommodation can family members of migrants and Irish nationals access?

Family members of migrants and Irish nationals are entitled to access accommodation in the same manner as the migrant or Irish national they are accompanying. The three main options are:

- private rented accommodation
- local authority accommodation
- purchase

8.2.2.1 Private rented accommodation

Persons wishing to rent a house or apartment from a private landlord can do so directly themselves by replying to advertisements in newspapers or seek the assistance of a letting agency. Finding accommodation can be expensive and time-consuming, particularly in big cities. Prospective tenants should:

- Inspect the property before agreeing to move in and record the condition of the property and its contents in writing. Houses and apartments to let should comply with certain minimum standards.[46]

- Agree the amount of deposit and rent to be paid and the time of payment. A receipt should be obtained for all money paid to the landlord. The deposit should be returned to the tenant when s/he leaves the accommodation. However, the landlord may retain some or all of the deposit if: the tenant gives insufficient notice, damages the property or leaves without paying bills or rent.

- Find out whether the rent covers such items as electricity, gas and bin charges (where relevant).

- Agree on who is responsible for any repairs that need to be carried out in the future.

Tenants should be aware of their rights and duties as a tenant. The most important of these are:

- The landlord must provide a rent book. The rent book should contain the name and address of the landlord, amount of deposit paid, the amount of rent and the time and method of payment. All rent payments should be entered in the rent book. The rent book should also include the terms of the tenancy.

- The landlord is not permitted (except in cases of emergency) to enter the accommodation without making an appointment with the tenant.

- The landlord must give a minimum of four weeks notice in writing if they require the tenant to leave the accommodation. This is referred to as a 'notice to quit'. If the tenant does not leave by the end of the four-week period, the landlord can go to court to apply for an eviction order.

- The tenant must also provide notice to the landlord if they decide to move out.

8.2.2.2 *Local authority (council or corporation) Housing*

Local authority housing is available, generally for persons who do not have sufficient resources to provide their own accommodation. Practice with regard to eligibility for local authority housing varies. Priority is usually given to low-income families with children and to older persons. However, there is usually a long waiting list of people for local authority housing.

Persons who are interested in being considered for local authority housing should:

● Contact their nearest local authority (see Appendix E for a full list of local authorities in Ireland), and obtain a copy of the authority's scheme of letting priorities. This sets out the rules for the allocation of accommodation including such matters as how applicants are prioritised and what type of accommodation may be provided to different categories of applicants.

● If the person is still interested in local authority accommodation, they should complete the application form, which is provided by the local authority.

● There is no requirement to live in the area for a certain time in order to qualify for local authority housing. It is possible to apply to more than one local authority, but not all local authorities accept applications from outside their area.

● Non-nationals who wish to apply for local authority accommodation may be required to provide evidence that they intend, and are entitled, to live in Ireland permanently. The practice varies with regard to this requirement and persons should contact their local authority.

● When the application has been received, an official from the local authority or health board will usually visit the applicant. (However, practice varies between local authorities and they may visit the applicant only when suitable accommodation is available.)

● As most local authorities have insufficient accommodation to meet the demand, they will put the applicant's name on a list. Some local authorities have a 'points system' to assist them in determining the greatest need for accommodation among applicants. An applicant will be awarded points for issues such as overcrowding.

8.2.2.2.1 *Offer of accommodation:*

If the person is offered a house or flat by the local authority and decides to take it, they must sign a tenancy agreement.

● The tenancy agreement is legal document and both the tenant and the local authority must adhere to the terms of the agreement.

● In the case of a married couple or partners, the tenancy is usually in joint names.

● The amount of rent to be paid per week is based on the income of the household.

● It is important to ensure that rent is paid up to date as the tenant may be issued with a notice to quit if arrears of rent have built up.

● Tenants can apply to transfer to another area.

8.2.2.3 Purchase

There are no restrictions on non-nationals buying private residential property in Ireland.[a] However, there are requirements under the Land Acts and additional documents may be required. There are some restrictions with regard to farmland.[b]

However, persons should be aware that house purchase can be a lengthy and costly process, therefore, for some, renting a property may be a better option. It is important to note that a person's Certificate of Registration will not be extended simply because the person has bought property in Ireland, or is in the process of purchasing property.

Persons interested in buying a private house or apartment may find a suitable property through an auctioneer/estate agent or through advertisements in local and national newspapers.

- Persons who cannot afford to buy a property from their own resources need to get a mortgage from a building society or bank.
- Houses/apartments should be viewed and in the case of a second-hand house or apartment, a survey should be carried out to ensure that it is structurally sound.
- If the person is satisfied that they have found a property they wish to buy, they should make an offer, if the property is for sale by private treaty. If the property is for sale by auction, they must attend the auction and the highest bidder purchases the property.
- Generally, estate agents do not charge a fee to purchasers of property.
- The purchase of property can be complicated, and prospective buyers should always engage a solicitor to act for them.

8.2.2.4 What laws govern discrimination in the provision of accommodation?

The *Equal Status Act*, 2000, prohibits discrimination on the grounds of gender, marital status, family status, sexual orientation, religious belief, age, disability, "race" and membership of the Traveller Community in the provision of goods and services, the disposal of property and access to education. Discrimination on the nine grounds listed in the Act is prohibited in both the public and private sectors. The process for referring complaints is similar to that under the *Employment Equality Act*, 1998. Further information is available from the equality tribunal.[47]

8.2.3 What medical services are family members of migrants and Irish nationals entitled to?

Family members of migrants and Irish nationals, legally resident in Ireland, have two options with regard to medical care:

- public health care
- private health care

---

a *The Aliens Act*, 1935 states that "Real and personal property of every description in Saorstat Eireann or subject to the law of Saorstat Eireann may be taken, acquired, held and disposed of by an alien in like manner and to the like extend as such property may be taken, acquired, held or disposed of by a citizen of Saorstat Eireann".

b These restrictions apply to non-EU nationals wishing to buy land over five acres in size. They should contact the Department of Agriculture, Food and Rural Development, Agriculture House, Kildare Street, Dublin 2, telephone (01) 607 2000, Lo-call 1890 200 510.

8.2.3.1 Public health care

The public health care system, including primary and hospital services, can be accessed by any person resident in Ireland including those who are family members of migrants and Irish nationals. This system can be accessed for a nominal charge, or free of charge for medical card holders.

8.2.3.1.1 What services can be accessed for a nominal charge?

A range of services are available including the following:

- General Practitioner (GP) services (family doctor) with a charge of between €30 and €50 per consultation
- in-patient hospital treatment in a public ward subject to a daily charge of €40[a]
- all other out-patient services including consultants
- visits to hospital Accident and Emergency Departments subject to a charge of €40 (persons who are referred by their GP will not be charged)
- maternity and infant care

Generally, to get free medical care in Ireland a person needs a medical card.

8.2.3.1.2 Who is entitled to a medical card?

If the migrant, or Irish person, whom they are accompanying, is eligible for the medical card, the family member(s) will, in general, be eligible.

Entitlement to a medical card in Ireland is based on a person's residence and means. To be fully eligible for a medical card a person must:

- be 'ordinarily resident' in Ireland; this means that they must intend to live in Ireland for at least one year and be permitted to do so.
- satisfy the means test; a person will only be eligible for free medical care (Category A entitlement, that is medical card holders) if their gross income, less PRSI contributions is less than €138 and in the case of a married couple or single parent €200.[b]

8.2.3.1.3 What does a medical card entitle you to?

A medical card entitles you to the following free medical services:

- General Practitioner (GP) services but you must register with a GP (see Section 8.2.3.1.4)
- prescribed medicines
- in-patient hospital treatment in a public ward

---

a Up to a maximum of €400 in any twelve-month period (as of 1 January 2003).

b A married couple or a single parent must earn less than €200. These rates apply to persons under 66 years of age. Persons applying for the medical card are permitted to have the following amounts over the income level and still qualify for the medical card, as of 1 January 2003:
  - €25 for each child under 16 years of age
  - €26 for each child over 16 years of age with no income maintained by applicant
  - the amount by which the rent or mortgage paid each week exceeds €25
  - the amount by which the costs of travelling to and from work each week exceeds €22
  - weekly expenditure on medicines

- out-patient hospital treatment
- dental, ophthalmic and aural services
- community care services

8.2.3.1.4 Registering with a General Practitioner (GP)

Persons who qualify for the medical card must register with a General Practitioner (family doctor). Not all GPs accept medical card patients, so the medical card holder should obtain a list of doctors in their area who accept medical card patients:

- They can obtain this list from the local health board offices and health centre together with a registration form, which the doctor will be required to sign.
- General practitioners are only permitted to accept a certain number of medical card patients. Therefore, they will sometimes refuse to accept any further patients.
- If a person is unable to find a doctor who will accept them as a patient under the medical card scheme, one will be assigned to them by the health board office or health centre.

8.2.3.1.5 Applying for a medical card

Persons who wish to apply for a medical card should submit a completed application form, together with evidence that they are 'ordinarily resident' in Ireland and that they satisfy the means test, to their local health board offices or health centre.

8.2.3.2 Private health care

Persons can also take out private health insurance.[a] This insurance covers private care in public or private hospitals. There are two private health insurers in Ireland, VHI and BUPA.[48] Medical insurance will not cover pre-existing medical conditions and the cover may not, in any event, take effect for an initial period.

8.2.4 What social welfare entitlements do family members of migrants and Irish nationals have?

Irish social welfare legislation does not distinguish between nationals and non-nationals. Essentially, any person from outside the State who complies with the relevant laws covering entry, living and working here is entitled to seek social welfare payments in compliance with the normal conditions. For further information, contact the Information Service of the Department of Social and Family Affairs on (01) 704 3000.

8.2.5 What education are family members of migrants and Irish nationals entitled to?

8.2.5.1 EEA and Swiss nationals

8.2.5.1.1 EU nationals

All EU citizens are entitled to equal treatment in the educational sector in Ireland on the same basis as Irish citizens. Thus for example, migrant EU students are

---

a Persons who wish to avail of private health care and who have not taken out private health insurance will be required to pay for hospital treatment.

entitled to the same fee level (or none as the case may be) and maintenance grants as national students.[49]

8.2.5.1.2 EEA and Swiss nationals

EEA and Swiss nationals are generally entitled to education on the same basis as Irish nationals. However, EEA nationals (other than those belonging to the EU and Swiss nationals are not entitled to local authority/VEC education grants. Third-level education fees vary between educational institutions. Employees are also entitled to 'training in vocational schools and retraining centres'.[50]

8.2.5.2 Non-EEA and Swiss nationals

Non-EEA/Swiss national family members who are non-economically active, are entitled to access education on the same basis as their partner as long as the relationship is valid.

8.2.5.3 Children of family members of migrants and Irish nationals

All children and young people under the age of 18 in Ireland have the same rights irrespective of the child's or parent's/parents' or legal caregivers' race, colour, sex, language, religion, political or other opinion, national, ethnic or social origin, property, disability, birth or other status.[51] Children of non-EEA nationals can therefore access services on the same basis as an Irish child. Children of non-EEA nationals are registered on their parent's/parents' or legal caregivers' Certificate of Registration until the age of 16. However, children's birth certificates are usually required for identification and other purposes. Thereafter, they must register themselves, in their own name, with the registration officer in the area where reside. The local registration officer is a member of the Gardaí. Applicants should inquire at their local Garda station for the location of the registration officer for the area in which they reside. In Dublin, this is the Garda National Immigration Bureau.

All children and young people in Ireland must engage in full-time education until they are 16 years old. At first and second level, there are two main education sectors: primary school (first level), and post-primary and vocational training (second level).

Schools are managed by the State (Comprehensive, Vocational Education Committees [VECs]) and religious bodies (Catholic, Protestant, Muslim, Jewish) and governed by their own ethos/philosophy. Lists of schools are available from the Department of Education and Science.[52]

Children with language needs are generally placed in classes with other children/young people of a similar age. Government support is provided to allow schools to offer limited language support programmes for bilingual and multilingual children. To apply to a school or education centre parents or legal caregivers can follow the process below:

- The parents/legal caregivers contact the local school/education centre of choice by writing or telephoning the school principal or manager to arrange a meeting.
- At the first meeting, the parents/legal caregivers are provided with the formal school/education centre policy which outlines the ethos, selection criteria and other matters.

- The parents/legal caregivers are required to provide the school/education centre with basic information on the student.

- An informal education and linguistic assessment of the student may take place but there is no State interpretation facility for this process. Schools/education centres cannot refuse access to a student on the basis of their level of English.

- If there are no places, or if the school/education centre is unsuitable for the student, the school/education centre recommends another school/education centre in the locality.

- If the student is offered a place in a school, the parents/legal caregivers should obtain a letter of acceptance from the school/education centre.

8.2.6 How can family members of migrants and Irish nationals acquire Irish citizenship?

Family members of migrants and Irish nationals in Ireland can become Irish citizens in three ways:

- naturalisation

- post-nuptial citizenship

- descent

The *Irish Nationality and Citizenship Acts* 1956, 1986, 1994 and 2001 set out the criteria under which Irish citizenship is granted.

8.2.6.1 Acquiring citizenship by naturalisation

A person wishing to apply for a certificate of naturalisation must fulfil certain conditions including having legally resided in Ireland for five years out of the previous nine-year period. The Minister for Justice, Equality & Law Reform may grant an application for a certificate of naturalisation at their discretion if they are satisfied that the applicant:

- is of full age

- is of good character

- has had a period of one year's continuous residence in Ireland immediately prior to their application, and in the eight years immediately preceding that period has had a total residence of four years in Ireland

- intends in good faith to continue to reside in Ireland after naturalisation

- has made a declaration of fidelity to the nation and loyalty to the State, either before a District Court Justice or in such other manner permitted by the Minister

The Minister for Justice, Equality & Law Reform may waive these conditions in certain circumstances specified in the Acts. The number of circumstances in which the Minister may waive the conditions, has been reduced by the 2001, Act.[a]

---

a *Irish Nationality and Citizenship Act* 1956, Section 16 (as amended by *Irish Nationality and Citizenship Act*, 1986, Section 5). Since the coming into force of the 2001 Act, this no longer applies to persons married to a naturalised Irish citizen or persons married to a person who is an Irish citizen otherwise than by naturalisation.

8.2.6.2 Acquiring post-nuptial citizenship

A non-national who married an Irish national on or before 29 November 2002, and has been in a subsisting marriage with that person for a minimum of three years, may become an Irish citizen by making a post-nuptial declaration of citizenship. However, this is not possible if the Irish spouse has acquired citizenship by naturalisation, post-nuptial declaration, or was granted citizenship as a token of honour. Any such declarations will have to be made before 30 November 2005.

In the case of spouses of Irish nationals who got married on or after 30 November, 2002, the Minister may at his 'absolute discretion' grant an application for a certificate of naturalisation to the spouse of an Irish citizen if the applicant:

- is of full age
- is of good character
- is married to an Irish citizen for at least three years
- is in a subsisting marriage, recognised as being in accordance with Irish legislation
- is living together with the Irish citizen as husband and wife (the applicant must submit an affidavit to that effect to the Minister)
- has lived in Ireland for at least one year continuously prior to the application
- has been resident in Ireland for at least two years of the four years immediately preceding that period
- intends in good faith to continue to reside in Ireland after naturalisation
- has made a declaration of 'fidelity to the nation and loyalty to the State' in whatever manner may be prescribed[53]

The Minister for Justice, Equality & Law Reform may waive certain of the above conditions if satisfied that the applicant would suffer serious consequences in respect of his or her bodily integrity or liberty if not granted Irish citizenship.[54]

8.2.6.3 Acquiring citizenship by descent

Persons whose father or mother was an Irish Citizen at the time of their birth are automatically Irish citizens. However, if a person is born outside Ireland, and the parent through whom they are claiming citizenship was also born outside Ireland, they will not be entitled to citizenship except in certain limited circumstances.[55] Persons whose grandparents were Irish citizens can become Irish citizens by registering in the Foreign Births Register in the Department of Foreign Affairs or, if residing outside Ireland, at the nearest Irish Embassy or Consulate.

8.2.6.4 Acquiring permission to remain without condition as to time

Persons who have been legally resident in Ireland for ten years and who have not applied for naturalisation may obtain a residence stamp giving them 'permission to remain without condition as to time'.[56]

8.2.7 What do family members of migrants and Irish nationals need to open a bank account?

Banks require new customers to produce the following documents when opening a bank account:

- photo identification (a passport satisfies this requirement)

- proof of address in Ireland, for example a utility bill (electricity, gas or other utility) or lease agreement

- although not officially documented as a requirement, banks often request applicants to provide a personal introduction from an existing customer

8.2.8 Can family members of migrants and Irish nationals vote in elections?

Non-national residents in Ireland over 18 years old may vote in some elections:

Citizens of...	Permitted to vote at...
The UK	Dáil, European and local elections
EU states apart from the UK	European and local elections
Non-EU states	Local elections only

Those permitted to vote must have their name included in the Electoral Register if they want to vote. Application forms are available in post offices, libraries and council and corporation offices.

Endnotes

1   Ingoldsby, Brian *Regular Migration* to Ireland paper delivered at the Incorporated Law Society Seminar: 'Rights to Reside in Ireland' 14 May 2002, at Blackhall Place, Dublin p. 5.

2   Council Directive 90/336 (later replaced by Council Directive 93/96) on *Migrant Students* [1993] OJ L317/59; Council Directive 90/365 *Employed and Self-employed people who have Ceased to Work* [1990] OJ L180/28; Directive 90/364 [1990] OJ L180/26.

3   Case C-413/99 *Baumbast,* 17 September 2002.

4   Proposal for a European Parliament and Council Directive 29 June 2001 on the *Right of Citizens of the Union and their Family Members to Move and Reside Freely within the Territory of the Member States* COM(2001) 257 final [2001] OJ C270 E/23.

5   Case C-85/96 *Maria Martinez Sala v Freistaat Bayern* [1998] ECR I-2691.

6   *Ibid.*

7   *European Communities (Right of Residence for Non-economically Active Persons) Regulations* 1997, Regulation 2(1).

8   *Ibid,* Regulation 7 (1)(b).

9   *Ibid,* Regulation 2 (1).

10 *Ibid,* Regulations 7 (1)(a)(iii).

11 *Ibid,* Regulation 6 (2).

12 *European Communities (Aliens) Regulations* 1977, Regulation 2 (2).

13 Ingoldsby, Brian *Regular Migration to Ireland* paper delivered at the Incorporated Law Society Seminar: 'Rights to Reside in Ireland' 14 May 2002, at Blackhall Place, Dublin p. 5.

14 *Refugee Act* 1996, Section 18(1).

15 *Ibid,* Section 3.

16 Department of Social and Family Affairs, Gandon House, Amiens Street, Dublin 1, telephone
(01) 874 8444, website *http://www.welfare.ie/* The Department's leaflet SW100 P*ersonal Public Service Number*
provides additional information on obtaining a PPS.

17 Further information may be obtained on Revenue Publication RES 2 *Coming to Live in Ireland*
http://www.revenue.ie/

18 *Terms of Employment (Information) Act* 1994.

19 *National Minimum Wages Act* 2000.

20 This is provided for in the *National Minimum Wages Act* 2000, Section 15(1):

   "Subject to subsection (2) and Sections 16, 17 and 18, a person who:

   (a) enters employment for the first time after attaining the age of 18 years or

   (b) having entered into employment before attaining the age of 18 years, continues in employment on attaining that age

   shall be remunerated by his or her employer in respect of his or her working hours in any pay reference period at
an hourly rate of pay that on average is not less than :

   (i) in the case of an employee commencing employment for the first time after attaining the age of 18 years:

      (I) in his or her first year after commenced employment, 80% and

      (II) in his or her second year after having commenced employment, 90%

   (ii) in the case if an employee having entered into employment before attaining the age of 18 years and continuing
in employment on attaining that age

      (I) in his or her first year after having attained the age of 18 years, 80%

      (II) in his or her second year after having attained that age, 90%

   of the national minimum hourly rate of pay, notwithstanding that the employee, if he or she has changed his or
her employer during the relevant period, may have been remunerated at a higher rate by the previous employer."

21 *Payment of Wages Act* 1991

22 *Organisation of Working Time Act* 1997, Section 19.

23 *Ibid,* Section 14(1).

24 *Ibid,* Section 8.

25 *Ibid,* Section 9(1)(a) and (b).

26 *Ibid,* Section 10.

27 *Ibid,* Section 26.

28 *Parental Leave Act* 1998 Section 7 (1).

29 *Ibid,* Section 19 (3)(c).

30 *Ibid,* Section 13 (1).

31 *Ibid,* Section 13 (2).

32 *Ibid,* Section 13 (4).

33 *Ibid,* Section 13 (1).

34 This form may be downloaded from the Labour Relations Commission website
www.lrc.ie/rc_services/rights_commissioner.htm or can be obtained from the Secretariat, Rights Commissioner
Service, Labour Relations Commission, Tom Johnson House, Haddington Road, Dublin 4, telephone: (01) 613 6700.

35 Minimum notice is provided for in the *Minimum Notice and Terms of Employment Act* 1973, as amended by the
Work Protection (Regular Part-Time Employees) Act 1991.

36 According to the *Employment Equality Act* 1998,Section 2(1), (dealing with interpretation), 'marital status' means
"single, married, separated, divorced and widowed".

37 'Family status' is described in Section 2(1) of the Act as "responsibility

   (a) as a parent or as a person in loco parentis in relation to a person who has not attained the age of 18 years, or

   (b) as a parent or the resident primary carer in relation to a person of or over that age with a disability which is of
such a nature as to give rise to the need for care or support on a continuing, regular or frequent basis".

38 Discrimination on the basis of 'race' is described in the *Employment Equality Act* 1998, Section 6 (2)(h) as
"between any two persons that are of a different 'race', 'colour', nationality or ethnic or national origins".

39 'Religious belief' as defined in the *Employment Equality Act* 1998, includes religious background or outlook.

40 The *Employment Equality Act* 1998, Section 2(1) defines 'sexual orientation' as meaning "heterosexual,
homosexual or bisexual orientation".

41 'Disability' is defined in the *Employment Equality Act* 1998, Section 2(1) as:

"(a) the total or partial absence of a person's bodily or mental functions, including the absence of a part of the person's body,

(b) the presence in the body of organisms causing, or likely to cause, chronic disease or illness,

(c) the malfunction, malformation or disfigurement of a part of a person's body,

(d) a condition or malfunction which results in a person learning differently from a person without the condition or malfunction, or

(e) a condition, illness or disease which affects a person's thought processes, perception of reality, emotions or judgement which results in disturbed behaviour,

and shall be taken to include a disability which exists at present, or which previously existed but no longer exists, or which may exist in the future or which is imputed to a person".

42 *Employment Equality Act* 1998,Section 8(1).

43 The Equality Authority may be contacted at 2, Clonmel Street, Dublin 2, telephone (01) 417 3333, fax (01) 417 3366, email *info@equality.ie*

44 The respondent must also use the form provided by the ODEI - the equality tribunal to reply (Form ODEI 4). If the correct forms are not used, the provisions in the *Employment Equality Act* 1998, permitting the director to draw inferences from failure to supply information, do not apply.

45 *http://www.labourcourt.ie/labour/labour.nsf/LookupPageLink/formsDownload*

46 Details of these can be obtained from Threshold, 21 Stoneybatter, Dublin 7, email advice@threshold.ie.

47 Further information is available from the ODEI - the equality tribunal, 3 Clonmel Street, Dublin 2, telephone (01) 477 4100, website *http://www.odei.ie/*

48 Voluntary Health Insurance (VHI), VHI House, Lower Abbey Street, Dublin 1, telephone (01) 874 4499, Lo-call 1850 444 444.

BUPA Ireland, Mill Island, Fermoy, Co. Cork, telephone (021) 42121, or 12 Fitzwilliam Square, Dublin 2, telephone (01) 6627 662, Lo-call 1890 700 890.

49 Case C-184/99 *Grzelczyk v CPAS* [2001] ECR I-6193.

50 Council Regulation 68/1612/EEC, 15 October 1968, on *Freedom of Movement for Workers within the Community* (as amended by Regulations 312/76, Article 7.3).

51 Refer to the *International Convention on the Rights of the Child* 1989, Article 2(1), signed by Ireland, 30 September 1990 and ratified 28 September 1992.

52 Department of Education and Science, Marlborough Street, Dublin 1, telephone (01) 873 4700, website *http://www.education.ie/*

53 *Irish Nationality and Citizenship Act* 1956, Section 15A (1), as amended by the *Irish Nationality and Citizenship Act* 2001, Section 5.

54 *Irish Nationality and Citizenship Act* 1956, Section 15A (2), as amended by the *Irish Nationality and Citizenship Act* 2001, Section 5.

55 *Irish Nationality and Citizenship Act* 1956, Section 7 (3), as amended by the *Irish Nationality and Citizenship Act* 2001, Section 5.

56 Further information available on the Department of Justice, Equality & Law Reform website *http://www.justice.ie/*

Persons Residing in the State without Permission

PERSONS RESIDING IN THE STATE WITHOUT PERMISSION

There is little concrete information in Ireland, or globally, on illegal immigration due to its clandestine nature, but it is generally agreed that the following constitute the main categories of undocumented migrants:

- Persons who have entered the host State, without authorisation, and are residing there illegally, but have not yet come to the attention of the authorities. They may be living in the host State voluntarily or may have been trafficked for the purposes of prostitution, or other purposes, and may not be in a position to leave without the assistance of State authorities or voluntary organisations.

- Persons who have entered the host State legally, for example, as tourists or students, and continue to reside there after their permit has expired, but who have not yet come to the attention of the authorities.

- Former asylum seekers and persons who have applied for other forms of international protection, who have not been found to be in need of protection. Such persons will have had a final negative decision regarding their application and may be subject to a deportation order.

Non-EEA and Swiss nationals who are residing in Ireland without authorisation are liable to be deported from the State.

An EEA and Swiss national may be required to leave the State if they have been refused a residence permit, if they have refused to apply for a residence permit or to undergo a medical examination after having been required to do so, or if their conduct or activities are such that it would be contrary to public policy, or it would endanger public security or health to permit the person to stay in the State.

9.1   On what Grounds Can the Minister Propose to Make a Deportation Order?

Section 3 of the *Immigration Act* 1999, permits the Minister for Justice, Equality & Law Reform to order certain non-nationals to leave the State. The Minister may make a deportation order in respect of the following:

- a person who has served or is serving a term of imprisonment imposed by a court of the State

- a person whose deportation was recommended by a court in the State before which a person was indicted for or charged with any crime or offence

- a person who has been required to leave the State under Regulation 14 of the *European Communities (Aliens) Regulations*, 1977

- a person to whom Regulation 19 of the *European Communities (Right of Residence for Non-Economically Active Persons) Regulations* 1997 applies

- a person whose application for refugee status has been transferred to another country under the Dublin Convention

- a person whose application for asylum has been refused by the Minister

- a person to whom leave to land in the State has been refused

- a person who has contravened a restriction imposed on him/her in respect of landing in or entering into or leave to stay in the State

- a person whose deportation would be conducive to the common good in the opinion of the Minister

9.2 *Responding to Notification that the Minister Proposes to Make a Deportation Order*

Persons who are notified in writing that the Minister proposes to make a deportation order may:

- make representations in writing to the Minister within 15 working days (from   the date of the letter) setting out the reasons why they should be allowed to remain in the State

- leave Ireland voluntarily (if the person agrees to leave voluntarily, they must inform the Minister of their travel arrangements)

- consent to the making of a deportation order

9.2.1 *Making representations to the Minister*

Before deciding the matter, the Minister will take into consideration any representations duly made to him/her under Section 3 (6) of the *Immigration Act*, 1999 as amended in relation to the proposal to make a deportation order.[1]

- Persons should make representations in writing to the Minister.

- It is advisable to avail of legal advice and representation, particularly in cases where the person may fear torture, inhuman or degrading treatment if returned to his/her country of origin. In such cases, Ireland's commitments under international law, in particular the *European Convention on Human Rights* and the *International Covenant on Civil and Political Rights* may be relevant.

- The person's reasons for wishing to remain in the State should be set out fully and any supporting evidence should be included.

- Representations on behalf of the person may be made by others who wish to support the person's application for permission to remain.

Section 3 (6)(a) of the *Immigration Act*, 1999 lists certain matters to which the Minister for Justice, Equality & Law Reform shall have regard in determining whether to make a deportation order. These are as follows:

- the age of the person

- the duration of residence in the State of the person

- the family and domestic circumstances of the person

- the nature of the person's connection with the State, if any

- the employment (including self-employment) record of the person

- the employment (including self-employment) prospects of the person

- the character and conduct of the person both within and (where relevant and ascertainable) outside the State (including any criminal convictions)

- humanitarian considerations

- any representations made by or on behalf of the person
- the common good
- considerations of national security and public policy

If the Minister considers that the person should not be deported, the person will be granted leave to remain in Ireland usually for a period of one year, which may be renewed.

Persons who have been granted leave to remain in Ireland must obtain a Certificate of Registration from their local registration officer. They must bring with them the letter informing them that they have been granted leave to remain. In addition, they should also bring a passport or other identity document.

Persons granted leave to remain will have to apply for the renewal of their Certificate of Registration thirty days in advance of the expiry date. They should report to their local registration officer to apply for the renewal. The local registration officer is a member of the Gardaí. Applicants should inquire at their local Garda station for the location of the registration officer for the area in which they reside. In Dublin, this is the Garda National Immigration Bureau. They may be required to make representations to the Minister for Justice, Equality & Law Reform providing details of their current situation in the State. Documentation that is normally required is evidence of employment/college attendance and evidence of financial circumstances. It is also recommended that information regarding the reasons for the person's unwillingness to return to their country of origin be updated at this point.

9.2.2 Leaving Ireland voluntarily

A person who decides to return to their country of origin or former habitual residence should inform the Repatriation Unit of the Immigration Division of the Department of Justice, Equality & Law Reform[a] of their intention. The Department will then seek to facilitate the person's departure from the State and make a record of their departure. Doing this ensures that if the person makes an application to come to Ireland at any time in the future, their prior presence in the State will not negatively affect the assessment of their visa application and/or application for leave to enter the State.

Generally, an appointment with a Department official will be made for the necessary arrangements to be put in place. The Department of Justice, Equality & Law Reform requires persons arranging their own voluntary departure to:

- withdraw any pending applications for residence permits before beginning the voluntary procedure
- journey by air
- buy a one-way ticket to their country of return (should a return ticket be bought, the Department of Justice, Equality & Law Reform will retain the return stubs)
- avoid transiting via the UK or any other country for which they do not have transit permission; they must verify that any State through which they intend

a The phone number for the Repatriation Unit of the Immigration Division of the Department of Justice, Equality & Law Reform is (01) 616 7700#5#1.

to transit will allow them to embark for their connecting flight (this can be verified by enquiring at the relevant Embassy in Dublin/London); the obligation is on the returnee to confirm and conform with such requirements

- give the Department of Justice, Equality & Law Reform at least five days notice of their flight

- show their tickets, or travel agent's receipt of payment with the flight details to the Department of Justice, Equality & Law Reform

- allow their passport to be retained by the Department of Justice, Equality & Law Reform until the day of their flight; the passport will be transmitted to the Airport before the flight

- arrive at the airport at least two hours before check-in time and go to the information desk on the ground floor and ask for an Information Officer; this officer will return their passport before they board the flight and will supervise their departure

- ensure the journey is finalised within a 24-hour period

The International Organisation for Migration (IOM) is an inter-governmental, yet independent organisation, with offices in over 120 countries worldwide. IOM works with governments and project partners to uphold the rights of migrants. The IOM Dublin office currently provides Voluntary Assisted Return Programmes, which aim to assist asylum seekers and irregular migrants who wish to return home but may not have the means or the necessary documentation to do so. IOM has, to date, assisted people to return to almost thirty countries of origin. For nationals of the CIS countries (these include all the former Soviet States, with the exception of the Baltic States), IOM's Voluntary Assisted Return and Reintegration Programme can provide reintegration assistance for returnees in their home country, facilitating sustainable return.[2]

9.2.3 *Consenting to deportation*

A person who consents to the making of a deportation order must to do so in writing by signing a consent form. If the Minister for Justice, Equality & Law Reform is satisfied that the person understands the consequences of their consent, s/he will issue a deportation order in respect of the person without further notice being required.[3] The Minister for Justice, Equality & Law Reform in co-operation with the person and the Garda National Immigration Bureau will then proceed to arrange for the removal of the person as soon as is practicable.

A person in respect of whom a deportation order has been issued, will generally not be permitted to return to Ireland once they have been deported unless the deportation order is revoked prior to the person's application for permission to return (visa application/application for leave to enter the State).[a]

Where a person who has consented in writing to the making of a deportation order is not deported within three months from the making of the order, the order shall cease to have effect.

---

a The *Immigration Act*, 1999 (as amended), Section 3 (1) provides that "the Minister may by order require any non-national specified in the order to leave the State within such period as may be specified in the order and to remain thereafter out of the State".

Persons in respect of whom a deportation order has been made, by the Minister, may be detained in order to ensure their deportation.[a]

Persons who are the subject of a deportation order may be required to comply with the following in order to ensure their deportation:[4]

- present themselves to a Garda, or Immigration Officer, at a date, time and place specified in the notice informing the person of the decision to issue a deportation order

- produce any travel document, passport, travel ticket or other document which may be required for the purpose of his/her deportation

- co-operate with Gardaí, or Immigration Officers, in order to obtain a travel document, passport, travel ticket or other document required for the purpose of the deportation

- reside, or remain, in a particular district or place in the State pending removal from the State

- report to a specified Garda Station, or Immigration Officer, at specified intervals pending deportation

- notify the Gardaí, or Immigration Officers, of any change of address

If a Garda, or Immigration Officer, 'with reasonable cause suspects' that a person who is the subject of a deportation order:

- has failed to comply with any provisions of the deportation order, or with a requirement in a notice informing the person of the decision to issue a deportation order;

- intends to leave the State and enter another State without permission;

- has destroyed their identity documents;

- is in possession of forged identity documents; or

- intends to avoid removal from the State;[5]

they may arrest the person without warrant and detain them in a prescribed place.[b]

If the Minister decides not to make a deportation order, the person will be granted leave to remain, usually for a period of one year initially.[c]

9.2.4 Challenging the deportation process

The validity of a notification of the Minister's intention to make a deportation order, the notification of the making of a deportation order, and of the deportation order itself, can only be questioned by way of an application seeking leave for judicial review.[6]

---

a *The Immigration Act,* 1999, Section 3 (1A) as amended by the Illegal Immigrants (Trafficking) Act, 2000, Section 10 (a)(i).

b The 'prescribed places' for the detention of persons awaiting deportation are as follows: Castlerea Prison; Central Mental Hospital; Cloverhill Prison; Cork Prison; Limerick Prison; Midland Prison; Mountjoy Prison; St Patrick's Institution; The Training Unit, Glengarriff Parade; and Wheatfield Prison. Immigration Act 1999 (Deportation) Regulations, 2000 SI No. 103 of 2002.

c See Chapter 7.

Section 5 (2)(a) of the *Illegal Immigrants Trafficking Act*, 2000, states that:

> *an application for leave to apply for judicial review in these cases, shall be made within the period of 14 days, commencing on the date on which the person was notified of the decision,...or making of the Order concerned, unless the High Court considers that there is good and sufficient reason for extending the period within which the application shall be made.*

If the High Court refuses an application for leave, this decision may not be appealed to the Supreme Court except with the leave of the High Court.[a]

9.3 *Regularisation*

There are very few avenues open to persons residing without authorisation in the State to regularise their status. Unlike many EU States, there is no provision in Irish legislation for undocumented persons to apply for regularisation.

9.3.1 *Leave to remain*

Leave to remain may be granted pursuant to Section 3(6) of the *Immigration Act*, 1999, at the discretion of the Minister for Justice, Equality & Law Reform, to persons in respect of whom the making of a deportation order has been proposed, after they have unsuccessfully applied for permission to remain in the State, but who may not be returned to their country of origin, due to war or some other compelling reason.[7]

a According to the *Illegal Immigrants (Trafficking) Act* 2000, Section 5 (3)(a), leave shall only be granted where a 'point of law of exceptional public importance' is involved and where it is desirable in the public interest that an appeal should be taken to the Supreme Court.

Endnotes

1 *Immigration Act* 1999 (as amended), Section 3 (3)(b)(i).

2 The IOM is located at 9 Marlborough Court, Marlborough Street, Dublin 1 telephone 01-878 7900, e-mail *varp@iomdublin.org*

3 *Immigration Act* 1999 (as amended), Section 3 (5)(a).

4 *Immigration Act* 1999 Section 3 (9)(a)(i), as amended by the *Illegal Immigrants (Trafficking) Act* 2000.

5 *Immigration Act* 1999 Section 5 (1) as amended by the Illegal Immigrants (Trafficking) Act 2000.

6 *Illegal Immigrants (Trafficking) Act* 2000,Section 5 (1)(a), (b) and (c).

7 See Section 6.1.

Visitors

VISITORS

Each year thousands of persons come to Ireland on a short-term basis as tourists and other visitors. The rights and entitlements of persons who come to Ireland on a short-term basis, and the rules regarding their entry to the State, are dependent mainly on whether they are EEA or Swiss nationals.

10.1 EEA and Swiss Nationals

10.1.1 EU nationals

The status of Citizenship of the Union was introduced by the Treaty of Maastricht (1992). Article 17 of the *EC Treaty*[a] states:

> *Citizenship of the Union is hereby established. Every person holding the nationality of a Member State shall be a citizen of the Union. Citizenship of the Union shall complement and not replace national citizenship.*
>
> *Citizens of the Union shall enjoy the rights conferred by this Treaty and shall be subject to the duties imposed thereby.*

Article 18(1) of the *EC Treaty* states:

> *Every Citizen of the Union shall have the right to move and reside freely within the territory of the Member States, subject to the limitations and conditions laid down by this Treaty and by the measures adopted to give it effect.*

The right to move and reside referred to in Article 18(1) may be subject to limits and conditions. For non-economically active migrants, these conditions include various financial conditions and are set out in a series of Community Directives.[1] However, the competent authorities and, where necessary, the national courts must ensure that these limitations and conditions are applied in compliance with the general principles of Community law and, in particular, the principle of proportionality.[2]

The Commission has proposed replacing these Directives with a general all-embracing Directive to deal with Citizens' migration rights, but this not been adopted yet.[3] However, it is clear that the effect of Article 18(1) is such that once a Citizen of the Union is lawfully resident in the territory of another Member State, they are entitled to equal treatment with nationals of that State in most circumstances. For example, regarding welfare rights, equal treatment extends to all EU migrants, regardless of whether they are workers, service providers or simply visitors, provided they are lawfully resident.[4] Regarding political rights, Citizens of the Union have the right to vote and stand in both municipal and European elections, when resident in another Member State.

10.1.2 EEA nationals

In 1994, the European Economic Area Agreement was signed between the European Union and Norway, Iceland and Liechtenstein. Nationals of these states enjoy certain rights within the EU. EEA nationals do not need a visa to enter Ireland to take up employment or for any other purpose.

---

a Unless otherwise stated, all references to the *EC Treaty* refer to the *EC Treaty* as amended by the Treaties of Amsterdam and Nice.

10.1.3 *Swiss nationals*

The *European Communities and Swiss Confederation Act*, 2001, came into force in June 2002. As a result, Swiss nationals now have the same rights as EEA nationals in Ireland. EEA and Swiss nationals do not need a visa to enter Ireland to take up employment or for any other purpose.

10.2 *Non-EEA and Swiss Nationals*

Non-EEA and Swiss nationals may come to Ireland on a short-term basis. They are required to comply with immigration formalities including obtaining a visa if they are nationals of states whose citizens are required to possess a visa in order to travel to Ireland.

10.3 *Applying for Visas*

Persons coming to Ireland as visitors and who are nationals of a state whose passport holders require a visa in order to travel to Ireland, must obtain a visa.[a] Applications can be made:

- through the Irish Embassy/Consulate in the applicant's country of residence
- through any Irish Embassy or Consulate if there is none in the applicant's country of residence
- by post, directly to the Visa Office, Department of Foreign Affairs, 13/14 Burgh Quay, Dublin 2, if there is no Irish Embassy or Consulate in the applicant's country of residence

Applicants must include the following documentation with their application:

- a completed visa application form
- evidence of their stay in Ireland and their intention/obligation to return
- a valid passport (or a full copy of the passport if the application is being made by post, or directly to the Department of Foreign Affairs)
- the visa application fee[b]
- two passport photographs of the applicant

If insufficient information is provided, the applicant may be asked to furnish the required information. However, some applications may be refused without any further information being sought.

If a person travels to Ireland to visit a particular person or family, the applicant will be asked to provide the name of the contact person in Ireland, who may be asked to supply further information.

---

a Under the provisions of the *Aliens (Visas) Order* 2002 (SI No. 178 of 2002), certain non-nationals are not required to possess a visa to travel to Ireland. Persons from states not listed are required to have a visa (see Appendix A).

b Visa application processing fees are currently: €25 for a single journey and €50 for a multiple entry visa. Citizens of the following countries are exempt for the visa application fee: Bosnia, Bulgaria, Ecuador, Indonesia, Ivory Coast, Kirghizstan, Morocco, Peru, Slovak Republic, Sri Lanka, Tanzania, Tunisia, Uganda, Yugoslavia and Zambia (as of 1 January 2002).

10.4 Appealing Visa Applications that Have Been Refused

A person whose application for a visa has been refused may apply to the Visa Section of the Department of Justice, Equality & Law Reform to have the application reviewed by a more senior official. Before doing so, they should request the reasons for the initial refusal of the visa application; these are not automatically provided but in most cases contain important information relevant to the appeal.

10.5 Registering with the (Garda) Registration Officer

10.5.1 EEA and Swiss nationals

EEA and Swiss nationals visiting Ireland are permitted to remain in Ireland without being required to register with the Gardaí. However, if persons intend to remain in Ireland for more than three months, it is recommended that they apply for a residence permit. An application for a residence permit should be made to the local registration officer who is a member of the Gardaí. Applicants should inquire at their local Garda station for the location of the registration officer for the area in which they reside. In Dublin, this is the Garda National Immigration Bureau. (Spouses and dependents of EEA and Swiss nationals are permitted to reside in Ireland for the duration of the residence permit.)

10.5.2 Non-EEA and Swiss nationals

Non-EEA/Swiss nationals who are nationals of states whose passport holders are required to possess a visa in order to travel to Ireland must be in possession of a valid visa on arrival. At point of entry, permission to remain is normally granted for an initial period of one month even if the validity of the visa extends beyond this. Non-EEA and Swiss nationals are permitted to remain in Ireland for a maximum period of three months without being required to register with the Garda registration officer. However, they must satisfy Immigration Officers at the port or airport of entry that they have sufficient funds to support themselves during their stay and that they do not intend to contravene Irish immigration laws.

If non-EEA and Swiss nationals wish to remain in Ireland longer than three months they must obtain the permission of the Minister for Justice Equality & Law Reform. An applicant will be required to state the proposed length of their stay in Ireland and to demonstrate that they have sufficient funds for the duration of the stay. Permission may be obtained from the registration officer in the area where the person resides. The local registration officer is a member of the Gardaí. Applicants should inquire at their local Garda station for the location of the registration officer for the area in which they reside. In Dublin, this is the Garda National Immigration Bureau.

The person is then issued with a Certificate of Registration by the registration officer. The Certificate of Registration contains a photograph of the holder and states the duration of their permission to remain in Ireland. It also contains a stamp,[a] the number of which indicates the basis on which the Certificate of Registration was provided.

a See Appendix D.

10.6 What Rights and Entitlements Do Visitors Have?

10.6.1 Are visitors entitled to work?

10.6.1.1 EEA and Swiss nationals

EEA and Swiss nationals may take up work while in Ireland as a visitor. In this case, the *European Communities (Aliens) Regulations*, 1977 will apply to them.[a]

10.6.1.2 Non-EEA and Swiss nationals

Non-EEA and Swiss national visitors are not entitled to work in Ireland. If persons wish to work here, they must return to their country of origin and make the necessary applications from there.[b] Generally persons may not change their immigration status while in Ireland.

10.6.2 What types of accommodation can visitors access?

Persons who come to Ireland on a short-term basis usually reside in hotels, hostels, other short-term accommodation, or with persons they are visiting. However, visitors are not prevented from accessing private rented accommodation.

10.6.2.1 Private rented accommodation

Persons wishing to rent a house or apartment from a private landlord can do so directly themselves by replying to advertisements in newspapers or seek the assistance of a letting agency. Finding accommodation can be expensive and time-consuming, particularly in big cities. Prospective tenants should:

- Inspect the property before agreeing to move in and record the condition of the property and its contents in writing. Houses and apartments to let should comply with certain minimum standards.[5]

- Agree the amount of deposit and rent to be paid and the time of payment. A receipt should be obtained for all money paid to the landlord. The deposit should be returned to the tenant when s/he leaves the accommodation. However, the landlord may retain some or all of the deposit if: the tenant gives insufficient notice, damages the property or leaves without paying bills or rent.

- Find out whether the rent covers such items as electricity, gas and bin charges (where relevant).

- Agree on who is responsible for any repairs that need to be carried out in the future.

Tenants should be aware of their rights and duties as a tenant. The most important of these are:

- The landlord must provide a rent book. The rent book should contain the name and address of the landlord, amount of deposit paid, the amount of rent and the time and method of payment. All rent payments should be entered in the rent book. The rent book should also include the terms of the tenancy.

- The landlord is not permitted (except in cases of emergency) to enter the accommodation without making an appointment with the tenant.

a See Chapter 2.
b See Chapter 2.

- The landlord must give a minimum of four weeks notice in writing if they require the tenant to leave the accommodation. This is referred to as a 'notice to quit'. If the tenant does not leave by the end of the four-week period, the landlord can go to court to apply for an eviction order.

- The tenant must also provide notice to the landlord if they decide to move out.

10.6.3 What medical services are visitors entitled to?

10.6.3.1 EU nationals

EU nationals are entitled to free hospital treatment in a public ward. They should obtain an E111 from before they leave their country of origin. In the event of illness, this should be presented, together with a form of identification, if required, to the doctor or hospital treating the person.

10.6.3.2 Non-EU nationals

Non-EU nationals should take out insurance before leaving their country of origin to cover illness or accidents while in Ireland, as they will not be entitled to free medical care. They should seek advice from their travel agent.

10.6.4 What social welfare entitlements do visitors have?

Irish social welfare legislation does not distinguish between nationals and non-nationals. Essentially, any person from outside the State who complies with the relevant laws covering entry, and living and working here is entitled to seek social welfare payments in compliance with the normal conditions. For further information, contact the Information Service of the Department of Social and Family Affairs on (01) 704 3000.

10.6.5 What education can visitors access?

Visitors are generally not permitted to attend educational courses while in Ireland. It may be possible to attend short-term courses such as a weekend course. EEA and Swiss nationals may commence study while here as a visitor. However, non-EEA and Swiss nationals generally may not change their immigration status while in the State. If they are interested in pursuing a course in Ireland, they must return to their country of origin and make the necessary application from there.

Endnotes

1   Council Directive 90/336 (later replaced by Council Directive 93/96) on *Migrant Students* [1993] OJ L317/59; Council Directive 90/365 *Employed and Self-employed People who have Ceased to Work* [1990] OJ L180/28; Directive 90/364 [1990] OJ L180/26.

2   Case C-413/99 *Baumbast,* 17 September 2002.

3   Proposal for a European Parliament and Council Directive 29 June 2001 on the *Right of Citizens of the Union and their Family Members to Move and Reside Freely within the Territory of the Member States* COM(2001) 257 final [2001] OJ C270 E/23.

4   Case C-85/96 *Maria Martinez Sala v Freistaat Bayern* [1998] ECR I-2691.

5   Details of these can be obtained from Threshold, 21 Stoneybatter, Dublin 7, email *advice@threshold.ie*

VISA REQUIREMENTS

Passport holders of the following countries do not need to have a visa to travel to Ireland:[a]

Andorra	Guatemala	Norway
Antigua and Barbuda	Guyana	Panama
Argentina	Honduras	Paraguay
Australia	Hong Kong (SAR) •	Poland
Austria	Hungary	Portugal
Bahamas	Iceland	St Kitts and Nevis
Barbados	Israel	Saint Lucia
Belgium	Italy	St Vincent & the Grenadines
Belize	Jamaica	
Bolivia	Japan	San Marino
Botswana	Korea (Republic of South)	Seychelles
Brazil	Kiribati	Singapore
Brunei	Latvia	Slovenia
Canada	Lesotho	Solomon Islands
Chile	Liechtenstein	South Africa
Costa Rica	Lithuania	Spain
Croatia	Luxembourg	Swaziland
Cyprus	Macau (SAR) •	Sweden
Czech Republic	Malawi	Switzerland
Denmark	Malaysia	Tonga
Dominica	Maldives	Trinidad and Tobago
El Salvador	Malta	Tuvalu
Estonia	Mauritius	USA
Fiji	Mexico	UK and Colonies
Finland	Monaco	Uruguay
France	Nauru	Vanuatu
Germany	New Zealand	Vatican City
Greece	Netherlands	Venezuela
Grenada	Nicaragua	Western Samoa

• SAR - Special Administrative Region

a Available from the Department of Foreign Affairs *http://www.irlgov.iveagh.ie/*

RESTRICTIONS ON ENTRY FOR EEA AND SWISS NATIONALS

In accordance with the *European Communities (Aliens) Regulations*, 1977, EEA and Swiss nationals may only be refused leave to land if: "... his or her personal conduct has been such that it would be contrary to public policy or would endanger public security",[1] or if the person is suffering from a scheduled disease which include:[2]

A Diseases which might endanger public health

(1) Diseases subject to the International Health Regulations for the time being adopted by the World Health Assembly of the World Health Organisation

(2) Tuberculosis of the respiratory system in an active state or showing a tendency to develop

(3) Syphilis

(4) Other infectious or contagious diseases in respect of which special provisions are in operation to prevent the spread of such diseases from abroad

B Diseases or disabilities which might justify decisions on grounds of public policy or which might endanger public security:

(1) Drug addiction

(2) Profound mental disturbances, manifest conditions of psychotic disturbances with agitation, delirium, hallucination or confusion.

Endnotes

1   *European Communities (Aliens) Regulations* 1977, Regulations 4 (i) and 4 (ii), SI No. 393.

2   *The European Communities (Aliens) Regulations* 1977, Schedule 2, sets out these 'scheduled diseases and disabilities'.

RESTRICTIONS ON ENTRY FOR NON-EEA AND SWISS NATIONALS

Non-nationals (not including EEA and Swiss nationals) will be refused leave to land if they:[a]

- do not possess a employment permit if coming to Ireland to take up employment
- are suffering from certain disabilities
- are not in possession of a visa if they are nationals of a state whose passport holders are required to possess a visa to travel to Ireland
- belong to a class of persons prohibited from landing
- are prohibited from landing by order of the Minister
- have been convicted whether in Ireland or another jurisdiction of a crime punishable by at least one year imprisonment
- are not in possession of a passport or other document that:
  - establishes their identity and nationality
  - was issued on behalf of an authority recognised by the Government
  - does not purport to have been renewed otherwise, than by, or on behalf of, that authority
- are the subject of a deportation order
- intend to travel to the UK or Northern Ireland and the Immigration Officer is satisfied that they would not qualify for admission there
- have arrived in Ireland as part of the crew of an aircraft or ship and remain in the State without authorisation after the departure of the ship or aircraft

APPENDIX C

a *Aliens Order* 1946 (as amended), Section 5 (3).

RESIDENCY STAMPS

The names of the various residency stamps, and to whom they refer, are outlined below:

Stamp name	Refers to...
Stamp No.1	people who are entitled to work if they are in possession of an employment permit, work visa or work authorisation. This stamp is also issued to people with a business permission
Stamp No.2	students who are entitled to work 20 hours per week
Stamp No.3	visitors and they are not entitled to work
Stamp No.4	people entitled to work without a employment permit. This stamp is issued to persons with leave to remain, and those with refugee status.
Stamp A	medical practitioners who are entitled to work
Stamp B	spouses of medical practitioners who are not entitled to work

ADDRESSES

Government Departments and Agencies

Immigration and Citizenship Division Department of Justice, Equality & Law Reform
13/14 Burgh Quay
Dublin 2
(01) 616 7700

Passport Office
Setana House
Molesworth Street
Dublin 2
(01) 671 1633

Visa Office Department of Foreign Affairs
13/14 Burgh Quay
Dublin 2
(01) 663 1000

Garda National Immigration Bureau
13/14 Burgh Quay
Dublin 2
(01) 666 9193

Work Permits & Employment Rights Department of Enterprise, Trade and Employment
Davitt House
65A Adelaide Road
Dublin 2
(01) 631 2121
Work Permits Section:
(01) 631 3308
(01) 631 3333
Employment Rights Information:
(01) 631 3131

FÁS
27 Upper Baggot St
Dublin 4
(01) 607 0500

National Consultative Committee on Racism & Interculturalism
26 Harcourt Street
Dublin 2
(01) 478 5777

The Office of the Ombudswoman
18 Lower Leeson St
Dublin 2
(01) 639 5600
Locall: (1890) 223030

Garda Racial & Intercultural Office
Community Relations
Harcourt Street
Dublin 2
(01) 666 3150

Tourism Victim Support
Garda Headquarters
Harcourt Street
Dublin 2
(01) 478 5295

Equality Authority
2 Clonmel St
Dublin 2
(01) 417 3336
Locall: (1890) 245 545

ODEI - The Equality Tribunal
3 Clonmel St
Dublin 2
(01) 477 4100
Locall: (1890) 344 424

Employment Appeals Tribunal
Davitt House
65A Adelaide Road
Dublin 2
(01) 631 2121
Locall: (1890) 220 222

Labour Court
Tom Johnson House
Beggar's Bush
Dublin 4
(01) 613 6666
Locall: (1890) 220 228

Labour Relations Commission
Tom Johnson House
Beggar's Bush
Dublin 4
(01) 613 6700
Locall: (1890) 220227

Employment Rights Information Unit
Room GO5
Davitt House
65A Adelaide Road
Dublin 2
(01) 631 3131

Reception and Integration Agency Department of Justice, Equality & Law Reform
Block C, Ardilaun Centre
112-114 St Stephen's
Green West
Dublin 2
(01) 418 3200

Department of Education and Science
Marlborough St
Dublin 1
(01) 873 4700
International Section:
(01) 889 2379

Department of Social and Family Affairs
Áras Mhic Dhiarmada
Store St
Dublin 1
(01) 704 3000

Health Boards

East Coast Area Health Board
Southern Cross House
Southern Cross
Business Park
Bray, Co Wicklow
(01) 201 4200
Customer Services
Freephone: (1800) 520 520

Midland Health Board
Arden Road
Tullamore
Co. Offaly
(0506) 21868

Mid-Western Health Board
31/33 Catherine St
Limerick
(061) 301 111

North Eastern Health Board
Kells, Co Meath
(046) 80500

North Western Health Board
Manorhamilton
Co Leitrim
(071) 982 0400

Northern Area Health Board
Head Office
Sword Business Campus
Swords
Co. Dublin
(01) 813 1800
Customer Services
Freephone: (1800) 520 520

South Eastern Health Board
Lacken
Dublin Rd
Kilkenny
(056) 84100

South Western Area Health Board
Oak House
Limetree Avenue
Millenium Park
Naas
Co Kildare
(045) 889 100
Customer Services
Freephone: (1890) 737 343

Southern Health Board
Wilton Road
Cork
(021) 454 5011

Western Health Board
Merlin Park Regional Hospital
Galway
(091) 757 631

Professional Bodies

This list includes bodies that represent the employment sectors for which a working visa/work authorisation may be obtained (see 2.5.5.1 page 31 for the list of employment sectors). This list is sorted in the same order as the list of employment sectors.

Irish Computer Society
17/19 St. John
Rogerson's Quay
Dublin 2
(01) 672 7998

The Royal Institute of Architects Ireland
8 Merrion Square
Dublin 2
(01) 676 1703

Institute of Engineers in Ireland
22 Clyde Road
Dublin 4
Ireland
(01) 668 4341

Society of Chartered Surveyors
5 Wilton Place
Dublin 2
(01) 676 5500

Irish Planning Institute
8 Merrion Square
Dublin 2
(01) 662 8807

Medical Council
Lynn House
Portobello Court
Lower Rathmines Road
Dublin 6
(01) 496 5588

**An Bord Altranais
(Nursing Board)**
31 Fitzwilliam Square
Dublin 2
(01) 639 8500

Dental Council
57 Merrion Square
Dublin 2
(01) 676 2069
(01) 676 2226

**National Social Work
Qualification Board**
8 -11 Lower Baggot
Street
Dublin 2
(01) 676 6281

Validation Unit
Personnel Management
and Development
Department of Health
and Children
Hawkins House
Dublin 2
(01) 635 4041

**Society of Hearing Aid
Audiologists**
20 O' Connell Street
Limerick
(061) 414 917

**Association of Clinical
Biochemists**
c/o Clinical Biochemistry
Department
St. Vincent's Hospital
Elm Park
Dublin 4
(01) 269 4533

**Association of
Cardiological Technicians**
Cardiac Department
Beaumont Hospital
Dublin 9
(01) 837 7755

**Irish Institute of
Radiography**
28 Millbrook Court
Kilmainham
Dublin 8
(01) 679 0433

**Irish Nutrition and
Dietetic Institute**
Ashgrove House
Kill Avenue
Dun Laoighaire
Co. Dublin
(01) 280 4839

**The Pharmaceutical
Society of Ireland**
18 Shrewsbury Road
Dublin 4
(01) 218 4000

**Association of Physical
Scientists in Medicine**
c/o Department of
Medical Physics & Bio
Engineering
University College
Hospital
Galway
(091) 524 222

**Academy of Medical
Laboratory Science**
31 Old Kilmainham Road
Dublin 8
(01) 677 5602

**Association of
Occupational Therapists**
29 Gardiner Place
Dublin 1
(01) 878 0247

**Irish Association of
Orthoptists**
Eye Department
The Children's Hospital
Temple Street
Dublin 1
(01) 809 5462

**Psychological Society of
Ireland**
CX House
2A Corn Exchange Place
Poolbeg Street
Dublin 2
(01) 671 7048

**Irish Society of
Chartered
Physiotherapists**
Royal College of
Surgeons
St Stephen's Green
Dublin 2
(01) 402 2148

**Irish Association of
Speech and Language
Therapists**
29 Gardiner Place
Dublin 1
(01) 878 0215

Migrant Organisations

Afghan Community of Ireland Association
20 Ashington Garc
Off Navan Rd
Dublin 7
(01) 868 3577

Africa Solidarity Centre
Terenure Enterprise
17 Rathfarnham Rd
Dublin 6W
(01) 490 3237

African Cultural Centre
12 Upper Crescent
Belfast
BT7 1NT
North Ireland
(00 44 48) 902 38742

African Refugee Network
90 Meath Street
Dublin 8
(01) 473 4523
Fax: (01) 454 0745

AKIDWA
19 Belvedere Place
Dublin 1
(01) 855 2111

Algerian Solidarity Group
10 Upper Camden St
Dublin 2
(01) 478 3490

Bosnian Community Development Project
40 Pearce Street
Dublin 2
(01) 671 9202

Children of Zimbabwe
10 Camden Street
Dublin 2
(086) 328 7711, after 5:30pm

Chinese Information Centre
3 Beresford Place
Dublin 1
(01) 888 1355

Congolese Irish Partnership
19 Belvedere Place
Dublin 1
(01) 855 2111

Congolese Solidarity Group
10 Upper Camden St
Dublin 2
(01) 478 3490

Cuban Support Group Ireland
15 Merrion Square
Dublin 2
(01) 676 1213

Galway One World Centre
The Hall
Quay Street
Galway
(091) 581 688

Irish Chinese Welfare Association
63 Fitzwilliam Square
Dublin 2
(01) 611 4666

Irish Croatian Association
25 Merrion Square
Dublin 2
(01) 668 6165

Irish South African Association
10 Arnold Park
Glenageary
Co Dublin
(01) 285 1867

Irish Sudanese Association
3 Belgrave Rd
Rathmines
Dublin 6
(01) 498 3926

Islamic Cultural Centre
19 Roebuck Rd
Clonskeagh
Dublin 14
(01) 208 0000

Islamic Foundation of Ireland
163 South Circular Rd
Dublin 8
(01) 453 3242

Latin American Solidarity Centre
5 Merrion Row
Dublin 2
(01) 676 0435

Nigerian Support Group
10 Upper Camden St
Dublin 2
(01) 478 3490

Roma Support Group
Pavee Point
46 North Great Charles
Dublin 1
(01) 878 0255

Society of Russian Speakers
4 Merchant Quay
Dublin 8
(01) 677 1128

Vietnamese Irish Association
45/46 Hardwicke St
Dublin 1
(01) 874 2331

Human Rights Organisations

Amnesty International
48 Fleet Street
Dublin 2
(01) 677 6361

Comhlamh
10 Upper Camden Street
Dublin 2
(01) 478 3490

Human Rights Commission
17-19 Lower Hatch Street
Dublin 2
(01) 647 2562

Integrating Ireland
10 Upper Camden Street
Dublin 2
(01) 478 3490

Irish Commission for Justice and Peace
169 Booterstown Avenue
Blackrock
Co. Dublin
(01) 288 4713

Irish Council for Civil Liberties
Dominick Court
41 Lower Dominick Street
Dublin 1
(01) 878 3137

Sports Against Racism
135 Capel St
Dublin 1
(01) 873 5077
Fax: (01) 873 1924

Advice Organisations

Comhairle (Information for All)
7th Floor
Hume House
Dublin 4
(01) 605 9000

Emigrant Advice Centre
1a Cathedral Street
Dublin 1
(01) 873 2844

Free Legal Advice Centre
13 Lower Dorset Street
Dublin 2
(01) 679 4239

Irish Centre for Migration Studies
NUI Cork
Western Road
Cork
(021) 490 2889

Irish Immigrant Support Centre (NASC)
St. Mary's of the Isle
Sharman Crawford Street
Cork
(021) 431 7411

Irish National Organisation for the Unemployed
Araby House
8 North Richmond Street
Dublin 1
(01) 856 0088

Irish Refugee Council
40 Lower Dominick Street
Dublin 1
(01) 873 0042

Law Society of Ireland
Blackhall Place
Dublin 7
(01) 671 0711

Longford Women's Centre
Willow house
Ardnacassa Avenue
Ballinalee Rd
Longford
(043) 41511

Migrant Advice Centre
3 Beresford Place
Dublin 1
(01) 888 1355

Refugee Information Service
27 Annamoe Terrace
Dublin 7
(01) 838 2740

Refugee Legal Service (Solicitors)
48/49 North Brunswick Street
Georges Lane
Smithsfield
Dublin 7
(01) 646 9600
Freephone: (1800) 238 343

**Refugee Legal Service
(Registration Office for
new clients)**
Timberlay House
79-83 Lower Mount St
Dublin 2
(01) 631 0800

**Tallaght Intercultural
Project**
16 Glenshane Lawns
Brookfield
Tallaght
Dublin 24
(01) 452 2533

**Vincentian Refugee
Centre**
St. Peter's Church
Phibsboro
Dublin 7
(01) 810 2580

Trade Unions

City Bridges Project
Liberty Hall
Dublin 1
(01) 878 7272

ICTU
Head Office
31/32 Parnell Sq
Dublin 1
(01) 889 7777

International Organisations

**European Commission
Representation in Ireland**
18 Dawson Street
Dublin 2
(01) 662 5113

Irish Red Cross
12 Merrion Square
Dublin 2
(01) 676 5135
(01) 676 5136
(01) 676 5137

UNHCR
Liaison Office for Ireland
27 Fitzwilliam Street
Upper
Dublin 2
(01) 632 8679

**International
Organisation for
Migration**
9 Marleborough Court
Marleborough Street
Dublin 1
(01) 878 7900

Women's Organisations

Cherish
2 Lower Pembroke
Dublin 4
(01) 662 9212
Locall: (1890) 662 212

**Ruhama Women's
Project**
Senior House
All Hallow's College
Drumcondra
Dublin 9
(01) 836 0292
Email: admin@ruhama.ie

Women's Aid
Everton House
47 Old Cabra Road
Dublin 7
(01) 868 4721
Freephone: (1800) 341 900

Educational Organisations

An Síol
19 Manor Street
Dublin 7
(01) 677 5741

**Catherine McCauley
Centre**
23 Herbert Street
Dublin 2
(01) 638 7500

**CDVEC Curriculum
Development Unit**
Sundrive Road
Crumlin
Dublin 12
(01) 453 5487

Educate Together
75 Park West Road
Dublin 12
(01) 626 3089

**Integrate Ireland Language
& Training (IILT)**
Unit 4A
Trinity Enterprise Centre
Grand Canal Quay
Dublin 2
(01) 677 5344

**Irish Council for
Overseas Students**
41 Morehampton Road
Dublin 4
(01) 660 5233

**Irish Vocational
Education Association
(IVEA)**
McCann House
99 Marlborough Road
Dublin 4
(01) 496 6033

**Kerry Action for
Development Education**
11 Denny Street
Tralee
Co. Kerry
(066) 718 1358

Meitheal
35 Exchequer Street
Dublin 2
(01) 671 9803

MEI~RELSA
107 South Circular Road
Dublin 8
(01) 475 3122

**National Centre for
Guidance in Education**
1st Floor
42/43 Prussia Street
Dublin 7
(01) 869 0715

SPIRASI
Spiritan House
213 North Circular Road
Dublin 7
(01) 838 9664

Accommodation Organisations

**Clann Housing
Association**
18 Dame Street
Dublin 2
(01) 677 5010

Threshold
21 Stoneybatter
Dublin 7
(01) 6786098

Health Organisations

(See also Health Boards on page 226.)

**Cairde Healthwise
Project**
19 Belvedere Place
Dublin 1
(01) 855 2111
Fax: (01) 855 2089

**Centre for the Survivors
of Torture**
Spiritan House
213 North Circular Road
Dublin 7
(01) 838 9664

**Refugee and Asylum
Seeker Service**
Department of
Psychology
St. Brendan's Hospital
Rathdown Road
Dublin 7
(01) 868 0166

Religious Organisations

Dominican Justice Office
38 Iona Road
Glasnevin
Dublin 9
(01) 882 7484

DORAS
c/o Redemptorists
Community Limerick
Mount St. Alphonsus
Mission House
Limerick
(061) 310 328

Irish Missionary Union
Orwell Park
Rathgar
Dublin 6
(01) 496 5433

Gay and Lesbian Organisations

Gay and Lesbian Equality Network
c/o Outhouse
105 Capel Street
Dublin 1
(01) 873 4932

Gay Community News
Unit 2 Scarlet Row
Essex St West
Dublin 8
(01) 671 9076

Lone Parent Organisations

Cherish
2 Lower Pembroke Street
Dublin 2
(01) 662 9212

TREOIR
14 Gandon House
Lower Mayor Street
ISFC
Dublin 1
(01) 670 0120

Children's Organisations

Children's Rights Alliance
13 Harcourt Street
Dublin 2
(01) 405 4823

National Children's Office
Floor 3
94 St. Stephens Green
Dublin 2
(01) 418 0582

Youth Organisations

National Youth Council of Ireland
3 Montague Street
Dublin 2
Ireland
(01) 478 4122

National Youth Federation
20 Lower Dominick Street
Dublin 1
(01) 872 9933

Youth Action Against Racism and Discrimination
3 Montague Street
Dublin 2
Ireland
(01) 478 4122

Local Authorities - City Councils

Cork City Council
City Hall
Cork
(021) 496 6222

Dublin City Council
Civic Offices
Wood Quay
Dublin 8
(01) 672 2222

Galway City Council
City Hall
College Road
Galway
(091) 536 400

Limerick City Council
City Hall
Limerick
(061) 415 799

Waterford City Council
City Hall
The Mall
Waterford
(051) 309 900

Local Authorities - County Councils

Carlow County Council
Athy Road
Carlow
(0503) 70300

Cavan County Council
Courthouse
Cavan Town
Co. Cavan
(049) 433 1799

Clare County Council
New Road
Ennis
Co. Clare
(065) 682 1616

Cork County Council
County Hall
Cork
(021) 427 6891

Donegal County Council
County House
Lifford
Co. Donegal
(074) 72222

Dun Laoghaire/Rathdown County Council
Town Hall
Marine Road
Dun Laoghaire
Co. Dublin
(01) 205 4700

Fingal County Council
PO Box 174
Fingal County Hall
Main Street
Swords
Co. Dublin
(01) 890 5000

Galway County Council
PO Box 27
County Hall
Galway
(091) 509 000

Kerry County Council
Áras an Chontae
Tralee
Co. Kerry
(066) 712 1111

Kildare County Council
St Mary's
Naas
Co. Kildare
(045) 873 800

Kilkenny County Council
County Hall
John Street
Kilkenny
(056) 779 4000

Laois County Council
Portlaoise
Co. Laois
(0502) 64000

Leitrim County Council
Áras an Chontae
Carrick-on-Shannon
Co. Leitrim
(078) 20005

Limerick County Council
79/84 O'Connell Street
Limerick
(061) 38477

Longford County Council
Áras an Chontae
Great Water Street
Longford
(043) 46231

Louth County Council
County Hall
Millenium Centre
Dundalk
Co. Louth
(042) 933 5457

Mayo County Council
Áras an Chontae
Castlebar
Co. Mayo
(094) 24444

Meath County Council
County Hall
Railway Street
Navan
Co. Meath
(046) 21581

Monaghan County Council
County Offices
The Glen
Monaghan
(047) 30500

North Tipperary County Council
Couthouse
Nenagh
Co. Tipperary
(067) 3 1771

Offaly County Council
Áras an Chontae
Charleville Road
Tullamore
Co. Offaly
(0506) 46800

Roscommon County Council
Courthouse
Roscommon
(0903) 37100

Sligo County Council
Riverside
Sligo
(071) 915 6666

South Dublin County Council
Town Centre
Tallaght
Dublin 24
(01) 414 9000

South Tipperary County Council
Áras an Chontae
Clonmel
Co. Tipperary
(052) 34455

Waterford County Council
Civic Offices
Dungarvan
Co. Waterford
(058) 22000

Westmeath County Council
County Buildings
Mullingar
Co. Westmeath
(044) 32000

Wexford County Council
County Hall
Wexford
(053) 42211

Wicklow County Council
County Buildings
Station Road
Wicklow Town
Co. Wicklow
(0404) 20100

Borough Councils

Clonmel Borough Council
Town Hall
Parnell Street
Clonmel
Co. Tipperary
(052) 83800

Drogheda Borough Council
Corporation Offices
Fair Street
Drogheda
Co. Louth
(041) 983 3511

Kilkenny Borough Council
City Hall
High Street
Kilkenny
(056) 94000

Silgo Borough Council
Town Hall
Sligo
(071) 914 2141

Wexford Borough Council
Municipal Buildings
Wexford
(053) 42611

GLOSSARY

ACELS	Advisory Council for English Language Schools
Alien	A non-Irish national is referred to as an alien in the *Aliens Act*, 1935.
An Bord Altranais	The Irish Nursing Board.
APC	Asian, Pacific and Caribbean
BUPA Ireland	A private medical insurer.
C Study Visa	The type of visa a student wishing to study in Ireland for months should apply for.
CAO	Central Applications Office. Persons who want to apply for third-level undergraduate courses need to apply via the CAO. The CAO provides a handbook and application pack for courses on offer at the Irish universities and institutes of technology.
CEEA	The European Centre of Enterprises with Public Participation, and of Enterprises of General Economic Interest
Comhairle	The national support agency responsible for the provision of information, advice and advocacy to members of the public on social services.
Conference (EU)	EU conferences analyse the major problems arising in their sectors and foster ongoing contact between ministries dealing with the same subjects in Member States.
Convention (EU)	A practice or custom followed in government although not explicitly written in the constitution or in legislation. European Conventions and Agreements are not statutory acts of the organisation; they owe their legal existence simply to the expression of the will of those states that may become parties thereto, as manifested *inter alia* by the signature and ratification of the EU Treaty.
Council of Europe	The Council of Europe is a political organisation, founded in 1949, to defend the principles of democracy, human rights and the rule of law. Membership is open to all European states which undertake to abide by the organisation's principles. At present, the Council of Europe has 45 member states.
D Study Visa	The type of visa a non-EEA national wishing to study for less than three months should apply for.
Dáil	Lower house of parliament.
EAT	Employment Appeals Tribunal
EC Treaty	European Community Treaty
ECHR	European Convention on Human Rights. The ECHR guarantees civil and political human rights.

ECJ	European Court of Justice The Court of Justice comprises 15 judges and 8 advocates general. The judges and advocates general are appointed by common accord of the governments of the Member States and hold office for a renewable term of six years. They are chosen from jurists whose independence is beyond doubt and who are of recognised competence.
EEA	European Economic Area Agreement. In 1994, the EEA was signed between the European Union and Norway, Iceland and Liechtenstein. Nationals of these states enjoy rights within the EU that are similar to those of nationals of EU Member States and include those set out in the *European Communities (Right of Residence for Non-Economically Active Persons) Regulations*, 1997.
EEC	European Economic Community (later became the EU).
Employment Permit	The term used for what, until recently, was called a work permit.
Enterprise Ireland	An enterprise development agency dealing mainly with the food, drink and timber industries.
Equality Authority	The Equality Authority works towards the elimination of discrimination in employment, in the provision of goods and services, education, property and so on.
Equality Tribunal	The equality tribunal is an independent body established to investigate claims of discrimination under the *Employment Equality Act*, 1998 and the *Equal Status Act*, 2000. The official title is ODEI - the equality tribunal.
ETUC	The European Trade Union Confederation
EU	European Union (formerly the EEC)
EU *Social Charter*	The EU *Social Charter* guarantees social and economic human rights. It was adopted in 1961 and revised in 1996.
EURES	EURopean Employment Services (EURES) is a European labour market network aiming at facilitating the mobility of workers in the European Economic Area (EEA).
FÁS CALLNET	A service, where employers nationwide may register job vacancies by calling the FÁS number. Vacancy details are taken by trained staff who can help in drafting the most appropriate advertisement and can advise on relevant legislation. FÁS CALLNET takes vacancies from employers over the phone and via the Internet.
GP	General Practitioner (family doctor).
HEA	Higher Education Authority in Ireland

Health Boards	The statutory bodies responsible for the provision of health and personal social services in their respective areas.
ICOS	Irish Council for International Students
IDA	Industrial Development Authority. An organisation set up to provide assistance to persons wishing to establish a business in Ireland.
IEBI	International Education Board of Ireland
ILO	International Labour Organisation. It is a specialised UN agency which promotes social justice and internationally recognised human and labour rights. The ILO formulates international labour standards in the form of conventions and recommendations setting minimum standards of basic labour rights.
Labour Court	The Labour Court provides a free, comprehensive service for the resolution of disputes about industrial relations, equality, organisation of working time and national minimum wage matters.
Labour Relations Commission	The Labour Relations Commission was established in 1991 to Commission promote the development and improvement of industrial relations policies, procedures and practices in Ireland.
Local Authority	The name of the state authority responsible for local government in local areas.
MEI~RELSA	Marketing English in Ireland ~ Recognised English Language Schools Association
Member State	These are European countries that are members of the EU. They are currently 15 of them.
MPG	Minority Protection Group
NGO	Non-governmental Organisation
ODEI-the equality tribunal	ODEI stands for the Office of Director of Equality Investigations. ODEI-the equality tribunal is the official title for what is often referred to as the equality tribunal. See entry for equality tribunal.
P60	At the end of each tax year, employers in Ireland give their employees a P60. It is a form on which the details of gross pay and all deductions made during the year for an employee are recorded.
PAYE	Pay as You Earn. Tax deducted from an employee's salary at source.

PPS No.	Personal Public Service Number. This is an individual's unique reference number for dealing with the Public Service. Many government departments and public service agencies request you to supply your PPS No. before you can use their services.
Programme for Prosperity and Fairness	The Programme for Prosperity and Fairness is a government programme structured as a set of five 'operational frameworks'. The Programme contains a very extensive list of measures across a wide range of issues - such as housing, public transport, industrial policy and rural development - as well as the primary trade union concerns of pay, taxation and social inclusion.
PRSI	Pay-related Social Insurance. All employees in continuous permanent employment, between the ages of 16 and 66 years old, whether casual or contract, compulsorily contribute to the Social Insurance Fund of the Department of Social Welfare.
Revised Social Charter	The *Revised Social Charter* has taken the place of the EU *Social Charter*. It has been amended to add new rights, to take account in particular of the fundamental social changes which have occurred since the original EU *Social Charter* was adopted.
Rights Commissioner	Rights Commissioners investigate disputes, grievances and claims that individuals or small groups of workers refer under labour-related legislation.
RSI No.	See the entry for PPS No. which replaces the earlier number known as the RSI No.
Saorstat Eireann	Irish Free State.
SI	Statutory Instrument. It is generally held that statutory instruments, often referred to as 'secondary legislation' or 'delegated legislation', are 'law' in the strict sense of that term. It would follow, therefore, that the making of such instruments constitutes law-making. For a number of reasons this may be an incomplete description, and there are arguments to support the view that statutory instruments might not constitute 'law' in the strict sense of that term.
Social Welfare	Supports and services provided by the government to people at various stages of their lives.
Third-country Nationals	Term used to refer to any person who is not a national of an EU Member State.
UK	The United Kingdom of Great Britain (England, Scotland, and Wales) and Northern Ireland.

UN	United Nations
UNICE	Union of Industrial and Employers' Confederations of Europe
VAT	Value Added Tax
VEC	Vocational Education Committee
VHI	Voluntary Health Insurance. A private medical insurer.
Work Permit	The term used until recently for what is now referred to as an employment permit
WP3	FÁS form necessary for employers applying for an employment permit
WP6	FÁS form necessary for employers applying for an employment permit

BIBLIOGRAPHY

Barrett, G. *The Rights of Third-country Family Members under European Community Law*, available from the Irish Centre for European Law, TCD (2000).

Department of Enterprise, Trade & Employment *Guide to Labour Law* *http://www.entemp.ie/*

Department of Enterprise, Trade & Employment, Information Leaflet *Working Visas for Employment in Ireland* 11 February 2003, Department of Enterprise, Trade & Employment (2003).

Department of Enterprise, Trade & Employment, Press Release *Department of Enterprise, Trade & Employment and FÁS Clarify Operational Arrangements of Work Permit Procedures* Department of Enterprise, Trade & Employment(2003) *http://www.entemp.ie/press03/070403a.htm*

Department of Justice, Equality & Law Reform Information Leaflet *New Immigration Procedures in Relation to Swiss Nationals* available on the Department's website *http://www.justice.ie/*

Department of Justice, Equality & Law Reform Information Leaflet *Student Visa Requirements* available on the Department's website *http://www.justice.ie/*

Department of Justice, Equality & Law Reform *Integration: A Two Way Process* Government Stationery Office, Dublin (1999).

Department of Justice, Equality & Law Reform *Report of the Public Consultation on Immigration Policy* available on the Department's website *http://www.justice.ie/*

Department of Social, Community and Family Affairs, Information Leaflet *SW100 Personal Public Service Number* *http://www.welfare.ie/*

European Council for Refugees and Exiles (ECRE) *An Overview of Proposals Addressing Migrant Smuggling and Trafficking in Persons* ECRE Background Paper July 2001, ECRE, London (2001) *http://www.ecre.org/policy/research/smuggle.shtml*

Guild, Elspeth, *A Guide to the Right of Establishment under the Europe Agreements* Bailey Shaw and Gillett, London (1996).

Guild, Elspeth and Staples, Helen 'Inside Out and Outside In: Third-country Nationals in European Law and Beyond' in *European Union Law and Policy on Immigration and Asylum* Universite Libre de Brussels, Brussels (2001).

Harney Mary (An Tánaiste) Press Release, *Tánaiste Announces New Immigration Rules for Accession Countries* 24 March 2003 *http://www.entemp.ie/press03/240303.htm*

IBEC Press Release *IBEC Expresses Concern with Work Permit Procedures* 7 April 2003 *http://www.ibec.ie/ibec/press/presspublicationsdoclib3.nsf/wvTopTwoNews/72D99 9E6FCA0591080256D01005E33DD?OpenDocument*

Immigration Law Practitioners Association (ILPA) and Minority Protection Group (MPG) *The Amsterdam Proposals* ILPA, London (2000).

Ingoldsby, Brian *Regular Migration to Ireland* paper delivered at the Incorporated Law Society Seminar: 'Rights to Reside in Ireland' 14 May 2002, at Blackhall Place, Dublin.

International Organisation for Migration *International Comparative Study of Migration Legislation and Practice* commissioned by the Department of Justice, Equality & Law Reform, April 2002 *http://www.justice.ie/*

Irish Congress of Trade Unions (ICTU) *Migration and Immigration: Changing the Face of Irish Society* ICTU, Dublin (2001).

Irish Times 1 March 2000 'Employers Back Plan to Bring 200,000 into State'.

Irish Times 3 April 2002 'Law Change on Workers Without Permits is Welcomed'.

Irish Vocational Education Association (IVEA) *Policy on Educational Provisions for Asylum Seekers, Refugees and Other Non-nationals* IVEA, Dublin (2001).

National Consultative Committee on Racism and Interculturalism (NCCRI) 'Issues and Recommendations Concerning the Employment of Migrant Workers in Ireland' Submission from the NCCRI to the Department of Enterprise, Trade & Employment, February 2001.

Duran Seddon (Ed.) *Joint Council for the Welfare of Immigrants, Immigration, Nationality & Refugee Law Handbook* 2002 Edition.

The Chambers of Commerce of Ireland (CCI) *Labour Force 2001: Economic Immigration CCI*, Dublin (2001).

UN High Commissioner for Human Rights, Fact Sheet No 24 *The Rights of Migrants http://193.194.138.190/html/menu6/2/fs24.htm*

UNHCR Discussion Paper 'Reconciling Migration Control and Refugee Protection in the European Union: A UNHCR Perspective'. October 2000 *http://www.unhcr.ch/cgi-bin/texis/vtx/home*

United Nations Press Release, 15 December 2000 *http://www.un.org/news/press/docs/2000/20001215.pil305.doc.html*

Ward, Eilis, 'Ireland and Refugees/Asylum seekers 1922 - 1996' in *The Expanding Nation: Towards a Multi-ethnic Ireland* Proceedings of a conference held in Trinity College Dublin 22-24 September 1998, pp 41-48 *http://www.tcd.ie/sociology/mphil/dwnl/expanding_nation.pdf*

Ward, Tanya *Immigration and Residency in Ireland* City of Dublin VEC, Dublin (2000).

INDEX

NOTES

NOTES

NOTES